Of Scholars, Savants and their Texts

Of Scholars, Savants, and their Texts

Studies in Philosophy and Religious Thought

Essays in Honor of Arthur Hyman

Editor: Ruth Link-Salinger
Advisor to Editor: Sol Roth
Associate Editor: Robert Herrera

PETER LANG
New York • Bern • Frankfurt am Main • Paris

Library of Congress Cataloging-in-Publication Data

Of scholars, savants, and their texts : studies in
philosophy and religious thought : essays in honor of
Arthur Hyman / editor, Ruth Link-Salinger ; advisor to
editor, Sol Roth ; associate editor, Robert Herrera.
 p. cm.
 Includes bibliographies and indexes.
 1. Philosophy. 2. Philosophy, Jewish. 3. Judaism—
Doctrines—History. 4. Hyman, Arthur, 1921- .
I. Hyman, Arthur, 1921- . II. Hyman, Ruth Link-
Salinger, 1926- . III. Roth, Sol. IV. Herrera, Robert
A.
 B29.04   1989   100—dc20   89-31590
 ISBN 0-8204-0834-4   CIP

CIP-Titelaufnahme der Deutschen Bibliothek

Of scholars, savants, and their texts : studies in
philosophy and religious thought ; essays in
honor of Arthur Hyman / ed.: Ruth Link-Salinger. – New York; Bern; Frankfurt am Main;
Paris: Lang, 1989.
 ISBN 0-8204-0834-4

NE: Link-Salinger, Ruth [Hrsg.]

© Peter Lang Publishing, Inc., New York 1989

All rights reserved.
Reprint or reproduction, even partially, in all forms such as microfilm,
xerography, microfiche, microcard, offset strictly prohibited.

Printed by Weihert-Druck GmbH, Darmstadt, West Germany

Contents

1. Ruth Link-Salinger, University of Luzern — 1
   Of Scholars: Study, Community, Civility, and Restraint (Fragments of a Preface)

2. Bernardo Carlos Bazàn, University of Ottawa — 9
   On "First Averroism" and its Doctrinal Background

3. Bernard Berofsky, Columbia University — 23
   The Role of Power in a Theory of Freedom

4. Ivan Boh, The Ohio State University — 35
   Frachantian's Debt to Heytesbury

5. Alexander Broadie, The University of Glasgow — 47
   Maimonides and Divine Knowledge

6. Hubert Dethier, Vrije Universiteit Brussel — 57
   Maimonides and German Idealism

7. J.M. Dillon, Trinity College, Dublin — 69
   The Theory of Three Classes of Men in Plotinus and in Philo

8. Jude P. Dougherty, The Catholic University of America — 77
   Maritain on Creative Intuition

9. Louis Finkelstein, Jewish Theological Seminary of America — 97
   Simeon the Righteous

10. Lawrence E. Frizzell, Seton Hall University — 103
    Education by Example: A Motif in Joseph and Literature of the Second Temple Period Maccabee

Contents

11. Robert A. Herrera, Seton Hall University — 113
    Augustine's Manichaean Turn: The Physical World in the New Creation

12. Jaakko Hintikka, Florida State University and University of Helsinki — 123
    On the Role of Modality in Aristotle's Metaphysics

13. Ephraim Kanarfogel, Stern College/ Yeshiva University — 135
    Compensation for the Study of Torah in Medieval Rabbinc Thought

14. Jacob Jay Lindenthal, University of Medicine and Dentistry– New Jersey Medical School and Yeshiva University — 149
    Perspectives on Health in the Judaic and Islamic Traditions

15. Bernard McGinn, University of Chicago — 163
    Platonic and Christian: The Case of the Divine Ideas

16. Larry B. Miller, The Catholic University of America — 173
    A Brief History of the Liar Paradox

17. Olaf Pluta, Ruhr Universität Bochum — 183
    The Question of Immortality in Lawrence of Lindores's *Quaestiones in Aristotelis libros De anima*

18. Sol Roth, Yeshiva University — 201
    The Halakha as a Theoretical Construction

19. Menahem Schmelzer, Jewish Theological Seminary of America — 209
    Two Philosophical Passages in the Liturgical Poetry of Rabbi Isaac Ibn Giat

20. Fadlou Shehadi, Rutgers University — 217
    Art and Imitation: Plato and Ibn Sina

21. Edward A. Synan, Pontifical Institute, University of Toronto   229
    Peter Bradlay: "No" to Scotist Univocity?

22. David Winston, Graduate Theological Union   239
    Theodicy in Ben Sira and Stoic Philosophy

23. Walter S. Wurzburger, Yeshiva University   251
    The Centrality of Virtue-Ethics in Maimonides

Publications of Arthur Hyman   261

Of Scholars: Study, Community, Civility, and Restraint (Fragments of a Preface)

Ruth Link-Salinger

On the occasion of the celebration of thirty years of active service to the Columbia University Philosophy Department, colleagues the world-over have joined in a common effort to honor a scholar of note in the fields of the History of Philosophy, the Philosophy of Religion and Semitics. The result of this joint venture is the *Festschrift* here presented. Editorial Board and contributors send the fruits of their learning, the encouragement of their shared scholarship, and the warm felicitations of the profession. As Columbia University and its Philosophy Department have been a home of the spirit for Professor Hyman for three decades, so has the association of devoted peers and students brightened and deepened his coherence in and commitment to academe and study. As we tender this tribute of our discipline in written work and intellectual search, we greet him in warmth, friendship, and respect. The models for this jubilee volume were the Festschriften edited by Professors Lieberman and Hyman for Professors Wolfson of Harvard University and Baron of Columbia University, both published by the American Academy for Jewish Research, in which Professor Hyman has been an officer for many years.

To mark this happy occasion in a still more significant way, it has been decided to honor Professor Hyman with the publication of some of his own work. Dean Jude Dougherty of the School of Philosophy of Catholic University has invited Professor Hyman's essays in Semitic Philosophy for his series in the History of Philosophy. This volume to be entitled *Essays in Jewish and Islamic Thought* will be published by Catholic University Press, which, in 1988 presented *A Straight Path: Essays in Medieval Philosophy and Culture (Essays in Honor of Arthur Hyman)* on the occasion of the celebration of the silver jubilee year of service to Yeshiva University. It has been Professor Hyman's expressed wish that neither *Festschrift* carry an explicit analysis or appreciation of his work, and that he be permitted to summarize his own path and goals in scholarship in a "Nachwort" to the collection of his essays. Professor Dougherty and Professor McGonagle of Catholic University Press have invited this assessment of the honoree of his own work, and the Editorial Boards of both *Festschriften* have reluctantly but respectfully accepted this limitation of their function. One of Professor Hyman's learned doctoral students, now a respected professor at Israel's most prestigious university, has, however, decided to publish, in Hebrew, the intended contribution to the present volume as a separate tribute to Professor Hyman. This projected essay will carry a description of Professor Hyman's methodology and contribution to the various traditions of established learning.

We would be remiss, however, in our chosen task as celebrants of the chosen path of one of our colleagues, were we not to mention those of our craft who brought Professor Hyman to his present eminence and effectiveness. Professor James Gutmann, then the Chairman of the Philosophy Department, invited Professor Hyman to teach Medieval Philosophy. Professor James Walsh, for many years Chairman and Advisor to Graduate Students, invited Professor Hyman to collaborate in *Philosophy in the Middle Ages*, the leading textbook in this field for two decades in 130 American universities and colleges.

The late Professor John H. Randall invited the collaboration of his younger colleague in the publication of his book on Aristotle and graciously acknowledged the help in the "Introduction." To recapture in print the many ties to Professor Paul and Professor Edith Kristeller is to do violence to their quietude. Finally, to do justice to the devotion of support, which Arthur Hyman enjoyed in shared work and in continuous interest in his teaching and research, mention must be made of the ever-present help of the Littauer Foundation in the decades that have passed. It was the wish, honored by the Littauer Foundation on two campuses, expressed by the late Professor Wolfson at Harvard, that the Chair at Harvard be made secure in its efforts to disseminate its program in Jewish Learning and that the Department of Philosophy at Columbia receive the necessary funds to underwrite the program of instruction in Comparative Medieval Philosophy and Jewish Philosophy, which has been the core of Professor Hyman's service to the entire learned community on Morningside Heights. The foundation of support for Professor Hyman's service at Columbia has also enabled students at Barnard, Union Theological and Jewish Theological Seminaries to study with and to be granted graduate degrees by Professor Hyman in the areas of his scholarly competences. The many years of shared collegial study and discussion in the University Seminar on the History of Religion brought Professor Hyman into regular contact with colleagues in the Religion Department, with whom he was very often to "share" degree candidates in that area of study.

A recent monograph published in Germany, analyzes with great care the goals and aspirations which motivated educators, scholars, and statesmen in their plans for an unusual modern university for the city of Berlin, at the end of the European Enlightenment period (at the beginning of the 19th century). Discussions called for the actualization of "Bildungsideale", of "Wissenschaft", and of the primacy and centrality of the Philosophy Faculty, hoped to be second to none in Europe. Unusual discussions took place on the role and function of the productive scholar, as regards his function of teacher and disseminator of knowledge in the halls of the university, and of his function as researcher and seeker of knowledge in the halls of the academy. It was projected that to have an elitist life of learning, it would be necessary to provide the institutionalization of learning in a "double track" elitist effort: university and academy for higher studies. The scholar would meet and encourage his students in the university. He would influence and broaden their studies and intellectual horizons. At the same time, he would broaden and deepen his own intellectual and academic searches in the mutual exchanges of insights in the world of learning of the academy and its chosen, carefully selected members and fellows. While the institutionalization of the modern university, in this case Berlin, lies very clearly in the transmission of culture, historically recorded in the ancient academies, the medieval universities, and the various royal academies, the monograph also calls attention to the rights of the modern scholar. These, to cite the German original of the text, are "Einsamkeit und Freiheit". These were thought to have been the basic rights of the craft of the modern scholar.

In a very peculiarly accurate way, Professor Hyman has had these privileges to freedom of work and reticence or privacy of scholarly attainment at Columbia. Deeply attached to the work of the American Academy for Jewish Research and its leadership in the team of Professor Salo Baron of Columbia University and of Professor Saul Lieberman of the Jewish Theological Seminary of America, Professor Hyman found there an anchor for search, quietude, and scholarly seriousness. The life of the productive scholar, the "holiness" of revealed and of transmitted texts, the importance of integrity of interpretation, the value of classical and ancient languages as a tool to research, the joy in discovery of one's own new interpretations of earlier materials, the sharp criticism of colleagues, and the shared civility of equals and superiors in learning were institutionalized in the Academy and became another home for both honoree and editor. We aspired to become-and later did become-heirs to our predecessors and mentors. As they became immortals on Morningside Heights, their examples fructified our work.

In a volume for the Institute of Social and Religious Studies of the Jewish Theological Seminary, now called the Finkelstein Institute, Dean Judith Berlin Lieberman, many years ago, wrote an article about the life of her father, the founder of Bar-Ilan University in Israel. One of the many memorable passages in that book records the appreciation and gratitude Judith Lieberman felt for having been a faculty wife on Morningside Heights, privileged to have made the contact of its wealth of learned personages. This above all else, has also made the life and work of Professor Hyman and his whole family an inheritance of richesse and blessing.

This milestone to a generation of learning of a coherent community of higher education is made possible by the trust and affection of many. The Advisor to the Editor, Professor Sol Roth, Hirsch Professor at Yeshiva University, student for the doctorate of his late much lamented great teacher, world-renowned for his pioneering work in the Philosophy of Science, which still inspires the modes of study of this generation of philosophers at Columbia, symbolizes, in this jubilee volume, the friendship, which Professor Nagel felt for the whole Hyman household. Though a colleague of Arthur Hyman's, Ernest Nagel, husband and father of scholars, never ceased to call attention to the projected career in philosophy of our own oldest son, Jeremy Saul, and to nurture it with suggestions and good advice. Professor Roth, specialist in the Philosophy of Science and the traditions of Jewish Law and Metaphysics, has helped to shape the book, sustained the Editorial Board with his sagesse, and funded the costs of the Volume in both "free" and "reticent" ways and sums. The Littauer Foundation has followed his request and advice to set in print this appreciation to Professor Hyman's work on campus for posterity. The Vice Presidents of Yeshiva University: Israel Miller, Egon Brenner, and Herbert Dobrinsky have kindly aided the Editorial Board by serving as receiving agents for the publication funds, which have been raised.

Rabbanit Judith Kramer Neuberger of the Administration of the Ner Israel Rabbinical College in Baltimore and Professor Judith Ochs Bleich of the Jewish History Department of Touro College in New York have spent valuable and memorable hours of discussion with the Editor to guide her in that exercise of Memory-and-Recollection of a period in history after the Destruction of European Jewish Life and Learning, which is here being given honor and meaning. Both honoree and editor have been intensely conscious of the high duty and demands of their path and their vocation, and it is a desideratum that the *Festschrift* serve as a vehicle of responsibility as well as a celebration of young dreams dreamt and seen fulfilled and of early sights set and mature work accomplished. These two ladies, daughters of dynastic learning, institution-builders of note, and mothers of scholars of present and future have helped the editor to set the tone for this project and to subdue most of the emotion which is best exhibited in pregnant silence.

The career of Professor Hyman as Visiting Professor at The Hebrew University in Jerusalem, at Yale University, the University of California at La Jolla, at Dropsie University, and at Bar Ilan University, also took him, for many years, to the Graduate Faculty of the New School for Social Research. There he worked intimately with Professor Aron Gurwitsch and with Professor Hans Jonas, who did not then imagine that one of his doctoral students would many years later serve as Editor for Professor Hyman's Jubilee Volume and honor the man who had so conscientiously served as reader of his dissertation. Professor Herrera, now of the Philosophy Faculty of Seton Hall University, will have owed his senior colleague no debt of devotion and service. The care, love, and affection which he has shown to honoree and to editor have no match and the many academicians here represented by so many interesting areas of research and dissemination of learning are well-honored as well by his trust in their manuscripts.

For many years, in Professor Hyman's presence, it has been unusually useful and diplomatic to relearn the Goethe saying, so popular in the days of my youth in Berlin: "Entsagen sollst Du" (You shall renounce). It is a strong command and demand, left in a fragmentary state, harsh in rhetoric and in content. In my own personal experience, it has always had to fend off the older tradition of the Stoics, calling for the open *expression* of gratitude as the basis for all human civility and moral life in society. How then best to honor a man, whose public posture in alma mater has been one of freedom and reticence and deep humility? Professor Hyman supervised my M.A. dissertation in Political Philosophy and History at Columbia in a six-week period, in a time in which the first sponsor, Professor Franz Neumann, had passed away and Professor Wuorinen had fallen seriously ill. No man was ever harder to please nor more rigorous in the styling of the work. It was difficult for Professor Hyman to lead to the task-at-hand a student so bitterly orphaned by her respect for her earlier mentor. Neumann, master of men, of scholars and of humanists, himself the reticent of reticents. Perhaps this is indeed the time to recollect that Professor Hyman put himself at the head of that challenge, as he has on so many other occasions for so many other graduate students in so many other universities. The manuscript of this M.A. was, for many years, not to be found at Columbia; until, on a peculiar occasion Professor Hyman, himself, found it deposited by the University in the Rare Book Collection, assigned reading for the Honors Students in German History, by a faculty member of that department. Professor Hyman has had a rich career in *help* in all areas of academe at all times and fulfilled these also to high excellence and strange effectiveness.

For this reason and for so many others, best committed to silence in over-radiant memory, the undersigned would like to close this *Festschrift*, which was gathered in the semester in which Professor Hyman was Lady Davis Visiting Professor at the Hebrew University, in the same manner and from the same text, which served so well as the close of *A Straight Path: Studies in Medieval Philosophy and Culture (Essays in Honor of Arthur Hyman)*

On this *Derekh Yeshara*, this straight path of devotion to learning and dignity of bearing, on which I have encountered Professor Hyman again and again, one text-from Hosea 2:21-22-stands out as a special personal marker:

And I will betroth thee unto me forever;
And I will betroth thee unto me in righteousness, in justice, and in loving kindness, and in compassion.
And I will betroth thee unto me in faithfulness;
And thou shall know the Lord.

>R. Link-Salinger
>Theology Department-University of Luzern (Switzerland)

P. S.

We want to acknowledge our inability to standardize the form and style of the work of our colleagues who produce scholarship in so many diversified fields and cultures. We want to celebrate the work of Mr. Kevin McMahon, President of *Laserset*, whose craftsmanship enabled us to publish this *Festschrift* with references in eight languages.

>R. L. S.

On "First Averroism" and its Doctrinal Background

Bernardo Carlos Bazán

1. The idea of a "first averroism" or "primitive averroism", recently reintroduced by Fr. F.-A. Gauthier,[1] is used to designate that particular moment in the history of Thirteenth Century philosophy when latin thinkers favourably received Averroes' writings, and used them freely in order to reach a better understanding of Aristotle's philosophy, without suspecting in them the existence of any major doctrinal danger arising from what is known now as "averroistic monopsychism". Neither the expression nor the idea of a "first averroism" is new. As early as 1937, Fr. D. Salman pointed out that before 1250 there was no sign of mistrust with respect to Averroes.[2] The same notion was proposed several times by F. Van Steenberghen, who emphasized the fact that "before 1250 the influence of Averroes was by no means in the direction of monopsychism".[3]

2. If the idea is not a new one, Gauthier has presented it in a framework of sources which makes it possible to study for the first time its real content. Twenty years ago only a couple of writings were available to study the teachings of the masters of Arts between 1250 and 1265. The situation is different today, and Gauthier has been able to draw up a list of ten commentaries on *De anima Vetus*, where the influence of Averroes is clear and can be assessed in its historical and doctrinal scope.[4] To those ten documents we can also add a few others which are also of significance to our subject. On one extreme, the treatise *De anima et de potenciis eius* (circa 1225), seems to be the first witness to the ingenuous use of Averroes' *Long Commentary On the Soul* by the Latins.[5] On the other extreme, the *Quaestiones*

in tertium De anima of Siger de Brabant, are undoubtedly the first witness to the radical interpretation of that text by a Master of arts (written before 1265, according to Gauthier,[6] or in 1269, according to myself and F. Van Steenberghen[7]). Between these years other commentaries and texts were published from which I will only call the attention to the four "Introductions to philosophy", published by Claude Lafleur.[8] With those documents in hand, an attempt can be made to understand why it took between twenty to thirty years for the Latin thinkers to denounce in Averroes' writings some kind of serious and dangerous doctrinal error.[9]

3. There seems to be a general consensus on what constitutes the main feature of "first averroism", although some differences around details remain among historians. Already in 1937 D. Salman pointed out that the first Latins who used Averroes attributed to the arab master the theory of the multiplicity of agent and possible intellects, and opposed this doctrine to Avicenna's separate Agent Intellect. The same idea was repeated by G. de Mattos in 1940,[10] by Miller in 1954[11] and by F. Van Steenberghen in 1966.[12] Finally, R.-A. Gauthier, on the basis of texts originated mainly in the Faculty of Arts, has singled out as the most important characteristic of the "first averroism" the doctrine of the agent intellect as a faculty of the human soul, which the Latin masters attributed to Averroes in opposition to Avicenna.[13]

We could not agree more with this picture even if it has to be adapted in each case to the particularities of the different masters to whom it applies. The question, however, is: does this characterization allow us to understand why the first Latin masters who read Averroes did not see any doctrinal error in his writings, the doctrine of "monopsychism"? We do not think so. We consider that the specific doctrine of "first averroism" is in itself a phenomenon that requires to be explained. The particular interpretation that the masters of arts gave of Averroes' doctrine between 1225 and 1250 was made possible by their own theoretical a priori, which constitutes the horizon of understanding where Averroes' text was "received". We would like to identify that context of understanding, or at least to point out in its direction.

4. By asking "how is it possible that the first readers of Averroes did not see in his *Long Commentary on De anima* the dreadful doctrine of monopsychism", we are assuming that such a doctrine is indeed in that text. Someone could say, as Gauthier has, that to see "monopsychism" in Averroes' writings is not the result of a "natural reading", and that the "second averroism", characterized by the affirmation of the unicity of the "material" intellect by some masters of arts after 1260, was nothing but the self fulfilling prophecy of some theologians who denounced that error since 1252. We have concluded elsewhere that the *Long Commentary* postulates monopsychism as a necessary consequence of the nature of the intellect, and that the "reading" proposed by the theologians is the correct result of a progressive awareness of all the implications of Averroes' philosophy of mind.[14] Having stated this assumption, we must turn now to the texts in order to see what they reveal as a valid explanation of their particular understanding of Averroes' noetics.

5. Our study will not cover the totality of the available documents originated in the Faculty of Arts between 1225 and 1260. We will concentrate instead in the analysis of the following eight:

    1. *De anima et de potenciis eius* (c. 1225).[15]
    2. *Philosophica disciplina* (c. 1245).[16]
    3. *Sententia super secundum et tertium De anima* (c. 1246-1247), mss. Oxford, Bodleian, Ms. Lat. Misc. c. 70, f. 1ra-25vb and Roma, Bibl. Naz. V.E. 828, f. 46vb, 49ra-52ra. We prepare the critical edition of this text.
    4. *Lectura in Librum de anima* (c. 1246-1247), edited by Gauthier.[17]
    5. *Arnulfi Provincialis, Diuisio scientiarum* (c. 1250-1260).[18]
    6. *Questiones super librum De anima* (c. 1250), ms. Siena, Com. L. III, 21, f. 134ra-177va27. Fr. Gauthier made available to us a first draft of this text; we express here to him our gratitude.

7. *Questiones in tres libros De anima* (c. 1260), edited by J. Vennebusch.[19]
8. *Questiones in II et III De anima* (c. 1260), mss. Erfurt, Amplon. Q. 312, f. 43ra-60rb; Oxford, Merton 272, f. 242ra-253vb (Liber III only); Siena Com. L. III, 21, f. 177va27-191ra3 (Liber III only). We prepare the critical edition of this text.

To make our references shorter, these texts will be referred to by their number in this list. They all assert that the agent intellect is part of the soul. Not all of them belong, however, equally to the "first averroism", if by that we understand lack of awareness of "monopsychism" as a consequence of Averroes' principles. Text 6 shows no longer innocence when he poses the question: "utrum intellectus sit *unus numero in omnibus hominibus secundum quod uult Commentator*, uel non" (L. III, q. 2, f. 177rb). Text 7, which, as Gauthier has proven, depends on Text 6, is also aware of Averroes' monopsychism: "ad hoc solebat respondere *Averrois* et Emphace et omnes *sustinentes unitatem intellectus possibilis*..." (L. III, q. 65, p. 280, lin. 35-55).[20] We have kept however texts 6 and 7 in our list of sources, because they are still clear witnesses of the doctrine that in our opinion better explains why the masters of arts did not grasp, at first glance, the theory of monopsychism in Averroes' writings.

A few explanations could be and have been advanced to explain that fact: the enormous difficulties and ambiguities of Averroes' *Long Commentary*, where, as R. Miller has shown so well, a great number of texts can objectively explain why the "first averroists" read in it the theory of the agent intellect as a part of the soul;[21] the lack of philosophical training of the Latins, who only after the "invasion" of Aristotle and his arab commentators started the exploration of the great complexities of natural philosophy, often having to slow down this task due to ecclesiastical opposition. All these theoretical and historical explanations are appropriate, especially when put together as a complex situation. We think, however, that still another element should be added to the picture in order to explain the

Latins' blindness in seeing monopsychism, and the long time it took them to perceive it.

6. Reflecting on the main orientation of pre-thomistic anthropologies, we realized, some time ago, that "pluralism of forms" was an insufficient characterization of them, because that doctrine was nothing but an instrument to give a better or more fashionable explanation of a deeper thesis, one which was held by every latin master before S. Thomas, namely, anthropological *dualism*.[22]

The study of the texts produced by the masters of Arts before 1260 leads to a remarkably similar conclusion. Anthropological dualism and the substantiality of the intellectual soul constitute the theoretical general background against which are to be understood all the particular psychological or anthropological theses of these masters, as well as their interpretation of the different new sources which became available to them through the movement of translations.

7. The first *thesis* of dualism is a strong affirmation of the substantiality of the soul, with its *corollary*, the existence of a particular activity that belongs exclusively to the soul. There is much textual evidence of the existence of such a thesis in all the texts produced by the masters of arts listed above. Here is a sample:

Text 1.: "Anima uero rationalis dicitur *substancia* quia potest *esse per se*, id est *separata* (p. 32, lin. 127-128).

Corollary: "alique forme sunt in intellectu possibili quas non abstrahit intellectus agens a fantasmatibus, set anima adquirit eas per rectam operationem...et alique ...per superiorem illuminationem" (p. 53-54, lin. 483-487).

Text 2.: "de anima absolute determinare in quantum est *aliquid in se*, non est naturalis philosophi, set potius methaphisici, cuius est considerare *substantias spirituales separatas*" (p. 264, lin. 139-141).

Text 3. Thesis and corollary: "sicut nauta a naui separabilis est secundum substantiam, similiter anima intellectiua separabilis est a corpore, quia non est actus alicuius partis corporis. ... anima intellectiua non dependet a corpore secundum esse <neque> in quantum ad aliquas sui operationes, ut intelligere prout est operatio intellectus agentis..." (f. 2ra). The agent intellect and its operation belong to the intellectual soul as a substance *per se*; the possible intellect is a derivative and precarious faculty, linked to the equally precarious union of the soul to the body : "Anima enim intellectiua...in quantum est forma, sic unitur corpori, et ex unione ipsius cum corpore *contrahit* intellectum possibilem... in quantum autem anima est hoc aliquid, sic est motor corpori et sic debetur sibi intellectus agens" (f. 20v). In this dualistic framework, the specific thesis of the "first averroism", acquires a very special configuration, quite different both from aristotelian and averroic noetics : "nota quod intellectus agens et possibilis *idem sunt secundum substantiam*, differunt tamen, quia *intellectus possibilis debetur anime a parte sue unionis cum corpore*, et ideo separata anima a corpore corrumpitur ... Intellectus *agens debetur anime in quantum est hoc aliquid*, et iste intellectus in quantum agens est, est perpetuus et incorruptibilis" (*ibid.*).

Text 4: "forma substantialis que est anima habet esse per se, est hoc aliquid, et est aliquid ens in actu antequam perficiat materiam... sicut nauta <est> de se hoc aliquid, similiter erit anima de se hoc aliquid" (p. 145, lin. 290-305). "Ipsa tamen separata, anima non est, set substantia spiritualis : est enim anima nomen officii, sicut angelus" (p. 146, lin. 333-334).

Corollary: "secundum quod separatus est (intellectus) non intelligit in recipiendo, quoniam intelligibilia semper sunt sibi presencia" (p. 46, lin. 336-338).

Consistent with his strong dualism, this master does not hesitate to say that "philosophically" he can accept the transmigration of the soul : "Et dico quod *secundum naturam* non est inconueniens animam separatam ab uno corpore ingredi corpus aliud dispositum ad susceptionem anime intellectiue". The only obstacle is a theological one : "Tamen secundum ordinem et dispositionem diuinam esset inconueniens : unitur enim anima intellectiua corpori ad hoc ut ibi mereatur uel demereatur" (p. 127, lin. 257-270). It is within this framework of theological considerations that the opposition to transmigration in pp. 457-458, must be understood.

Text 5: The philosophical explanation of why our intellectual soul is like a *tabula nuda* given by Arnulfus Provincialis, implies the substantiality of the soul and its operational independence, both characteristics having been hindered by the union with the body : "unio eius cum corpore qua fit distantior a suo Creatore intelligentia... corpus interpositum prohibet erectionem intellectus in Primum" (p. 301, lin. 59-63).

Text 6: "de anima contingit loqui dupliciter : aut ut est *quedam substantia in se*... aut... ut est actus et forma corporis" (f. 136vb). As a substance, its intellectual faculty is the agent intellect, which is full of intelligible forms; as perfection of the body it has a receptive intellect: "agens est pars formalis ipsius intellectiue, siue uirtus eius formalis et nobilior, scilicet qua habet scientiam in actu ab instanti sue creationis, cum sit forma separata a materia de se; et secundum istam habet anima omnem scientiam in actu sicut intelligentia. Alia est eius pars materialis, que est sicut tabula nuda et in potentia ad scientiam. Secundum primam non est (uel *ms.*) actus corporis nec unibilis ei, set separata secundum esse et substantiam, sicut homo a capa sua" (f. 135vb).

Corollary: "duplex est cognitio anime : una...per exempla sibi concreata...hec autem cognitio est intellectus agentis... et sub hac ratione non est nobis coniunctus. Unde Averroys 3° De anima ...(dicit) quod sub ratione agentis non copulatur nobis, et ideo non communicat nobis intelligentiam... Alia est cognitio anime per formas acquisitas, que lumine intellectus agentis abstrahuntur a uirtute fantastica...et sic intelligit intellectus noster prout nobis copulatus est" (f. 138vb).

Text 7: "intellectiva est substantia quedam penitus separata que advenit sensitive sicut forma materie... sensitiva et intellectiva nunquam sunt eadem essentia ... anima hominis (est)... totum aggregatum" (p. 176). "In intellectu est considerare potentiam duplicem : unam qua convenit cum substanciis separatis et differt a formis inseparabilibus, secundum quod potest separari et existere per se; aliam secundum quam tanquam per differentiam specificam differt a substanciis separatis, per quam habet quandam habilitatem ut uniatur cum corpore" (p. 164). As was the case in Text 6, it is within this dualistic conception that the doctrine of the substantial coincidence of the agent and receptive intellects must be understood : "ista duo, **agens et possibilis**, radicantur in una substantia anime, quarum una sicut forma, altera sicut materia... possibilitatem *contrahit* ex coniunctione sui cum corpore." (p. 275; cf. p. 312).

Corollary: "intelligere quod debetur homini per intellectum, aliud est ab intelligere quod debetur intellectui ut est separatus" (p. 170).

Text 8: "intellectus potest considerari prout coniunctus corpori et recipiens ab ymaginatione...et sic est "possibilis" differentia essentialis ipsius... Vel potest intellectus considerari in quantum est *substantia ens per se, non relata ad corpus* uel ad ymaginationem... et sic (non) est "possibilis" eius differentia (set "agens") (f. 179vb). "Intellectus possibilis solus (est) corruptibilis secundum operationem quam habet in homine" (f. 181vb).

Corollary: "duplex intellectus, scilicet coniunctus et separatus; intellectus coniunctus nichil sentiens <nichil> intelligit uel addiscet; intellectus autem separatus nichil sentiens *omnia intelligit siue addiscit*" (f. 187rb).

A dualism as strong as the one shown by the masters of arts demands a few complementary doctrines, as it was the case with the masters of theology. If the soul is a substance, it must have some sort of composition which will allow to distinguish it from the absolute simplicity of the First Cause. The need for such a composition is present in the texts of the masters of arts, although the kind of composition varies in some cases : cf. for example, *Text 4*, p. 214, lin. 311-317 and p. 455, lin. 259-260; *Text 6*, f. 172va; *Text 7*, p. 270, lin. 85-87 and p. 305, lin. 35-40; *Text 8*, Siena ff. 184va-vb. Another complementary doctrine is the need for *intermediaries*, capable of assuring a link between the substance soul and the substance body: cf. *Text 1*, p. 49, lin. 425; *Text 4*, p. 156, lin. 226-233 and p. 231, lin. 285-290; *Text 5*, p. 333, lin. 498-499; *Text 6*, f. 150vb and f. 156va; *Text 7*, p. 142, lin. 55-61, etc.

We would like to argue here that this highly spiritualistic anthropology is to account for the sympathetic reading of Averroes by our masters of arts. In the final analysis, Averroes' noetics is itself a strong reaction against Alexander's materialism, and this feature of being an aristotelian spiritualism fitted with the deep tendencies of Latin anthropologies. The typical averroic thesis, for instance, that the definition of the soul given in *De anima* is an analogical one, perfectly suited the needs of a dualistic anthropology willing to ensure the ontological completeness and independence of the intellectual soul without endangering it by a very strict and univocal interpretation of the notion of substantial form. That is why many of our masters adopted such a thesis:

Text 3: "anima intellectiua non est eiusdem rationis cum sensitiua et uegetatiua" (f. 3ra); "non solum debemus specificare... (diffinitionem communem) animabus, set etiam oportet specificare diffinitionem propriam cuiuslibet anime" (f. 4rb). *Text 4*: "sicut et in figuris est ratio communis figure que nulli speciali figure est propria, similiter erit communis anime diffinitio nulli differencie anime propria" (p. 197, lin. 113-115). *Text 6*: "Et si queratur utrum conueniat hec diffinitio equaliter uegetatiue, sensitiue et intellectiue, dicendum quod non, immo secundum prius et posterius, secundum Commentatorem" (f. 155 ra.). *Text 8*: "Vnde dicit Commentator quod hec diffinitio aut non uniuoce conuenit partibus anime, sicut estimauit Alexander, aut ad minus dicitur de partibus anime secundum prius et posterius. Vnde *minime* uere conuenit anime rationali" (Siena 178ra; Erfurt 51va; Oxford 242va). *Text 7*, after giving partial approval to Averroes' analogical conception, ends up proposing the univocity of the definition within a context that is so dualistic, and implies so clearly the pluralism of forms, that this opposition to Averroes does not invalidate our previous conclusions.

The first readers of Averroes approached his writings with a dualistic a priori, and they found in them what they were seeking: arguments confirming the substantial character of the intellectual soul, its ontological and operational independence. Some of these arguments were linked to Averroes' most dangerous theses, but his first readers only saw in them ways to ensure that the intellect's function as perfection of the body could not jeopardize its spirituality and immortality. Due to limitations of space, we will give only two examples of this naive use of central averroic ideas.

1) The corruptible *pathetikos nous* of *De anima* 430 a 24, identified by Averroes with the highest sensitive faculty (the cogitative), and considered by him to be the true substantial form of human beings ("Et per istum intellectum differt homo ab aliis animalibus", *Long Commentary*, III, 20, 315-316), is the key to grasping the union of the separate and unique "material" intellect and the individuals, as well as the multiplication of the acts of understanding. The same idea of a sensitive faculty being the substantial form of human beings is found in *Text 1* (p. 49, lin. 423-430) where it is called "rationalitas" and is considered as a "potencia media" between the intellect and the sensitive faculties. It is also clearly stated in *Text 6*: "intellectus non est forma reponens hominem in specie, set sensitiua particularis" (f. 161ra). There is no question, however, of relating this idea with monopsychism : for our masters it is simply an aspect of their pluralism of forms concerning the body, where the highest sensitive, but material form plays the role of "forma completiva", and of their dualism, which links the body, once completed in its order, with the intellectual soul - a personal and spiritual substance.

2) For many of the masters of arts, the agent and possible intellects are two faculties of one substance in the sense that the "possibility" is a state that affects the spiritual substance insofar as it is linked with the body ("possibilitas est anime secundum quod est in corpore" *Text 4*, p. 465, lin. 153-155), while the "agent" or actual dimension represents the true and noble nature of this substance when considered separate and in itself. The agent intellect, is full of intelligible forms, but its innate knowledge is obscured by the union with the body ("offuscatur", *Text 4*, p. 46, lin. 331-340; "obnubilatur", *Text 7*, p. 275, lin. 75; "cognitionem discretam amisit", *Text 5*, p. 302, lin. 74-75). It is only after the union with the body that the intellectual substance becomes receptive. It is in this dimension as "possible" that the intellect can be called "ours", although the highest form of knowledge exercised by the spiritual substance as "agent intellect" cannot truly be called "ours" : "intellectus autem possibilis *secundum quod huiusmodi noster est,* non autem intellectus agens" (*Text 4* p. 475, lin. 452-456). All these texts have an un-

mistakable averroistic flavour, but as of yet there is no question of monopsychism : it is still a strong anthropological dualism expressing the relationship between our "true" being as spiritual substances, and the state that affects "us" while united with our bodies. It is their anthropological dualism, that made our Latin masters accept many of Averroes' arguments without realizing that what for them was a means to justify the complex structure of man, was for Averroes a means to explain a highly more complex dualism involving men and a substance which belong to another realm.

This state of affairs is revealed by the way one master uses the sophisticated explanation of the union between the unique Material Intellect and the individual humans elaborated by Averroes in *Long Commentary* III, 20, lin. 132-144, to justify merely his own theory of the "double consideration" of the human intellect and of its way of understanding : "dicendum quod, secundum Commentatorem, intellectus potest dupliciter considerari : aut secundum comparationem ad indiuiduum singnatum, ut Sortem uel Platonem, aut prout est aliquid in se et absolute et in uniuersali. Et hoc dicit ipse de toto intellectu composito ex parte materiali et formali. Si primo modo, sic nec semper intelligit nec omnia, set quandoque et aliqua; si autem consideratur in sua uniuersalitate, prout absque omni glosa significant illa uerba Aristotilis 'et hoc intellectus separatus immixtus et impassibilis substantia actu est', sic intelligit omnia sicut iam patebit" (Siena f. 182va; Erfurt f. 53va; Oxford f. 246va; variants ommitted). Our master sees in the *Long Commentary* only what supports his spiritualistic conception of the soul and his dualistic conception of man, and he puts aside what complicates his project (as the eternity of species, stated by Averroes, *loc. cit.*, lin. 142-144). A selective reading and careful nuancing transformed Averroes' noetics in a strong support for such an anthropology. Everything, after all, was there : the intellect is a substance in itself, the body has its own substantial form, the union between the two realities could be explained in a very analogical way as the union between matter and form. Even the need for intermediaries (the images) was an idea to which the Latin masters were accustomed.

A dualistic conception of human beings explains, in my opinion, why the first readers of Averroes were so receptive to his writings and why it took them so long to discover that there was more than what met the eye in the *Long Commentary*.

Notes

1. R.-A. GAUTHIER, *S. Thomae Aq. Sentencia Libri De anima* (Opera Omnia, XLV, 1), Roma-Paris, 1984, Préface, p. 221*.

2. D. SALMAN, "Note sur la première influence d'Averroès". *Revue Néoscolastique de Philosophie*, 1937 (40), p. 203-212.

3. F. VAN STEENBERGHEN, *Aristotle in the West. The Origins of Latin Aristotelianism*. Louvain, 1955, p. 171. Cf. also *La Philosophie au XIIIe siècle*, Louvain 1966, p. 115, 279-281.

4. R.A. GAUTHIER, *op. cit.*, pp. 236*-267*.

5. R.A. GAUTHIER, "Le traité *De anima et de potenciis eius* d'un maître ès arts (vers 1225)", *Revue des sciences philosophiques et théologiques*, 1982 (66) p. 3-56. Before the publication of this text the historians accepted R. de Vaux's thesis according to which there was no sign of Averroes' influence before 1230. Cf. R. DE VAUX "La première entrée d'Averroès chez les Latins", *Revue des Sc. phil. et théol.*, 1933 (22), pp. 193-245 (cf. particularly p. 242).

6. R.A. GAUTHIER, "Notes sur Siger de Brabant 1. Siger en 1265, *Revue des Sc. phil. et théol.*, 1983 (67), p. 212.

7. B.C. BAZAN, *Siger de Brabant. Quaestiones in tertium de anima. De Anima intellectiva. De aeternitate mundi* (Philosophes médiévaux, XII). Louvain-Paris, 1972, p. 74*. F. VAN STEENBERGHEN, *Maître Siger de Brabant* (Philosophes médiévaux, XXI). Louvain-Paris, 1977, p. 52.

8. Cl. LAFLEUR, *Quatre introductions à la philosophie au XIIe siècle* (Publ. de l'Institut d'Études Médiévales, XXIII). Montréal-Paris, 1988.

9. For the history of the progressive discovery of Averroes' errors cf. F. VAN STEENBERGHEN, *La Philosophie au XIIIe siècle...* p. 281-285; R.A. GAUTHIER, *S. Thomae Aq. Sentencia...* pp. 221*-222*.

10. G. de MATTOS, "L'intellect agent personnel dans les premiers écrits d'Albert Le Grand et de Thomas d'Aquin", *Revue Néosc. de Philosophie* 1940 (43), p. 149.

11. R. MILLER, "An aspect of Averroes' influence on St. Albert", *Mediaeval Studies*, 1954 (16) p. 59 et p. 61.

12. F. VAN STEENBERGHEN, *La Philosophie au XIIIe siècle...* p. 280-281.

13. R.-A. GAUTHIER, "Le traité *De anima*..." (1982), p. 18. Cf. also, *S. Thomae Aq. Sentencia...* (1984), Préface, p. 221*.

14. B.C. BAZAN, "La noética de Averroes", *Philosophia* (Mendoza, Argentina), 1972 (38), pp. 19-49; cf. A. HYMAN, "Aristotle's Theory of the Intellect and its interpretation by Averroes", *Studies in Aristotle*, The Catholic University of America, 1981, pp. 161-191, and B.C. BAZAN, "Le commentaire de S. Thomas sur le *Traité de l'âme*. Un événement: l'édition critique de la commission Léonine", *Revue des Sc. phil. et théol.*, 1985 (69), p. 521-547 (particularly, p. 528-531).

15. Cf. *supra* n. 5.

16. Cf. *supra* n. 8.

17. R.A. GAUTHIER, Anonymi, *Magistri Artium Lectura in librum De anima* (Spicilegium Bonaventurianum XXIV) Grottaferrata 1985.

18. Cf. *supra* n. 8.

19. J. VENNEBUSCH, *Ein Anonymer Aristoteleskommentar des XIII. Jahrhunderts. Questiones in tres libros de anima.* Padernborn, 1963.

20. We cannot subscribe then to Gauthier's opinion when he states, talking about *Text 6*, that "rien n'indique que le maître soupçonne la doctrine du second averroïsme" (*S. Thomae Aq. Sentencia Libri De anima...* Préface, p. 255*). Neither can we accept without qualification the idea that *Text 7* still represents the interpretation of Averroes "qui avait régné à la faculté des arts de 1225 à 1250" (*ibid.* p. 263*).

21. R. MILLER, *op. cit.*, p. 61 sqq. For Miller, however, Averroes did in fact propose "monopsychism".

22. B.C. BAZAN, "Pluralisme de formes ou dualisme de substances" *Revue philosophique de Louvain*, 1969 (67), pp. 30-73.

The Role of Power in a Theory of Freedom

Bernard Berofsky

A philosophical theory must be sensitive to the uses to which that theory is to be put. In recent decades, the hierarchical theory of freedom has denied the importance to an agent's freedom of his ability to act otherwise. But Frankfurt, a principal exponent of that doctrine, concluded early on that there is a bona fide sense of freedom which is the power to do otherwise.[1] One is *free to do* A only when one has the power to do A. What he has stressed is the irrelevance of this sense to moral responsibility, since one should be blamed for a heinous action one could not have avoided doing so long as one still would have done it even if one could have avoided it.

Theodicy provides a context in which freedom is of interest independent of its relation to responsibility. God gave human beings freedom, so the defense goes, in the knowledge it would be abused just because beings with freedom are ipso facto more elevated than ones without it. Freedom is a value regardless of its relation to moral responsibility. Let us then distinguish freedom$_r$, freedom as a necessary condition of moral responsibility, from freedom$_d$, freedom as a dignity-conferring property. Freedom$_h$ will designate the hierarchical theorist's conception of freedom as some sort of harmony in which no facet or level of the self fails to endorse the action. (Evidently, the identification of different senses of freedom is not precluded.)

What is freedom$_d$? Although animals choose, human beings also engage in independent reflection which is often efficacious. So freedom$_d$ includes something like critical and independent self-regulation or, as we shall call it, autonomy.[2] My powers of critical reflection will help me effect my moral and nonmoral values by enabling a determination in a given situation of the applicable norms and the most appropriate action.

Autonomy also provides us with a central value, the capacity for individuality. For the recognition that a decision has been au-

23

tonomously generated enables us to see it as truly ours. Thus, a world which limits our power to realize an autonomous decision frustrates the deep desire to make *our* mark, to leave a trace, for better or worse, that reveals the sort of person we are.³ Since, therefore, a creature is worse off to the extent that he cannot effect a choice autonomously arrived at, we suppose that our dignity is enhanced insofar as we are at liberty to realize our desires. For we will then display our individual natures, moral or nonmoral, original or hackneyed. Freedom$_d$ then includes at least autonomy and power, where the latter is a function of one's internal makeup and the physical and social environment one happens to be in.

But why, asks the hierarchical theorist, should we need the power to effect choices we would *not* make? Freedom is not a means to an end such as the good life or action in accordance with value, but is rather an end itself. We are free$_h$ when we are pleased with our motivations or are inclined to act in ways we judge right or valuable.⁴ As tranquil, we have no reason to change. The power to change is important if we *lack* freedom!

Perhaps it would be clearer to set aside a fourth sense, freedom$_p$, the power to act differently from the way we do act. The hierarchical theorist's attitude towards freedom$_p$ is that it is often irrelevant to freedom$_r$ and freedom$_d$, and when it *is* relevant, it is only as a means to freedom$_r$ or freedom$_d$.

To evaluate the hierarchical theorist's view of power, we shall look at three sorts of cases: (a) the person who can but does not change for what she regards as the better; (b) the moral compulsive, powerless to do evil and content with this state of affairs; (c) the willing addict, powerless to change, but, like the moral compulsive, not disposed to do so if she could.

Frankfurt has been criticized by me and others for being unable to deal with type (a).⁵ In cases of weakness of will, an agent surely *may* act freely--and, by the way, may well be morally responsible--if he fails to live up to his own standards, not because he cannot do so, but just because it is difficult. But if his freedom is not freedom$_h$, it must be freedom$_p$. For the discovery that he is in truth an unwilling addict would change our view of his freedom.

One may convert this observation into a deeper objection to the hierarchical approach.⁶ Since an agent who succumbs to temptation may act freely in spite of internal conflict, why should one be sympathetic to the hierarchical idea that freedom *requires* the absence of conflict? Tranquility is an ideal; but it is dubious as a *requirement* on freedom. Consider, for example, a successful struggle against temptation. How uncharitable to deny the person freedom and perhaps moral credit. From the point of view of dignity a creature who happens to be subject to frailty surely is ennobled when he successfully overcomes his weakness. He makes the mark on the world he would choose to and evidently deserves moral praise. So we appear to have both $freedom_r$ and $freedom_d$ because we have $freedom_p$ and in spite of the absence of $freedom_h$.

A hierarchical theorist might argue that this agent *is* $free_h$ because his action is in accordance with the aspects of his nature he most identifies with, even if the *path* to $freedom_h$ was turbulent. Arthur, who recently kicked his nicotine habit, is now thought of as *free of* the habit, even if his struggle was arduous. This formulation does not solve the problem of the akratic, however. Albert's similar struggle failed; yet Albert may be free in all senses other than $freedom_h$.

Since Arthur overcame his addiction, we may have good reason to believe that Albert could have too. Since Albert was $free_p$, therefore, he may now be morally blameworthy for his failure. Suppose that Albert's continued employment is necessary to the survival of his large family and by continuing to smoke, he jeopardizes his job. So Albert is also $free_r$.

Albert may also be free in another sense. On behalf of the hierarchical theorist, we may note that it is contrary to the ordinary sense of the concept to say after a truly arduous and unsuccessful campaign that Albert continues to smoke freely (or of his own free will). We may see this more clearly if we think about cases in which the powerful coercive force is imposed from without. A guard who is forced to reveal secrets after the infliction of lengthy and painful torture surely does not succumb freely. Why should the situation be any different if the coercive force is just as powerful, but within the agent?

The reason this is so, as several authors have noted,[7] is that the concept of freedom that is ordinarily invoked is partly value-laden. An agent is regarded as unfree when the forces against which he is struggling are *so* powerful that it would be unreasonable to require that he expend the energy or strength to overcome them. Call this freedom$_v$. If Arthur quit smoking, it follows that he was free$_p$ to quit smoking; but if we think his addiction so severe as to render his act supererogatory, we would not say that he quit freely$_v$.

Notice how freedom$_v$ interacts with freedom$_r$. For the reasonableness of our expectations is obviously a function of conditions which bear on our responsibility. In the guard case above, although normally we would excuse a person who reveals secrets under lengthy and painful torture, we would be less inclined to absolve the guard if the facts which incline us to blame him--he was **aware of the potential dangers**, he promised not to talk, he knew that **revelation would result in enormous suffering**, he could have held out a little longer, he had reason to believe help was on the way--are the same facts which make it reasonable to increase our expectations of him. So he is free$_v$ *because* he is free$_r$. If he is blameworthy, it cannot be unreasonable to expect him to have acted otherwise. Thus, the mere dissonance between first and second levels is relatively unimportant to Albert's freedom. Given his freedom$_p$, circumstances dictate whether freedom$_r$ and freedom$_v$ are present *and they may well be*. So Albert is also free$_v$.

What about Albert's freedom$_d$? We may suppose that, like Arthur, Albert acknowledges the virtues of a nicotine-free life and is attracted to it. His reflections may be quite similar to Arthur's and he too has the power to effect whatever decisions on this matter he arrives at. But at some point he experiences weakness of will. He either fails to reach a firm decision to desist or fails to carry out what he may have thought to be a firm decision. Having said earlier that Arthur is ennobled by his display of strength, it seems only fair to say that Albert is disgraced. So even if he is blameworthy (free$_r$), he appears to lack freedom$_d$.

But we must be careful. If freedom (freedom$_p$ as a component of freedom$_d$) ennobles a human being, it does so even if he abuses it. The wise use of freedom also ennobles, but for a different reason--the person shows himself to be virtuous or prudent.

So if Albert is not free$_d$, it is not in virtue of what he does, nor in virtue of his abilities (for he can desist). Nor can we find fault in the manner of psychological processing, his critical skills, or his preference orderings. We are left either with the fact of the failure or his propensity towards such. But even if Albert is prone to weakness of will, we must recall that in this case his tendency is no stronger than Arthur's. So we are left with the failure or perhaps the irrationality implicit in displays of weakness of will. Albert knowingly acts contrary to his overall interests.

However we decide this matter, the hierarchical theorist's case is not strengthened. On the theory, Albert should be unfree; yet he is not. Even if we decide he is unfree$_d$, the decision is based not on a lack of harmony, but perhaps on the distinct fact of his irrationality. And if our only worry about Albert's freedom is grounded in his irrationality or weakness, there is *no* reason to deny that Arthur is free in spite of his similar unfreedom$_h$ *during*, not *after*, his struggle.

* * *

For Wolf, cases of type (b) are a vindication of an approach to freedom in which power plays a minor role. For a person who cannot do wrong deserves credit and must, therefore, be acting freely.[8] The only sort of power he need possess is second-order. Had there been good and sufficient reason to do otherwise, he would *then* have to have been able to do otherwise.

Since the sole reason we have to regard the 'moral compulsive' as free has to do with the moral credit to which he is entitled, Wolf must be arguing from his praiseworthiness to his freedom. The example of the blameworthy guard, call him "Abner," supports this argument to some extent. If the circumstances are such as to warrant a reprimand in spite of the duress under which the secret was extracted, Abner is free$_r$ and, therefore, both free$_v$ (it is reasonable to expect him to have retained the secret) and free$_p$ (he had the power to retain the secret). And since we would retract our judgment against Abner were we to discover that his rationality is defective, his decision-making apparatus is malfunctioning, or even that his self is disintegrating, so long as the defect explains the decision to reveal the secret, perhaps responsibility also presupposes freedom$_d$. (If Abner is free in these four senses-- he is, of course, not free$_h$--it is tempting to add a sixth since we would never *say* that Abner is revealing the secret freely. Even though the duress is not such as to permit Abner's act under the circumstances-- he is free$_v$--it is unusually great. So relative to the norms of interpersonal transactions, Abner is responding to abnormal duress and is in that sense unfree.)

The moral compulsive, unlike Abner, lacks freedom$_p$ and, therefore, freedom$_v$. He is, Wolf insists, praiseworthy (free$_r$) because he is free in the sense that his action is determined-in-a-satisfactory-way, i.e., by the right and the good.[9]

Alicia has received an admirable upbringing and has been well-trained to seek the good in all her endeavors. Moreover, suppose that Alicia's good is *the Good*. If she strays, she acts objectively wrongly. Alicia is not a saint; in fact she develops powerful impulses to abandon morality, to discard the chains that bind and inhibit total personal gratification. Although she identifies with her selfish impulses, she also sees the error of her potential ways and, in the end, does not veer from the path of duty. The struggle is a constant one, making Alicia feel that life is passing her by as she presses on to do her duty. She is further frustrated by the realization that she *is* doing what is overall the morally best thing to do--for in her special circumstances, that does *not* coincide with the most enjoyable thing to do.

So Alicia is moved by the right because it is right, but is neither content (free$_h$) nor, let us suppose, able to do otherwise (free$_p$). She satisfies neither the power nor the hierarchical conception of freedom. She is in a sense a good person; but why say she is a free person (or acts freely) just because she cannot be faulted for her actions?[10] Alicia is unable to express her deepest self, the aspect of her being she would, if she could, display to the world as the manifestation of her individuality. She is frustrated, an actress playing the role of goodie-goodie. She lacks freedom$_d$ and since she also lacks freedom$_p$, she cannot be expected to do otherwise and thus lacks freedom$_v$ as well.

Although Wolf is mistaken to regard determination by the right as sufficient for *freedom*, therefore, I will not judge whether Alicia is really morally praiseworthy for her acts. If she is, then perhaps that is what Wolf has in mind and we would have here a case of responsibility without freedom. (We would not necessarily have to retract our conclusions regarding Abner. Wolf believes that there are key asymmetries between praise and blame and would require freedom$_p$ for blame only. Since Abner can do otherwise, we can expect him to, and may then blame him for his failure.) If Alicia deserves no moral credit, on the other hand, then Wolf is wrong to regard Alicia as either free or morally responsible. The reason may be that Alicia cannot do what she deeply wants to do. In either case, Alicia is not free because she cannot do otherwise.

* * *

In vindicating the importance of power to freedom, we turn finally to (c) cases, i.e., willing addicts. We have already noted that the intuition Frankfurt relies upon concerns the moral responsibility of one who would do what he is doing even if he could do otherwise.

An implicit argument for the *freedom* of the willing addict may be formed from the suggestion that he is akin to the agent freely setting out on a course of action, unaware that a powerful force would compel him to do what he is doing were he to choose a different course. The willing addict similarly would be unable to desist were he to try, but is anyway disinclined to do so. In both cases, you have overdetermination and the irresistible nature of the addict's motivation should be discounted, just as we discount the potential intervener who actually does nothing. Given that the person may not even be aware he is addicted--since he is willing, he has never bothered to try to desist-- the case is even closer to that of the counterfactual intervener.

If we ignore the irresistibility, all we see is a willing, i.e., free agent. But if the irresistibility is to be ignored because it is causally irrelevant, what gives us the right to acknowledge the endorsement? This feature is crucial since it confers freedom on the hierarchical account, but is causally irrelevant since the willing addict is, after all, an addict.

If we are influenced by the thought that the willing addict would anyway do what he is doing were he cured of his addiction, why should we not be influenced by the thought that he would be doing what he is doing were he unwilling? If we were so influenced, we could hardly judge the addict as free; all we would see is one who can only do what he actually does--his endorsement is disregarded. The reason, I think, is that we describe the character of an agent in terms of questions like the first, not the second. We have a greater insight into the nature of a person when we know what he would do when he has control than when we know what he would do if we imagine some key component of his character to be different. The fact that he endorses his desire is a central feature of his character, whereas the strength of his desire is less so. If addictive behavior is a bad thing, the endorsement is a more serious condemnation of the person than the addiction. If a paradigm free agent is uncoerced and willing, deviation from the paradigm by introducing coercion changes *abilities*, whereas deviation by modifying endorsement changes *character*. So if our interest is *moral* evaluation, we change our judgment for the latter, not the former.

Even if this is still just about moral responsibility or freedom$_r$, it seems to me we should not blame a willing addict because of the way he *would* behave in a hypothetically different situation. He may not be as nice a chap as the unwilling addict, in which case we may wish to cast aspersions on his character. But the issue is the moral responsibility for an *action* and if we condemn the willing addict for his action, we might just as well blame him for an instance of addictive behavior he tries as hard as he can to prevent, not because he is really unwilling, but only to test his addiction. We may even suppose he is pleased to discover he is addicted; but he is surely not morally responsible for having done something he took all possible steps to prevent. The judgment of a person's character must be different from the judgment of his actions. Thus, just as Frankfurt disregards irresistibility when he appraises the actions of willing addicts, so must we discount their endorsement.[11]

Thus, a willing addict, whether or not he is aware of his addiction, may be as devoid of personal worth as the agent who is paradigmatically free and acts just like the addict; but he is not necessarily as free. He may be as unaware of his unfreedom as the victim of post-hypnotic suggestion.

These thoughts undermine the belief that willing addicts act freely; but they do not conclusively establish that they act unfreely. There remains the lingering feeling that we cannot just ignore the conception of freedom as an ideal. If a person, perhaps an addict, achieves his ideals and molds his character the way his ideals dictate, why should power be important to him at that point? If we insist that the feature which loses its interest must be designated freedom, we fail to do justice to that noble tradition emanating from the Stoics.

Earlier we noted that freedom can coexist with conflict and should point out in response to the above that the absence of conflict hardly suffices for freedom. Consider young children, lobotomized persons, the inhabitants of Brave New World, and those responding to post-hypnotic suggestion.[12] Moreover, if we remind ourselves that we are not gods, that our ideals change, we can see how valuable it is to retain a fund of underlying abilities which can be called into play when needed. The freedom to be other than what one is is also an ideal to be cherished by fallible beings like us.

Feinberg cites several values liberty (power) has even for a person (Martin Chuzzlewit) who achieves all he desires, but lacks the ability to obtain anything else.[13] He also *supposes* that Martin is a very narrow person. Martin's inability to pursue interests he lacks does not preclude his being a highly complex person with an enormous range of desires--and, therefore, related abilities--including perhaps complex desires which permit him to pursue 'new' interests. He may, for example, want to change his interests when their pursuit begins to bore him. (That he gets all he wants does not imply that he is satisfied with all he gets.) Martin need not be worried about the pointlessness of thoughts of change or of "wanting to develop new ones (interests) more harmonious with one's temperament or natural propensities."[14] If Martin is as described, since he *wants* to change, he *can*. Feinberg has stacked the cards by making Martin a simple robot. What Feinberg's Martin needs is not *liberty*, but a certain sort of *complexity*. To argue convincingly for the value of *liberty*, Feinberg must show how *it* can enhance the life of one who is blessed in other ways.

Similarly, Martin's low esteem may be due to his having been programmed and/or the simple nature he was provided by his programmer rather than the lack of liberty per se.

It may be interesting to extend this argument to the *other* virtues of liberty Feinberg cites. He notes the comfort one finds in the thought that there are no barriers to pursuits one *may someday* want to engage in, or the delight one experiences at the realization that there are more options than one will ever want to exercise, or simply the appreciation of liberty as one of the supreme values, irreducible to its extrinsic connection to other values its possession may promote in the way the beauty of the environment is a value which transcends the sum of one's actual experiences of that beauty.

If each of these interests is treated as a desire like any other, why can't we suppose again that the value of liberty presupposes its incorporation into the model of freedom as contentment? One who wants to have more options than she will ever want to exercise would not be content without those options. If one finds comfort in the thought that one can expand one's horizons without the threat of frustration, one wants this ability and would be unhappy to learn it does not obtain.

We have strayed from the issue. Liberty is a value for Martin only because it is assumed that he is sufficiently complex to respond to Feinberg's appeals on its behalf. The *value* of freedom is an issue separate from its *nature*. So even if the value of power (liberty) is grounded in its contribution to our satisfaction, the explanation may be that the *value* of freedom (constituted by power plus whatever) is the contribution it makes to our happiness.

To summarize. Without denying the bona fide character of freedom$_h$, its possession is unimportant in many interesting contexts. Moreover, in many of these contexts, the evaluation of an agent's action in terms of his responsibility and autonomy rests on his ability to do otherwise.

Notes

1. Harry Frankfurt, "Freedom of the Will and the Concept of a Person," *The Journal of Philosophy* January 1971: pp. 18-20.

2. This definition is advanced by Lawrence Haworth, *Autonomy: An Essay in Philosophical Psychology and Ethics* (New Haven: Yale UP, 1986).

3. See also Haworth, *Autonomy*, 188.

4. Gary Watson, "Free Agency," *The Journal of Philosophy* April 1975: pp. 205-220.

5. Bernard Berofsky, *Freedom from Necessity: The Metaphysical Basis of Responsibility* (New York: Routledge & Kegan Paul, 1987): pp. 43-44.

6. See also David Shatz, "Free Will and the Structure of Motivation," *Midwest Studies in Philosophy*, eds. Peter A. French, Theodore E. Uehling, Jr., and Howard K. Wettstein (Minneapolis: U. of Minnesota, 1986) 10: pp. 451-482.

7. Robert Audi, "Moral Responsibility, Freedom, and Compulsion," *American Philosophical Quarterly* 2 (1974): pp. 1-14; Patricia Greenspan, "Unfreedom and Responsibility," *Responsibility, Character, and the Emotions*, ed. Ferdinand Schoeman (Cambridge: Cambridge UP, 1987): pp. 63-80.

8. Susan Wolf, "Asymmetrical Freedom," *The Journal of Philosophy* March 1980: pp. 151-166.

9. Part of the motivation for this definition is the concern to avoid an indeterministic account of freedom. Wolf accepts the line of thought according to which such accounts implausibly reduce freedom to chance or randomness.

10. I thus agree with Benson who says, for different reasons, that Wolf's primary interest is not freedom, but moral responsibility. See Paul Benson, "Freedom and Value," *The Journal of Philosophy* September 1987: pp. 474-475.

11. See also Berofsky, *Freedom from Necessity*, pp. 39-55.

12. See also Shatz, "Free Will and the Structure of Motivation," pp. 455-457.

13. Joel Feinberg, "The Interest in Liberty on the Scales," *Rights, Justice, and the Bounds of Liberty* (Princeton: Princeton UP, 1980): pp. 30-44.

Frachantian's Debt to Heytesbury

Ivan Boh

In his exploratory article entitled "The Early Stages in the Introduction of Oxford Logic into Italy"[1] Professor William J. Courtenay presents us with a remarkable phenomenon in the history of logic. He traces the enormous influx of English logic across the Alps into northern Italy during the 14th and 15th centuries. His comprehensive work forms a suitable historical background for any further, more specialized studies, including the present one, which deals with a philosopher whose academic career overflows into the first years of the 16th century, but whose philosophical inspiration comes from the golden age of Oxford logic, the age of William Heytesbury and other *"Calculatores"*.

My effort here may be seen as an attempt to widen the picture drawn in Courtenay's article rather than to elaborate its details from within. For I explore the writings of an Italian logician, Antonius Frachantianus Vicentinus (= Frachantian), whose name is not even mentioned by Courtenay,--presumably because his intellectual activity is so much later--,but whose work clearly belongs to the tradition of those earlier Italian authors which did receive treatment in Courtenay's study.

Biographical data about Frachantian. Very little is known about the life and activities of this learned logician. First of all, it should be observed that C. Prantl, P. Boehner, I.M. Bochenski and E.J. Ashworth do not mention him at all in any of their comprehensive works, while W. and M. Kneale only mention an edition of a collection of logical works, the full title of which contains Frachantian's name and the title of his work appearing as part of the collection.[2] This edition is also the one mentioned by A. Maierù,[3] and the relevant part of the title is: "*...Questiones in Consequentias Strodi perutiles eximii artium doctoris domini Antonii Frachantiani Vicentini*", published in Venice in 1517. However, Frachantian's *Questiones in Consequentias Strodi* had in fact been published much earlier, in 1494, also in Venice, together with his *Questiones de sensu composito et diviso*. This latter work is a commentary, or better, an examination of the work *De sensu composito et diviso* by Paul of Pergula which, as Maierù reminds us, is itself based on Heytesbury's treatise by the same name.[4] No known manuscripts of either of these two treatises exist.

There are at least two other works attributed to Frachantian, the *Tractatus proportionalitatum*[5] and the *De casu et fortuna fatoque*.[6] Neither of these two works ever seems to have been printed.

Antonius Frachantianus came from a well to do Vicenza family of physicians and scholars. The date of his birth is not known, but we do know the date of his death,[7] i.e., April 26, 1506. We also know something about his education and teaching career. From the "Explicit" of his *Questiones in Consequentias Strodi ac De sensu composito et diviso* we learn that he had a dual title of "doctor of arts and medicine", and from the "Incipit" to the same work we know that he was at that time, around 1494, teaching "in gimnasio patavino", i.e., at what has become known as the University of Padua. We also know for certain that he was one of the two competitors of the famous Pietro Pompanazzi at that university in the first several years of the 16th century, and most certainly in 1504. The other "concurrens" was the bolognese scholar Tiberio Bachilieri.[8]

Aims of this study. In this paper I propose to establish (a) that several of Heytesbury's writings, including his *De sensu composito et diviso* greatly influenced the writings of Frachantian; (b) that the explicit references to and reliance upon Heytesbury's specific works by Frachantian show his thorough knowledge of Heytesbury's position on various points, and (c) that Frachantian once again re-asserted Heytesbury's endorsement of a version of the KK-thesis which seems to have been undermined by Peter of Mantua and which was explicitly rejected by Paul of Venice during the century and a half between Heytesbury's *Regule Solvendi Sophismata* (1335) and Frachantian's *Questiones*.

English logic in Italy. That Heytesbury's teaching and writings were very much present in Italy during the later 14th and 15th centuries, can be gathered from the data brought out by Courtenay in his study already mentioned. Even at the turn of the 14th century, the holdings at the Franciscan library in Padua changed remarkably. This 1396/97 inventory thus shows no works on English logic in the collection of 426 volumes. Only twelve years later, in the 1399 inventory, the collection of 1,025 volumes contained a number of important English texts, including W. Burley's *De puritate artis logice*, Ockham's *Summa logice*, Heytesbury's *Sophismata*, and Strode's *De consequentiis*. Courtenay believes that the expansion of English logic in the next decades can be accounted for primarily by the fact that so many Italian scholars in the 14th century regularly came to study at Oxford and almost all of them returned home. He observes that "at no time did they represent less than 20% of the foreign student population at Oxford, and by the end of the century they represented almost fifty percent of foreign students". Most, of course, were students of theology (including Paul of Venice) and of law, but some had undoubtedly been exposed to logic to a degree that made them discuss questions of logic in their own right.

While this spread of English logic in northern Italy was limited to interests of various philosophically and theologically oriented individuals, the introduction of it into the arts curricula -- Courtenay suggests -- "had to await the appearance of simpler school texts, such as those of Brinkley, Billingham, and Strode and the numerous texts on *insolubilia*, consequences, and obligations".[9]

Frachantian's examination of Strode's *Consequences* consists of forty questions (56 folios 4°) covering the whole spectrum of Strode's *Consequentie* and not only the most general rules of consequences as was the case, for example, with Sermoneta and Gaetanus. First, there are seven questions dealing with definitions of 'consequence'. Next, there are eight questions on the general rules of consequence. Thirdly, there is a discussion of rules that come from the second book of Aristotle's *On Interpretation* (3 questions). Next, there is an examination of special rules governing categorical propositions (14 questions); and finally there is a scrutiny of the rules for hypothetical propositions (4 questions).

Frachantian's examination of Strode's *Consequentie* as well as his discussion of the *De sensu composito et diviso* (=*DSCD*) of Paul of Pergula both take the form of *questiones*. There are eight questions coinciding with seven principal modes of composition and division, but with the eighth question added because Frachantian wanted to discuss whether there are more modes than seven of composition and division. Interestingly enough, one important reason why he wanted to discuss that question is precisely because Heytesbury had posited nine modes.

Origins of a special treatise on composite and divided senses of propositions. In a recent article,[10] N. Kretzmann argues that Heytesbury's treatise *DSCD* was either the first or among the first *separate* treatises on the subject (even though,--as he also points out--, the distinction itself goes as far back as Aristotle's discussion of the fallacies of composition and division in the *Soph. El.* 166a 22ff, and medievals never lost sight of the distinction). In Kretzmann's opinion, "Heytesbury's organization of the c/d [composition/division] distinction into number of modes is the most original and influential feature of *DSCD*; but, - he adds - surprisingly, in the treatise the number and order of modes are not easily determined..."[11] He also observes that in the early editions, *nine* modes are mentioned and characterized, but that in practice only eight modes of composition/division distinction are discussed and that in subsequent editions the ninth mode eventually disappears altogether.

Numerous first-rate logicians commented on this seminal specialized treatise introduced by Heytesbury, and Kretzmann examines the views on the question of the number of modes held by the following: Richard Billingham (fl. 1350; d. 1361 or later), two anonymous works, John Wyclif (ca. 1328-1384), Ralph Strode (d. 1387), John Venator Anglicus (d. 1428), Paul of Venice (d. 1429), Battista de Fabriano (d. 1446), Paul of Pergula (d. 1455), Alexander Sermoneta (d. 1486), Bernardino di Pietro Landucci (d. 1523) and Benedetto Vettori (d. 1561).[12] He observes (a) that these commentators never make a great deal of Heytesbury's original claim that there are nine modes; (b) that they make "reductions" of modes by combining the modes resulting from the uses of 'and' and 'or' into a single mode - as was already done in the later editions of Heytesbury, and (c) that they simply correct some mistakes without making a point that they are making a correction.

Frachantian is not commenting directly on the Heytesbury's *DSCD* but rather on the concise commentary written on Heytesbury's *DSCD* by Paul of Pergula a century later.[13] It turns out that both Pergula's text as well as Frachantian's discussion give a disproportionate amount of space to the seventh mode of composition and division. This is the mode resulting from the presence of epistemic/doxastic and volitional verbs in sentences in which they occur at various positions, i.e., at the beginning of the dictum, at the end of the dictum, or between the subject and the predicate of the dictum. Kretzmann noticed that this mode received a disproportionate attention already by Heytesbury. Although Paul of Pergula's own *DSCD* is supposed to be based on Heytesbury, Paul makes no reference, at least not by name, to him. On the other hand, there are no fewer than 49 explicit references to Heytesbury by name given in the Frachantian's *Questiones DSCD*. A majority of these references are to various *sophismata*, although there are also some references to *De incipit et desinit*, some to *DSCD*, and some to *De relativis*. There are 8 explicit references to *De scire et dubitare*, all of them, as one might expect, in the discussion of the seventh mode. Interestingly, Frachantian not only cited a given work, but also the specific part of it; e.g. in his "reply to the first principal problem". One could not fail to draw the conclusion that Frachantian knew Heytesbury's works well and it seems that he had copies of them in front of him.

Not only was Frachantian obviously acquainted with most works of Heytesbury; he was also convinced that Heytesbury's positions on various points are defensible and worthy of adoption. Frachantian is, of course, quite intent on remaining an impartial and considerate intellectual observer -- perhaps especially so because his *Questiones* were written for the young patrician Franciscus Bragadenus, the son of a prefect at the "patavian Gymnasium", to whom he wanted to give a good example of a strict intellectual inquiry. Yet, he does appear negatively predisposed toward Alexander Sermoneta and positively predisposed toward Heytesbury, and I do not recall a single case in which he would outright reject a Heytesbury's view, whereas there are many cut-short comments on Sermoneta.

Frachantian's uses of Heytesbury in the Questiones DSCD. Frachantian used the writings of the famous Englishman in various ways. First, he may simply have stated the view of Heytesbury as being opposed to a given position. The structure of this use is as follows: Some say that p; but Heytesbury rejected p. The implied conclusion is: Therefore one ought to seriously reconsider p (and p is likely to turn out to be false!). Observe the following text:

> In the tenth place, this is not valid: '*a* you know to be this something, therefore this something you know to be *a*'; and yet it is argued with the determination of a superior with respect to the predicate. For 'something' is superior to '*a*', and to 'this something'; therefore it is not legitimate to argue with those rules; but without these rules the consequence is legitimate. And so we have what was intended.[14]

Having stated this view (as well as several others before this), Frachantian pointed out that both Heytesbury in his reply to the first main point (*principale*) in the treatise *On Knowing and Doubting*, as well as the "Master" [i.e. Paul of Venice] in his *Logica Magna*, held another view on the matter, and Frachantian took this fact sufficient for a drastic revision.[15]

Secondly, Heytesbury's ideas may be used as definitive or the best-available clarification of a concept, so that all views incompatible with Heytesbury on that point are ruled out as defective or false. The following passage is instructive:

> What appellation of reason is I consider to be already known from other discussions. Appellation occurs when a term places a thing before the intellect under the proper concept of that thing, and this is indicated when a term importing an act of the mind or of will precedes, or when, appearing at the end, a verb of this sort follows [the subject]. Hence, if we say 'I know *a* to be true' the sentence signifies, and it is denoted, that this proposition is known by you, '*a* is true', which precisely and adequately signifies that *a* is true. It thus has appellation, because it denotes that *a* is true is known by you in the proposition '*a* is true' existing in your mind; and this is the thought of Heytesbury in the treatise On Knowing in the reply to the first principal question.[16]

Thirdly, Frachantian may simply have recommended Heytesbury's discussion of a certain point relevant to an issue in question, thereby implying that knowing Heytesbury was *generally* going to be helpful in understanding logical perplexities and in solving them:

> Note further that when this verb 'I know', and similar verbs, determine a complex (*complexum*), they undoubtedly effect this appellation. But when they determine a simple (*incomplexum*), we ought to consider whether that simple is a sign of a simple, such as 'man', or 'animal', or whether it is a sign of a complex, such as proposition '*a*'. If it is a sign of a simple, it has appellation, as when we say 'I know a man' (*Cognosco hominem*), 'I understand a rose' (*Intelligo rosam*), 'I apprehend a chimera' (*Apprehendo chimeram*). But if it is a sign of a complex, it does not have appellation, as in 'I know proposition *a*'; for it attempts to signify that I know the proposition which is *a* and which does not denote any replication

of the reason of *a*. Regarding this see Heytesbury in reply to the first principal argument of *On Knowing* who, in the case of the same argument which is the second argument of Paul, grants that you know *a*; do you, then, not think that every term which follows names the reason (*appellare rationem*)?[17]

Another indication that Frachantian highly valued Heytesbury is the explanation to his disciple as to why he went to such details on a point of textual analysis. He wrote: "I have dealt with this both clearly and fully, so that the first principal point of Heytesbury's *On Knowing and Doubting* should more easily be grasped."[18] Exegesis of Heytesbury's texts seems to be valued for its own sake.

As still another use of Heytesbury, we may cite a case of simply openly adopting Heytesbury's position on a given point and offering it as an adequate reply to a problem. This is a passage in which the distinction was made between "knowing a proposition" and "knowing that a proposition is true",--a distinction important both for philosophy in general and for dialectical disputation in particular:

> With respect to the eighth argument I reply in accordance with the view of Heytesbury in his second sophism that in order to know a proposition (it is not necessary) that one know how it is constructed and what a proposition is. It is enough that he who is supposed to know knows that it is so as the proposition signifies. However, in order to know that a proposition is true one must indeed understand what a proposition is and what truth is; and this is to say that when an incomplex sign is determined [70vA], the sign of a complex does not result from the former.[19]

Frachantian's Uses of Heytesbury in the Questiones in Consequentias Strodi. Moving now to Frachantian's major work, i.e., to his exhaustive commentary on Strode's *Consequentie*, we observe that there are no fewer than 65 explicit references to Heytesbury, including eleven or twelve to his *De scire et dubitare*. It is not by accident that all references to *De scire* occur in Question 14 in which Frachantian discussed the two epistemic rules of consequence, i.e. [R 13] If a consequence is sound and known by you to be sound and the antecedent is known, then its consequent is also known.[20] [$Ka(p \rightarrow q)$, $Kap/ \therefore Kaq$], and [R 14] If a consequence is sound and known by you to be sound, and its consequent is doubtful, then its antecedent is also doubtful or known to be false.[21] [$Ka(p \rightarrow q)$, $Daq/ \therefore Dap \vee KaF'p'$].

To illustrate the use of Heytesbury's *De scire et dubitare* by Frachantian, let us start with a case in which Heytesbury himself is charged with laxity of expression. There is an important theoretical distinction between *'consequence known to be sound'* and *'consequence being known'*, and Heytesbury knew it. However, the proper usage is not always employed, not even by Heytesbury. Frachantian notes:

> Although the two concepts are distinct, they are often used interchangeably. We say this because of a slip by Heytesbury in his treatise *De scire et dubitare*, in the solution to the second case (*casus*) where he says, 'I do not grant the consequence because I know it to be sound'. For at that place he takes 'known to be sound' for 'known', otherwise he would have misspoken (*male dixisset*). For by whatever reason the consequence in that case is true, by the same reason it follows that you know it to be true, since you indeed know the cause why it is true. However, he takes in that place 'consequence known to be sound' for '[consequence] known' (*consequentia scita*); and thus he says correctly that it is repugnant to the case for that consequence, i.e., '*a* is true, therefore this is true' - pointing to *a* -, to be known to be sound'.[22]

At another place at which he discussed five different senses of '*p* is doubtful', Frachantian used concrete examples given by Heytesbury, showing them to have been, as it were, paradigm cases. "In the second sense something is said to be doubtful, because I doubt it to be so as it signifies if I take it in the divided sense; and it is in this sense that this proposition, 'This is true' is doubtful in the second case (*casus*) of Heytesbury's *De scire et dubitare*, pointing to *a*, which says that one or the other of a pair of doubtful contradictories [(i.e. Dap and $Da \sim p$)] is true."[23]

Occasionally Frachantian found Heytesbury's statements, taken precisely as such, equally decisive in determination of his inquiry. "But what moves me most is an argument based on Heytesbury's statement in his fifth case. For he himself says: This inference is not sound, 'That proposition is doubtful, therefore it signifies as I doubt it to be'; rather, this one is sound: 'That proposition is doubtful to me, therefore it signifies as I doubt it to be or I doubt it to be as it signifies'."[24]

The KK-Thesis. It would be very easy to go on with concrete illustrations of Heytesbury's overwhelming presence in Frachantian's thought. Let me conclude with the final quotation, which I offer in proof of my contention - for which I argued in another paper elsewhere[25] - that Frachantian, even while discussing the epistemic rules of consequence, reasserted a version of KK-thesis, i.e., the proposition that if *a* known that *p*, then *a* knows that he knows that *p*. I believe this thesis is present in Heytesbury's *De scire et dubitare* as a provable (rather than self-evident) proposition and that Gaetanus of Thiene upheld it likewise, but that in the meanwhile Peter of Mantua seriously jeopardized it, and Paul of Venice outright rejected it. Although Frachantian's acceptance of the thesis comes out accidentally, as it were, in a passage in which he is rejecting a misleadingly similar thesis involving a *collective* use of the subject term, the clarity of his understanding of the issue comes out perfectly. He wrote: "I reject this inference, 'These persons know the seven liberal arts, therefore these persons know that they know the seven liberal arts'. For even though in singular number it is so that Whoever knows, he knows that he knows, in plural it is not so that If these men know, they know that they know."[26]

Frachantian, therefore probably relying upon Heytesbury's own sources but possibly also being influenced by his esteemed *concivis* Gaetanus, after a century and a half returned to the original insight of his English intellectual predecessor.

Conclusion. There is no doubt that Frachantian owed a big intellectual debt to the famous Calculator, a debt which he was eager to acknowledge in so many paragraphs and on so many different points.

Notes

1. In *English Logic in Italy in the 14th and the 15th Centuries*. Ed. Alfonso Maierù. (Napoli: Bibliopolis, 1982), 13-32.

2. Cf. W. and M. Kneale, *The Development of Logic* (Cambridge: University Press, 1962), p. 751.

3. A. Maierù, *Terminologia Logica della Tarda Scholastica* (Roma: Ateneo 1972), p. 31, n. 90.

4. Frachantian, Questiones *in Consequentiis Strodi ac de sensu composito et diviso* (Venetiis 1494, die X. mensis Ianuarii).

5. A. Maierù, *Op. cit.*, p. 35.

6. Cf. *Codices Vaticani Latini* (No. 10728).

7. Cf. B. Nardi, *Studi su Pietro Pompanazzi* (Firenze: Felice le Monnier, 1965), p. 291.

8. Cf. B. Nardi, *op. cit.*, p. 55.

9. Cf. A. Maierù, *English Logic*, p. 16.

10. "*Sensu Compositus, Sensus Divisus*, and Propositional Attitudes", *Medioevo* 7 (1981), 195-229.

11. N. Kretzmann, *op. cit.*, p. 200, n. 23.

12. Cf. N. Kretzmann, *op. cit.*, p. 210.

13. Cf. Paul of Pergula, *Logica* and *Tractatus de sensu composito et diviso*, ed. M.A. Brown (St. Bonaventure: The Franciscan Institute, 1961).

14. Frachantian, *Questiones* 1494, fol 68rB.

15. Frachantian, *Questiones* 1494, 68rB.

16. Frachantian, *Questiones* 1494, 68vA.

17. Frachantian, *Questiones* 1494, 68vA.

18. Frachantian, *Questiones* 1494, 70rB.

19. Frachantian, *Questiones* 1494, 70vA/B.

20. "Si aliqua consequentia est bona et scita a te esse bona et antecedent est scitum, ergo et consequens est scitum". *Questiones* 1494, 23rB.

21. "Si aliqua consequentia est bona scita a te esse bona, et consequens est dubium, ergo antecedens est dubium vel scitum esse falsum". *Questiones* 1494, 23rB.

22. Frachantian, *Questiones* 1494, 24rB.

23. Frachantian, *Questiones* 1494, 26vA.

24. Frachantian, *Questiones* 1494, 26rB.

25. Cf. I. Boh, "Epistemic and Alethic Iteration in Later Medieval Logic", *Philosophia Naturalis* 21 (1984), 492-506.

26. Frachantian, *Questiones* 1494, 25rB.

Acknowledgments. I hereby gratefully acknowledge the I.R.E.X. and the Fulbright (USEd) research grants to the German Democratic Republic and to Poland. My special thanks are due to Günter Schenk, dr.phil.sc., of Halle-Wittenberg University for his generous help in my research efforts.

Maimonides on Divine Knowledge

Alexander Broadie

In this paper I shall focus on a problem in Maimonides' account of divine knowledge. I shall argue that in Part III of *The Guide of the Perplexed* he adopts a position which does not conform with his basic doctrine presented in Part I.

For Maimonides, affirmative theology, that is, the doctrine that a given term has precisely the same signification when it is truly predicated of human beings and of God, implies anthropomorphism and therefore also idolatry. An alternative to affirmative theology must, therefore, be found. At least two alternatives remain. First is the claim that a term truly predicated of human beings and of God is amphibolous. Maimonides writes: "When two terms are used amphibolously they are predicated of two things between which there is a likeness in respect of some notion, which notion is an accident attached to both of them and not a constituent element of the essence of each one of them" [*Guide* I 56, p. 131].[1] In that case a term cannot be used amphibolously of human beings and God for if it were it would follow that some part of God would have merely accidental being, and this is absolutely to be ruled out, for, first, God's being is through-and-through necessary, and secondly, He does not have parts; internal complexity is a characteristic of created things only.

In the light of this consideration, Maimonides accepts that a term predicated truly of human beings and of God is used equivocally; that is, its signification on the one occurrence is wholly different from its signification on the other. What its signification is when predicated of God is something we cannot say, for we cannot think it; we can only say that the signification is wholly unlike its signification when applied to created things. In response to his self-directed question as to why certain terms, and not others, are appropriately used of God, he replies that there is a pastoral reason for this; if terms signifying what from our point of view are perfections are denied of God, then people will tend to lose their faith in Him. Their faith must be defended by whatever means are necessary.

Among those perfections is that of knowledge. Maimonides writes: '...it behooves those who believe that there are essential attributes that may be predicated of the Creator - namely, that He is existent, living, possessing power, knowing, and willing - to understand that these notions are not ascribed to Him and to us in the same sense...the terms "knowledge", "power", "will", and "life" as applied to Him, may He be exalted, and to all those possessing knowledge, power, will, and life, are purely equivocal, so that their meaning when they are predicated of Him is in no way like their meaning in other applications" [*Guide* I 56, p.130-1].

For the present, I wish to stress the uncompromising nature of Maimonides' position. Part I of the *Guide* contains as strong a statement as is to be found anywhere of the utter incompetence of the human intellect to secure cognitive grasp of God; the most that we can hope for is a clear insight into our incompetence. All we can know is that our knowledge is only negative; hence we cannot know what God's knowledge is like. Since His knowledge is identical with His essence, insight into the nature of God's knowledge is the same thing as insight into His essence. Such insight is absolutely debarred to us. We can say that God's essence is to exist, but that does not imply an ability to conceive what such existence is like.

As testimony to the uncompromising nature of Maimonides' position on the cognitive distance between Creator and creatures, I quote a brief passage on divine knowledge: "...if you say that, with one knowledge and with this changeless knowledge that has no multiplicity in it, He knows the multiple and the changeable things that are constantly being renewed without any renewal of knowledge in Him, and that His knowledge of a thing before it has come into being and after it has acquired reality as existent and after it has ceased to exist is one and the same knowledge in which there is no change, you have clearly stated that He knows with a knowledge that is not like our knowledge" [*Guide* I 60, p.144]. Elsewhere Maimonides tells us that "our intellect is unable to represent His knowledge" [*Eight Chapters*, ch.8],[2] and this phrase, though not repeated in the *Guide*, well describes the position adopted in Part I of the *Guide*. Hence our saying that God knows changeable things without any renewal of knowledge in Him, does not constitute a representation of His knowledge. Evidently, then, Maimonides believes that there are things that we find ourselves forced to say about God though we do not form a veridical concept corresponding to our words. Neither, as we have seen, is there, in Maimonides' view, any point in trying. Our creaturely nature debars us from such a concept.

That this metaphysical barrier is entirely impenetrable is what might be termed the "official doctrine" of Part I. But Maimonides evidently has difficulty maintaining it as he gradually unfolds the argument of the *Guide*. Indeed, as we shall see, he has some very helpful things to say about the nature of divine knowledge, which appear to be intended to help us represent it to ourselves, at least to some small extent. What he has to say is a good deal more helpful than anything we should have had the right to expect given the official doctrine. I shall begin my examination of those "helpful things" by rehearsing the chief reason that Maimonides had for investigating the concept of divine knowledge.

As is well known, a central topic in Part III of the *Guide* is divine providence. Some philosophers denied that there was such a thing, and on that basis drew large conclusions regarding the extent of God's knowledge. The starting point is the apparent fact that some who are unjust prosper and some who do not prosper are just. How is this possible? If God, knowing of human affairs, cannot order them better than that then He lacks power and if He can but does not care to then He is evil. The conclusion of "some philosophers" is that since God is neither evil nor lacking in power, the only remaining explanation for the fact that things are ordered as they are and not better is that God does not have knowledge of human affairs. Of course, this conclusion is intolerable to Maimonides: "See and marvel how they plunged into something worse than that which they tried to avoid...in trying to avoid imputing negligence to God, they decided that He is ignorant and that everything that is in this lowly world is hidden from Him, and He does not apprehend it" [*Guide* III 16, p.462]. What, however, of the fact that human affairs are ill ordered in the sense that some who are unjust prosper and some who do not prosper are just? Maimonides, however, denies the alleged fact. The appearance of ill-ordering is a product of a certain arrogance, by which a narrowly human perspective is treated as if sufficient to ground a universal truth. That some unjust people prosper at the start and that some just people do not, is no basis for forming a universal truth. For that, we require another perspective: "things should be considered in their final outcome and not in their beginnings" (*Guide* III 19, p.477].

If the argument from the apparent discrepancy between behaviour and recompense, falsely assumes that there is a discrepancy, two other arguments for the claim that God lacks knowledge of human affairs are not so easily dealt with. The first concerns a doctrine, due to Aristotle, according to which the faculties of intellect and sense perception are distinguished in part by the character of their proper objects. The proper object of the intellect is universal and that of the senses is individual or singular. An act of sense perception involves the exercise of a sensory receptor, and such a receptor is corporeal. God, who is pure spirit, and therefore in no respect corporeal, lacks sensory receptors. God, therefore, lacks the only means by which individuals can be known. We are individual, and therefore God can have no knowledge of our affairs. Thus runs the argument.

Maimonides is unimpressed, but in responding to it he makes a move which must puzzle us, given his teaching in Part I of the *Guide*, concerning the unknowability of God, and concerning the need, in consequence, to attach a purely negative signification to terms used of God. The ground principle employed in dealing with the argument just presented is this: "In the case of every one who makes any instrument, it is clear that unless he had a conception of the work to be done with that instrument, he would be unable to make it" [*Guide* III 19, p.478]. This is a plausible principle, and I do not wish here to raise a doubt about its validity in respect of human artificers. What, for our immediate purposes, is important about this principle is that Maimonides presents it as one which is universal in that it is true not only of human beings but also of God. Evidently Maimonides thinks that in enunciating that principle, he is saying something truly enlightening about God, and something that certain philosophers ought to have taken into account. He quotes the Psalmist: "He that planted the ear, shall He not hear? He that formed the eye, shall He not see?" [*Ps.* 94, v.9]. With this verse in mind, Maimonides argues as follows: "When, therefore, some of the philosophers thought that God does not apprehend these individual things because they are apprehended by the senses, whereas He, may He be exalted, does not apprehend with a sense but through an intellectual apprehension, he [sc. King David] argued against them by starting from the existence of the senses, saying: If the meaning of the apprehension of the sense of sight is hidden from Him and He does not know it, how did He bring into existence this instrument, which is disposed for visual apprehension?" [*Guide* III 19, p.478]. It is difficult to see how Maimonides is here remaining faithful to his negative theology. Admittedly he is not saying that without visual experiences similar to ours God could not have made the human eye, but he is saying that, as with human artificers, He must have had a conception of the work to be done with the eye. It is hard to see the point of that assertion; that is to say, hard to see what role the assertion could be playing in the argument, except as expressing a real similarity between God on the one hand and human artificers on the other in respect of the relation between conception and manufacture. It could be replied, of course, that Maimonides' claim about God's conception of what He makes has to be understood purely negatively (and therefore not really understood at all). If so, however, why did Maimonides think it helpful to make the claim? Certainly the mode of expression could hardly, in that case, have been more misleading.

I shall now turn to the third argument that Maimonides deals with which purports to support the claim that God cannot have knowledge of human affairs. As we shall see, it is, again, hard to understand the response of Maimonides except on the assumption that he is not remaining faithful to the doctrine of the *Guide*, Part I, concerning the signification of terms when they are predicated of God. The argument in question is that when a human act occurs a change takes place; hence as a person observes a human act the observer's cognitive faculty also undergoes change. But God is immutable, and hence cannot know any human act. There is apparently a dilemma here; immutability and knowledge of human acts seem to be mutually incompatible attributes. Maimonides, however, finds a way to reconcile them. He writes as follows: "...we say that He has known all the things that are produced anew before they have come about and that He has known them perpetually. For this reason no new knowledge comes to Him in any way. For seeing that a certain man is now nonexistent, but will exist at a certain time, will go on existing for such and such a duration, and will then again become nonexistent, there will be for Him no additional knowledge when that individual comes into existence as He had known beforehand. Nothing was produced thereby that was unknown to Him" [*Guide* III 20, p.481].

God's knowledge, thus described, seems an impossibility, and perhaps, on that account, the description should be rejected as false. There is a danger here, however, of seeking to anthropomorphize God's knowledge. That a certain kind of knowledge is impossible for beings living under the conditions of temporality, is no reason at all for saying that such knowledge is impossible for God. In this matter Maimonides appears to be following closely his strictures in Part I of the *Guide*. In the spirit of those earlier chapters, he writes: "For this knowledge [sc. God's] is not of the same species as ours so that we can draw an analogy with regard to it, but a totally different thing" [*Guide* III 20, p.482]. He does not, however, rest on that position; neither, as we shall now see, does he maintain it in practice.

The reason for saying that God's knowledge is "totally different" from ours is clear enough - our knowledge is essentially dependent knowledge. Our knowledge must have an object; what is known must have being if our knowledge of it is to have being. We cannot know that the object exists or what it is unless it does already have being. If instead we consider truth as the proper object of knowledge, then it should be said that our knowledge of the truth is dependent for its existence upon that truth. The knowledge is not independent of the truth, and neither is the truth dependent upon the knowledge, for we do not make something true by our cognitive act of knowing it to be true. Herein lies the "total difference" between divine knowledge and human. God, who created the world by an act of absolutely free will, must be an absolutely independent being. And the doctrine of the absolute independence of God, conjoined with the doctrine of His oneness, implies that His knowledge is likewise independent. God does not have to wait for something to exist, or to be true, for Him to know that it exists or that it is true. If He did have to wait it would follow that something other than God could cause a change in God, but neither can there be change in God, nor can God be other than absolute first cause - that is, He cannot be first cause in respect of something, but not in respect of everything. We must, therefore, say that in order to know any object or any truth God does not require to look beyond Himself.

That this is a difficult doctrine, is hardly a matter for dispute, and we should certainly expect Maimonides, in the light of his teaching in Part I of the *Guide*, to say that the doctrine is beyond our cognitive grasp, and that, in recognising that God's knowledge is utterly unlike ours, we have gone as far as we can - thus our knowledge of the nature of divine knowledge is itself to be understood negatively as recognition of our ignorance. Yet, having declared that "between our knowledge and His there is nothing in common, as there is nothing in common between our essence and His...there is a community only in the terms" [*Guide* III 20, p.482], he proceeds to point out a similarity between human knowledge and divine. The passage is of crucial importance for an appreciation of Maimonides' teaching on the names of God: "A great disparity subsists between the knowledge an artificer has of the thing he has made and the knowledge someone else has of the artifact in question. For if the artifact was made in a way conforming to the knowledge of its artificer, the artificer only made it through following his own knowledge. With regard to the other one who looks at that artifact, comprehending it with his knowledge, his knowledge follows the artifact...Such is the case with regard to that which exists taken as a whole in relation to our knowledge and His knowledge, may He be exalted. For we know all that we know only through looking at the beings...On the contrary, the things in question follow upon His knowledge, which preceded and established them as they are" [*Guide* III 21, pp.484-5]. An architect can, by consulting his idea of the house, know what is in the house. He does not need to go beyond his own thought in order to secure the knowledge. God, the architect of the universe, is likewise placed in relation to His artifact. Of course, the similarity is not perfect. One obvious difference is that a human architect cannot build a house merely by thinking it into existence - builders are required who will follow the blueprint, and they may not be entirely successful in their attempt to embody in bricks and mortar the architect's idea. Hence, the architect may be inaccurate if he relies only on his idea when he reports the details of the house. Nevertheless, the peculiar nature of the architect's knowledge in relation to the artifact which embodies that knowledge, does provide us with some means of grasping the concept of the independence of God's knowledge. My chief point here is that Maimonides' teaching on the peculiar nature of the artificer's knowledge is presented as having universal application, in that it is being presented as true both of human beings and also of God. What is the role of that teaching in the context of the argument of the *Guide* if it is not that of illuminating the nature of God's knowledge by indicating a similarity, however imperfect, between human knowledge and divine? In that case, however, it is hard to see how the very toughly worded teaching, in Part I of the *Guide*, on the negative interpretation of divine names, is being adhered to in the discussion, in Part III, on divine knowledge.

Given that contradictions are used in the *Guide* to conceal from the multitude truths which may harm their faith [see *Guide*, Introd., pp. 15-20], it is likely that what I have been discussing in this paper is one such intentional contradiction. If it is, then there is an interesting question concerning which side of the contradiction represents Maimonides' own position. That is, however, the subject of another paper.

Notes

1. All quotations from the *Guide* are taken from Moses Maimonides, *The Guide of the Perplexed*, trans. Shlomo Pines, with Introductory Essay by Leo Strauss (Chicago: U. of Chicago Press, 1963). In this paper each reference to the *Guide* states Part, chapter, and page.

2. Raymond L. Weiss and Charles E. Butterworth, *Ethical Writings of Maimonides* (New York: New York U. Press, 1975), 95.

Maimonides and German Idealism

Hubert Dethier

1. History as the actualization of divine purpose. - 2. The Platonizing Contention. - 3. Theoretical and Practical Reason. - 4. Characteristics Peculiar to Prophets. - 5. Love of God Achieved only through Knowledge of Divine Activity in the World. - 6. Characteristics Belonging Both to the Actions of God-Nature and to the Actions of Superior Statesmen. - 7. The Detour.

Some experiences described in Hegel's *Phenomenology of Mind* and also in the *Philosophy of Right* are also encountered in Maimonides' *Guide of the Perplexed*, though not in the same elaborate and complex form as in the *Phenomenology*. It is evident, however, according to Hegel's dialectic method, "that the lower level of development" can only be explained and understood by a considerably more sophisticated and elaborate level of development, which is the dialectical actualization of what was merely latent and implicit in the morality and stage of consciousness of a more ancient world: so the philosophical experience of Kant and Hegel can help us to better explain some latencies and possibilities contained in Maimonides' philosophical description of freedom and necessity. Hegel, for instance, presupposes that the whole of human history is a process through which mankind has been making a spiritual and moral progress; it is what the human mind has done in the course of its advance to self-knowledge; in other words, history has a plot, and the philosophers' task is to discern it. Many eminent historians have been unable to discern any plot and have contented themselves with recording what has happened; others have found the key to history in the operation of natural laws of various kinds. Hegel's attitude rests on the faith that history is the actualization of divine purpose, and that by the beginning of the 19th century man had advanced far enough to discern and observe what that purpose is. The purpose in question is the gradual realization of human freedom.

When reading Maimonides' *Guide of the Perplexed*, the historian of German Idealism will have his attention immediately aroused by a set of internally linked statements, choices and issues which were to reach a higher degree of complexity and development, and to find their actualization in the philosophies of both Kant and Marx. It will suffice here to point to the following item: the fact that a considerably portion of Maimonides' activity was devoted to legal doctrine is by no means irrelevant in a consideration of his philosophical attitude (1). In a sense this was a practical activity which may be assimilated to that of a statesman; it was accordingly consistent with Maimonides' Platonizing contention, later adopted by Marxism, that certain superior individuals are able to combine a mode of existence devoted to contemplation and intellection with a life of action. (Cf. Lenin's claim that "Bolsheviks have realized the dream of Plato: as philosophers they have seized the reins of political action".)

The difference between Theoretical and Practical Reason is a striking feature of Aristotelian tradition. For Kant, the failure of Reason to implement its claims in its theoretical capacity (2) does not entail that those claims be entirely abandoned. Practical (moral) reason may take over where theoretical reason fails. This does not mean (as Kant carefully explains in book II of the *Critique of Practical Reason*) that morality gives us insight into the supra-sensible. From a cognitive point of view the ideas remain as empty as before; it is only in moral contexts that they can be said to have significance, and even there it cannot be said that the ideas are made understandable in any very palpable sense. Fortunately, however, this is not only all that we can attain, but also all that we need. If Man enjoyed insight into the true nature of things, it might well destroy the essential value of moral actions, for then "God and eternity in their awful majesty would stand unceasingly before our eyes" and "most actions conforming to the (moral) law would be done out of fear, few would be done out of hope, none out of duty" (3).

Maimonides is evidently struggling with the same kind of problems. That he rejected the doctrine of the eternity of the world partly because it would have destroyed the foundations of religious law may appear to affirm the claim of religious belief to have a decisive voice in theoretical questions that are of paramount concern to it! This may appear as if the intellect is unable to reach a fully demonstrable conclusion with regard to most points. Clearly such a claim may have far-reaching implications. It could be argued that this position leads to the recognition of suprarational theoretical truths or, alternatively, to the assertion of validity of conclusions in the sphere of theory adopted only on the basis of practical reason (4). However, Maimonides himself does not at all countenance such a demotion and degradation of theoretical reason. In the *Guide* (Part I, Ch. 2) he explains the superiority of theoretical reason, which is concerned with the difference between truth and falsehood, over practical reason, which deals with the distinction between good and evil. It must be remembered here, that Kant made the opposite choice! Maimonides' allegorical interpretation of Adam's fall entails the conclusion that practical reason - not entirely in contradiction with Kant this time - has the comparatively lowly function of curbing the appetite to which man is prone when he is not given over to theoretical contemplation.

As for prophecy and divine revelation, they cannot be regarded as sources of supra-intellectual knowledge conceived as independent of, and superior to, the system of sciences produced by theoretical reason. This emerges clearly from Maimonides' description of the characteristics peculiar to prophets. According to him, prophets must show both an outstanding intellectual capacity and an outstanding imaginative capacity. Given these two prerequisites, in addition to suitable conduct, prophecy is a natural phenomenon; the gift of prophecy can be withheld from a person having the required qualifications only by means of a miracle! The intellectual capacity of prophets is similar, at least in kind, to that of the philosophers; it enables them to receive what Maimonides terms "divine overflow", an influx proceeding from the Active Intellect, which, according to the interpretation of the Aristotelian doctrine adopted by Maimonides, achieves the actualization of man's potential intellect. The Active Intellect is the last of the ten incorporeal Intellects; its special sphere of action is the sublunar world (5).

It must be remembered here that imagination is held to be inferior to intellect by Maimonides, who was on this point an orthodox Aristotelian. Imagination enables the prophet to see veridical dreams and visions, for the "divine overflow" spills over from the intellectual to the imaginative sphere. It certainly does not give access to a supra-intellectual truth. In fact, the superiority of Moses over all other prophets is, according to Maimonides' interpretation, partly the result of the circumstances that in his prophecy he did not resort to imagination (6).

Religious revelation does not procure any knowledge of the highest truth that cannot be achieved by the human intellect; it does, however, have an educational role - as well as a political one. Some specific problems in this field, in relation with the problem of the harmony between philosophy and religion, will be dealt with later on. We must now concentrate on the problem of historicity, historical necessity, and pre-Hegelianism, as we can call it, in Maimonides' moral and political philosophy.

We refer to what has been said about the difference between theoretical and practical reason, to the combination of theoretical life and a life of action, and to Maimonides' theory of negative theology, which will not be extensively developed in this paper. According to the point of view of negative theology (namely, that the only positive knowledge of which Man is capable deals not with God-in-Himself but with His governance of Nature, i.e. with the order obtaining in the cosmos and determining the events occurring in it), love of God can be achieved only through knowledge of divine activity in the world, i.e. the only knowledge of God available to finite Man (7). This supreme goal can be reached through a study of natural science and of metaphysics, which suggests that the highest perfection can be attained only by a man who leads a theoretical life - the man whose superiority was proclaimed by Aristotle. Maimonides, however, is at pains to show that the theoretical life can be combined with a life of action as evinced by the examples of the patriarchs, of Moses and of a Pythagorean philosopher like Plato!

The discussion takes a definite Hegelian turn at the point at which Maimonides states that a life of action may constitute an imitation of God. Some stratagems and characteristics of Hegel's cunning of reason appear fresh before our minds, i.e. the prophetic legislations and the statesman's endeavour to imitate the operations of nature or God (8). Maimonides emphasizes two characteristics that belong both to the actions of God-nature and to the actions of superior statesmen. First, however beneficial or destructive - or, in ordinary human parlance, however merciful or vengeful - the actions in question appear to be, neither God nor the prophetic statesman is actuated by passions; second, the activity of nature (or God) tends to preserve the cosmic order, which includes the perpetuity of the living species, but has no consideration for the individual. In the same way, the prophetic lawgivers and statesmen, who in founding or governing a polity should imitate this activity, should first and foremost have in mind the commonweal (or commonwealth), i.e. the welfare of the majority, and must not be deterred from following a politically correct course of action by the fact that it may hurt individuals!

The imitation of the works of God (or of nature) by the prophets means (9) that the prophets are to imitate in leadership the indirect and complicated way through which nature obtains its desired results as seen, for instance, in the extremely intricate mechanism of living organisms. Maimonides calls this indirect method a "gracious ruse" of God and his wisdom (10); he may have taken over the expression from Alexander of Aphrodisias' work *Principle of the All* (extant only in Arabic translation). It is reminiscent, not only on the verbal plane, of Hegel's cunning of reason. According to the *Guide*, Moses used the indirect method in making the sons of Israel wander for forty years in the desert instead of leading them straight to the land of Canaan, as he wanted the people to shed its slavish habits and acquire in the hard school of the desert the warlike virtues necessary for conquest. He also used it in adapting the commandments to the historical and geographical circumstances.

We will now examine, in greater detail, some implicit characteristics of the cunning of reason in their actualized Hegelian form, in order to gain a better understanding of what Maimonides - and Alexander of Aphrodisias before him - may possibly have had in mind. It must now be clear that charming cunning of reason is tightly connected to Maimonides' impressive approach of the "double truth", the ambiguity, the detour and the aberration. Thought usually takes a detour. Maimonides often emphasizes, much like Hegel will do later, the detour as being the cunning of reason, through which a person has the impression of acting toward a distinct purpose, whereas in reality he brings about something of a completely different nature.

The detour is, along with negation or irony, the second characteristic of dialectics. When one focuses all his attention directly on a target, one is not being sincere, but impudent and brazen, and very likely to miss his target. One will hunt it and, thereby, chase it away. If one aims for happiness too directly, one can never become happy (11). The detour implies that something is expressed indirectly by its opposite. It does not involve insincerity, but a train of thought that attains its aim and introduces its object indirectly into knowledge. By aiming for point A point B is reached. The detour is ethically so fundamentally important - as different chapters of the third book of the *Guide* amply show - that not only the true nature of man comes to the fore here, but his entire culture as well. Let's take a simple and obvious phenomenon: the act of sexual intercourse. The sexual act of mammals is practically identical to that of human beings. The animals, however, tend to accomplish this act more directly, as opposed to the human approach, in which a detour allows for sympathy, friendship, love, etc... The same detour, which in fact consists of the skill and guile of the hunter, also gives birth to the plastic arts, to poetry and music. Food, clothing, housing and resting-place originate in the same way. The detour spiritualizes what is material, and gives man the opportunity of transfigurating his physical life into an existence. His existence consists of the ability of reaching a goal via a detour, which is the aim of the ethical existence itself. The act is not performed suddenly or spontaneously, although this may appear to be the case, but it is the result of many different acts, which have been accomplished through the long detour of reflection. If one attempts to satisfy his needs directly, not only does one act brutally and revoltingly, but technically inefficient as well. The detour enhances patience, the ability to wait, the skill of preparation. Thus a pattern is formed, not a designated purpose or motivation, but an intricate element of the detour. In this context, Nietzsche referred to "the long patience"; he, too, considers the detour to be an attempt to escape from entanglement (which is the fundamental aim of philosophy). It never involves violence or impatient pushing and shoving, since this would terminate all thinking and create panic. It is obviously also closely linked to the "wanting" or "deciding". At a very specific moment in time, one decides to do something very specific. If one explains this in public, one is partially going back on his decision. One should not talk about it. One knows that one will have to face a large amount of detours, failures and wrong tracks in order to execute one's decision. If one keeps silent, one cultivates the long patience and thus one thinks and exists, and one acquires the courage of taking detours. Human existence, after all, is a detour toward death. The longer the detour, the more intense and profound the existence. A direct approach shortens the existence and plunges the individual into the abyss. The detour is life itself, which allows us to claim that a life of thinking is in no way equal to death or alienation of life. The detour is so fundamental to philosophy and ethics that they never attempt to approach a subject frontally. "Frontally" signifies: the exact definition, the generally accepted argumentation. The detour allows thought to take side-roads, to approach the problem from different unexpected angles (12). The solution will then, automatically, be revealed to the patient ones through the web of approximative detours. Thought, therefore, never resembles a frenetic effort, but has the appearance of a process of wandering along detours, in search of a solution, a solution that will, in turn, pose new problems. Anyway, thought never achieves a direct solution to a problem. The indirect approach includes the coincidence, the unexpected, the uncalculated and the unmeasured. The method of thinking runs along the pattern of a detour, a development of detours and finally of cunning, a cunning that outwits itself. Although thought consists of odysseic cunning, it is more than that. Cunning involves thought, but this thinking has its limits. Salomon's judgement was a type of cunning that involved a very acute argumentation. It stresses, once more, the ethical character of the detour. One follows the detour by including a datum into a larger context. Sensuality is fitted into a context, and man goes back to it via a detour. Thus it becomes acceptable and ethically good. Sexuality, which we already mentioned in this context, and the entire physical existence of man follows this pattern. Man achieves the physical realization of his body through a detour.

As for truth itself, the problem of detour and cunning is consistently present. When one has to choose between two possible roads, one cunningly avoids taking the road of truth, or the accordance between thought and object. According to Maimonides, one prefers the wrong track, the hard way, where this accordance is nowhere to be found. By forsaking the truth, one turns one's back to indolence and to lust, both of which are based on the accordance between thought and object, on usefulness. One does not live in accordance with others, who all live truthfully. The detour one takes is always a false track, but through one's cunning, one is taken toward the truth. In the state of accordance, everything is apparent, and therefore false. This does not mean that it is lost, since, one who is lost, keeps looking for the right track, whereas the false individual has already found it. He knows no cunning and no detour, everything is reduced to identity. He can make this identity appear to be very complicated. Maimonides' dialectics absorb the unreasonable, the dark, and incorporate it into the entity of reason. They display following characteristics:

- they are the philosophy of the detour;
- the irony consists of the discovery of negation and the negation of negation (cf. his negative theology);
- the reasoning not only involves the viewpoint of the spectator but also that of the participant;
- they are a poetic philosophy, since poetry looks for an entity and assumes an entity.

These dialectics originated at a moment of discrepancy between the individual and the universality. The excluded individual tried to adapt, but lost the naturalness, i.e. that which everybody accepts without giving it much thought. Zeno's apories express this frame of mind. Plato's dialectics attempted to harmonize the excluded individual and universality, after turning his back on the obvious. The rise of Christianity made the problem even more complex, because of the relationship between the truth of the church (religion) and the individual consciousness (knowledge). Dialectics can therefore be found in the work of several scholastics, such as Abaelardus or Thomas of Aquino. In a way, they lay the foundation for Pietro Pomponazzi's doctrine or theory of the "double truth"; however, the dialectics of all these philosophers are highly indebted to Maimonides, their great master.

The 17th century witnessed the problem of dialectics in relation to reason. Descartes is often presented as an undialectic philosopher, which is not true. Descartes' methods are dialectic in nature. The fourth rule requires the total approach of a problem, taking into account all known elements. Descartes discloses new, undiscovered phenomena: the unknown has to be filed among the "known". Similarly, Leibniz' idea of the infinitely small, his "petites perceptions", was conceived, as was Kant's "Ding an sich", by simultaneously eliminating dialectics. Dialectic pretense, however, surfaces. Within philosophy, dialectics get categorized, only to be developed in depth by Fichte, Schelling and Hegel according to Maimonides' methodology. This method centers around the detour, the shortest way. Detours can, however, also be wrong tracks. One may aim at a certain point and take a track that leads one away from it. One is following a wrong track and realizes this only after a lapse of time. One slides farther away from one's aim, until suddenly one realizes that one finds oneself at the very point at which one aimed to be.

Since philosophy takes detours, it cannot help wandering. Wandering is a substantial element in philosophy, and the more intense philosophy gets, the higher the chances of choosing wrong tracks. Those wrong tracks, however, incorporate the direction of truth. The wandering gets lost on the right track, which is a perfect definition of Maimonides' fundamental reasoning. Being prepared to take wrong tracks causes fear, not of an inhibiting or passive nature, but active fear, allowing, according to Maimonides, for temerity, boldness, risk and wager.

Notes

1. Cf. H.A. Wolfson, "The Platonic, Aristotelian, and Stoic Theories of Creation in Halevi and Maimonides", in I. Epstein, E. Levine, and C. Roth, eds., *Essays in Honor of the Very Rev. Dr. J.H. Hertz*, London, 1942, pp. 427-442.

2. The metaphysical sciences of rational psychology, rational cosmology, and natural theology turn out to be without foundation.

3. *Critique of Practical Reason*, in "Werke", Berlin Academy (1900-42), vol. V, p. 148.

4. Alexander Altmann, "Das Verhältnis Maimunis zur jüdischen Mystik", in *Monatschrift für Geschichte und Wissenschaft des Judentums*, vol. 80 (1936), pp. 305-330.

5. According to Maimonides the conclusions reached by the prophets through the use of the intellect are in no way different from those of the philosophers, though the prophecy may reach them more rapidly; all prophets are philosophers! This clearly applies also to Moses, in spite of a statement in the *Guide* that none of the author's assertions about the prophets pertain to Moses. In other writings Maimonides describes Moses as having attained union with the Active Intellect; according to the conception of certain Islamic Aristotelians, union with the Active Intellect represents the highest goal and is reached by the great philosophers.

6. Z. Diesendruck, "Maimonides' Lehre von der Prophetie", in G.A. Kohut, ed., *Jewish Studies in Memory of Israel Abrahams*, New York, 1927, pp. 74-134. H.A. Wolfson, "Halevi and Maimonides on Prophecy", in *Jewish Quarterly Review*, N.S. vol. 32 (1941-1942), pp. 345-370 and N.S. vol. 33 (1942-1943), pp. 49-82.

7. H.A. Wolfson, "Maimonides on Negative Attributes", in A. Marx and others, eds., *Louis Ginsberg Jubilee Volume*, New York, 1945, pp. 419-446.

8. The two are equivalent; the expression "divine or natural actions", which occurs in the *Guide*, may have been in Spinoza's mind when he first spoke of "Deus sive natura".

9. *Guide*, Part III, Ch. 32.

10. *La Guide des Egarés. Traité de Théologie et de Philosophie* par Moïse ben Maimoun, traduit pour la première fois (1856-66) sur l'original arabe et accompagné de notes critiques, littéraires et explicatives, par Salomon Munk, membre

de l'Institut, Nouvelle édition, Paris, Editions G.-P. Maisonneuve, MCMLX, tome troisième, chap. XXXII, pp. 252-253.

11. Cf. L. Flam, *Denken en Existeren*, 1964, p. 273: "What is happening to me now I tend to explain initially as a mishap or bad luck, but after giving the matter some thought, I must come to the conclusion that it is merely a detour on the way to greater happiness, a detour I have to take in order to get there. Much of what is happening to me thus acquires an ethical nature, and I include it into the major detour I take, while the preconceived aim is a detour leading to something else. Therefore I am, as long as I live, always following detours."

12. When thinking takes a detour, it poses being on the road as a problem. Objectivity implies a maximum diversity of viewpoints in relation to the same object. This is also a part of the detour. In reality, an object is approached from as many different angles as possible, and constructed similarly. The thinking individual experiences this attitude as a liberation from subjectivism, partiality and bigotry. Pedantic individuals always consider certain problems from their so-called true and unique point of view. They act "smartalecky" and pretend to be educationalists, and thus they deform everything they touch. They are not even liberated from themselves, which is a fundamental condition in each philosophical act.

The Theory of Three Classes of Men in Plotinus and in Philo

J.M. Dillon

I

Plotinus begins his early tractate, Ennead V 9 [5], On Intellect and the Ideas and Being, with a fine passage contrasting three classes of men. It runs as follows (in Armstrong's Loeb translation):

> "All men from the beginning, as soon as they are born, employ sense-perception before intellect, and sense-objects are necessarily the first which they encounter. Some of them stay here and live through their lives considering these to be primary and ultimate, and since they consider what is painful and pleasant in them to be evil and good respectively, they think this is enough, and pass their lives pursuing the one and contriving to get rid of the other. And those of them who claim rationality make this their philosophy, like the heavy sort of birds who have taken much from the earth and are weighed down by it and so are unable to fly high although nature has given them wings.
>
> Others have risen a little from the things below because the better part of their soul has urged them on from the pleasant to a greater beauty; but since they were unable to see what is above, as they have no other ground to stand on, they are brought down, with the name of virtue, to practical actions and choices of the things below from which they tried to raise themselves at first.
>
> But there is a third kind of godlike men (*theioi anthropoi*) who by their greater power and the sharpness of their eyes, as if by a special keensightedness, see the glory above and are raised to it as if above the clouds and the mist of this lower world, and remain there, overlooking all things here below and delighting in the true region which is their own, like a man who has come home after long wandering to his own well-ordered country."

Modern editors, such as Bréhier, Harder, Henry and Schwyzer, Cilento, and Armstrong, are united in their identification of these three classes of person with the Epicureans (the earthy birds that cannot fly), the Stoics (those that rise only a little above the ground), and the Platonists (the divine men) respectively, and I would not seek to dispute that[1]. Certainly Plotinus repeatedly begins an essay with a doxography of this sort[2], and he no doubt has Epicureans and Stoics primarily in mind in this passage. While granting this, however, I want to suggest here that another influence is making itself felt, in the form of the particular triadic structure which Plotinus is employing.

It is apposite in this connexion, I think, to turn back in the first instance to a similarly peculiar passage in the works of Philo of Alexandria, towards the end of his short treatise *On the Giants* (ss. 60-61)[3], where a three-fold division of humankind likewise appears:

> "So then it is no myth at all of giants that he (sc. Moses) sets before us; rather he wishes to show you that some men are earth-born, some are heaven-born, and some God-born. The earth-born are those who take the pleasures of the body for their quarry, who make it their practice to indulge in them and enjoy them and provide the means by which each of them may be promoted. The heaven-born are the votaries of the arts and of knowledge, the lovers of learning -- for the heavenly element in each of us is the mind, as the heavenly beings are each of them a mind. And it is the mind which pursues the learning of the schools and the other arts one and all, which sharpens and whets itself, aye and trains and drills itself solid in the contemplation of what is intelligible by mind (*ta noeta*).
>
> But the men of God are priests and prophets who have refused to accept membership in the commonwealth of the world and to become citizens therein (*kosmopolitai*), but have risen wholly above the sphere of sense-perception and have been translated into the world of the intelligible and dwell there registered as freemen of the commonwealth of Ideas (*ideōn politeia*), which are imperishable and incorporeal." (trans. Colson, Loeb Classical Library ed.)

Once again, it is an obvious suggestion that Epicureans, Stoics and Platonists (or rather, perhaps, 'Mosaics') are being referred to, but Philo's categories have a much broader reference than that. The 'men of Earth' are simply 'les hommes moyen sensuels', for whom the world of the senses is all that there is. The 'men of Heaven' are a more interesting category. They are those who are skilled in 'the wisdom of this world', in Paul's words (cf. I Cor. 1, 18-25) -- in all branches of *enkyklios paideia*. There is probably also a reference to the Stoic view that there is nothing that transcends the material world, but no sort of school philosopher is necessarily being referred to at all. These people value the life of the mind; they employ the 'heavenly' part of us, *nous*, but they use it for the amassing and enjoyment of this-worldly knowledge and skills -- they are 'lovers or sound and spectacle', in the words of Plato (Rep. V 475E).

The 'men of God', finally, are not said to transcend intellect, but they employ it to turn away from this world altogether, realising that Reality lies elsewhere. They do not deign even to become *kos-*

mopolitai -- a crack here, surely at the Stoics -- but depart mentally from this world, and take their place as citizens of the 'commonwealth of Ideas', a reference to the realm of the Platonic Forms.

This theme of withdrawal, of alienation, recurs, as we see, in Plotinus in very similar terms. Plotinus' divine men are portrayed, with a reference both to the allegorical interpretation of the *Odyssey* and, perhaps, also to Plato's use of *Iliad* 9, 363 in *Crito* 44B, as returning 'to their well-ordered country', the intelligible world. In the case of both philosophers, the myth of Plato's *Phaedo* (109Bff.) seems to be exercising an influence. Philo's description of the men of God as 'rising above' (*hyperkypsantes*) the sense-world echoes the *anakypsas* of *Phaedo* 109d2 (cf. also 109e3), while Plotinus talks of rising above the clouds and mists of this realm in language strongly reminiscent of *Phaedo* 109b5, where "water and mist and air have run together" into certain hollows in the real earth where we live, "like ants or frogs about a pond"[4].

But if this explains, as I think it does, the coincidence of imagery, it does not explain the triadic schema. Since I am not one of those who believe that Plotinus was acquainted with the works of Philo, I am under the necessity of supposing that any coincidence of doctrine or imagery between them is either just that, a coincidence, or that it betokens some third source, either common to both, such as Plato, the Old Academy, or the Stoics, or intermediate between them, such as, perhaps, Numenius of Apamea.

II

In the case of the three classes of men, the situation is rather troublesome. On the one hand, the idea of such a triadic division could be seen as going back to Pythagoras and his famous image of the three classes of people whom one may find attending a festival, as told by Plato's pupil, Heraclides of Pontus[5]. Heraclides presents Pythagoras as engaged in conversation with Leon, tyrant of Phlius. Being asked by Leon what was his profession, Pythagoras declares that he is a 'philosopher', and when Leon, who is not familiar with this Pythagorean coinage, asks what is meant by a philosopher, Pythagoras explains by way of an image:

71

"Pythagoras replied that life seemed to him like the gathering when the great games were held, which were attended by the whole of Greece. For there some men sought to win fame and the glory of the crown by exerting their bodies, others were attracted by the gain and profit of buying and selling, but there was one kind of man, the noblest of all, who sought neither applause nor profit, but came in order to watch and wanted to see what was happening and how. So too among us, who have migrated into this life from a different life and mode of being, as if from some city to a crowded festival, some are slaves to fame, others to money; but there are some rare spirits who, holding all else as nothing, eagerly contemplate the universe; these he calls lovers of wisdom (*philosophoi*); and as at the festival it most becomes a gentleman to be a spectator without thought of personal gain, so in life the contemplation and understanding of the universe is far superior to all other pursuits."[6]

There is considerable irony in this image, I should say, since it is precisely the humblest, and most *numerous*, element in any festival or games, the spectators, who are being singled out as the noblest and *rarest* element, while the competitors, who would naturally be regarded as the most noble by ordinary men, are relegated to the lowest rank, because they have paid attention to their bodies rather than their minds. Even the despised hucksters and assorted charlatans who attend to make money are preferred to them, since they are making at least *some* use of their minds.[7]

III

This Pythagorean account of the three types of life, however, only gets us part of the way. In that story, the philosophers are presented primarily as contemplators of this world and its wonders (though in Iamblichus' version, at least, such contemplation is linked with the contemplation of intelligible reality; but this may be Iamblichus' own contribution), whereas in the scheme which we are investigating, the second level of men, the 'heaven-born' of Philo, and the 'higher-flying birds' of Plotinus, are already contemplators of the beauties and the order of this world, while the highest level transcend it altogether.

The closest analogy, in fact, to the scheme of Philo and Plotinus is to be found in the well-known triadic distinction found in many Gnostic systems between 'corporeal' or 'material' (*sarkikoi, choikoi, hylikoi*), 'psychic' (*psychikoi*), and 'spiritual' (*pneumatikoi*) men[8], such as we find set out in Irenaeus, *Adv. Haer.* I 1, 14, or Hippolytus, *Ref.* X 9-10 (Naassenes and Peratae), but most clearly, perhaps, in the *Excerpta ex Theodoto* of Clement of Alexandria (preserved in Book VII of the *Stromateis*), which are notes of an account of Valentinianism "according to the oriental teaching" (i.e., as opposed to that of the Italian school), composed by a certain Theodotus[9]. Exc. 54 runs as follows:

> "From Adam three natures are begotten. The first was the irrational (alogos), which was Cain's, the second the rational and just, which was Abel's, the third the spiritual (pneumatikê), which was Seth's. Now that which is earthly (choikos) is 'according to the image' (Gen. 1:26), that which is psychical (psychikos) is 'according to the likeness' of God (ibid.), and that which is spiritual is 'according to the Form' (kat' idean, Gen. 5:3); and with reference to these three, without the other children of Adam, it was said: "This is the book of the generation of men" (Gen. 5:1). And because Seth was spiritual he neither tends flocks nor tills the soil but produces a child, as spiritual things do. And him, "who hoped to call upon the name of the Lord" (Gen. 4:26), who looked upward and whose "citizenship is in heaven" (Phil. 3:20) -- him the world does not contain."
>
> (trans. R.P. Casey)

Here, the natures of Cain, Abel and Seth are distinguished hierarchically, on the basis of Gen. 4. Philo, it must be admitted, knows nothing of a special ranking for Seth above Abel. For him, both Abel and Seth are representatives of virtue and *nous*, over against Cain, and Seth is simply a reincarnation of Abel (*De Post. Caini*, 172-3). The exaltation of Seth seems to be a distinctively Gnostic development. It is in respect of the quotation of *Philippians* 3:20 ("for our citizenship is in heaven") that a point of contact with Philo arises. The whole final section, with its reference to "looking upward" (*anô bleponta*) and transcending this world, is reminiscent of *Gig.* 61, where the Men of God rise into the intelligible world and become enrolled in the *politeia* of the Forms. Similar imagery is employed by Plotinus, the 'third class' being portrayed as coming home to their true fatherland outside this world.

IV

If some similarity be granted between these three passages, what are we to make of it? Where does this triadic division of mankind originate? Who is influencing whom? That Plotinus knew some Gnostic writings is attested by Porphyry (*Vit. Plot.* ch. 16), and at least two of these have turned up in the Nag Hammadi Corpus, *Zostrianus* (VIII 1) and *Allogenes* (XI 3), with which treatises another is closely connected in doctrine, *The Three Steles of Seth* (VII 5). While Plotinus emphatically disapproved of their doctrines, and of their general attitude to the world and to Hellenic culture (as we can see from his attack on them in *Ennead* II 9), it is quite possible that he was prepared to borrow from them a concept such as this, stripped of its objectionable aspects -- notably the exclusiveness of the pneumatic class, and the notion that the Elect are exempt from, as being superior to, conventional law and custom. In fact, Theodotus accepts (*Exc.* 56, 3) that, since the psychics have free will, some of them are capable of being saved, but the material men are beyond salvation. Of course, Platonists believed that very few people ever became 'godlike', but there is no predestined number or class of these, and nothing very terrible, in any case, happens to those who do not qualify, provided that they behave themselves reasonably.

Plotinus, then, could be seen as having borrowed this concept from Gnostic sources, but what of Philo? One can, of course, push the birth of Gnosticism back before Christianity, to dissident Jewish sects such as the Samaritans, the Essenes or the Therapeutae, all of whom had a belief in the salvation of a small body of the Elect, and with the latter two of whom Philo had some contact, as we know. The apostle Paul, after all, can be seen both to react to and to reflect these beliefs (e.g. 1 *Cor.* 8; 10, 15; *Rom.* 8), with a strong antithesis between those of the Flesh and those of the Spirit. This gives one the basic antithesis between pneumatic and sarkic man, though not the triadic distinction. If, however, you combine with this an antipathy to the 'wisdom of this world', represented both by the orthodox Jewish establishment and by the Greek philosophical tradition, one has, I think, the makings of the triadic distinction which we have before us. Whether the older Pythagorean schema had any influence on this is unclear, but it is not necessary, I think, to postulate that it did, well-known though it would have been to both Philo and Plotinus.

Philo, then, I would suggest, may have picked up this concept of the three levels of man from his contacts with the Essenes or Therapeutae, and Plotinus from a later stage in the Gnostic tradition. It is clear, admittedly, that whoever was an influence on Philo had not yet elevated Seth to the position of archetype of pneumatic man, since we find no sign of such a development in his writings, but that is no great problem. The triadic schema is not dependent on the status of Seth, though it fits the trio of Cain, Abel and Seth very well, even as it can be adapted to the sequence of Epicureans, Stoics and Platonists. In the hands of Philo and Plotinus, it constitutes an interesting case of cultural cross-fertilisation.

Notes

1. The reference, in particular, to practical actions and choices (*praxeis kai eklogai*), in the case of the second class of 'birds', is a pretty clear reference to Stoic terminology and doctrine, cf. *SVF* III 64; 118, but the reference to those who rationalise and philosophise pleasure-seeking also refers plainly enough to the Epicureans.

2. E.g. *Enn.* II 4, 1; III 1, 2; IV 7, 2-3.

3. Commented on recently by David Winston and myself, in *Two Treatises of Philo of Alexandria*, ed. David Winston and John Dillon, Scholars Press, Chico, 1983.

4. Although the word Plotinus uses for 'mist' (*achlys*, instead of *homichlē*), he borrows from a famous passage of the *Iliad* (5, 127), where Athena removes the mist from Diomedes' eyes, so that he can "discern both god and man".

5. Fr. 88 Wehrli, preserved by Cicero, in *Tusc. Disp.* V 3, 8-9. Cf. also Iamblichus, *Vita Pythagorica*, 58-59.

6. Trans. J.E. King (Loeb Classical Library). The form of this doubtless owes something to Cicero's stylistic elaboration, but there is no reason not to attribute the content to Heraclides.

7. In the version given by Iamblichus, the competitors, in their desire for fame, are ranked above those who are merely seeking material gain, but Cicero's version seems closer to Heraclides', whether or not *that* is the original version of the story.

8. There are also traces of this distinction in the Hermetic tradition, which does in general recognise a clear distinction between soul and 'spirit' (*pneuma*), or, in Platonic terms, intellect (*nous*), e.g. *CH* I passim, X 19-21. In IX 9, in fact, we find a triadic distinction of types of thing generated by God, "some exercising their activity through bodies, others that move themselves by means of psychic substance, and others that vivify themselves by means of spirit." This is not a division of classes of men, however, but something broader.

9. Edited by R.P. Casey, *The Excerpta ex Theodoto of Clement of Alexandria*, London, 1934.

Maritain on Creative Intuition

Jude P. Dougherty

I

That attitudes toward science and technology make a difference is widely recognized. If science is conceived as merely description and prediction and not as a search for causes and principles, it will surely be regarded as lacking in explanatory power. Adopting such a positivistic view of science, one automatically rules out certain time-honored disciplines simply because they do not fit the mold. Does something equally momentous flow from varying conceptions of art?

Given the ambiguities found in contemporary usage, that not all who use the term "philosophy of art" mean by it the same thing, one can nevertheless identify certain basic questions addressed by those who take up the discipline: What is the end of artistic production? Is or should art be a disinterested endeavor, serving no end beyond itself? What is the relation of art to beauty? To nature? Is art of its essence social? Are certain freedoms to be accorded to the artist which would normally be denied to others? Does artistic production raise a special set of epistemological problems? How describe the artistic process itself?

Maritain, over the period of a career extending from *Art and Scholasticism* to *Creative Intuition in Art and Poetry*, addresses all of these questions.[1] So, too, in this century, have thinkers as diverse as Leo Tolstoy, John Dewey and Ortega y Gasset.[2] Recognizing the ambiguity of the discipline and the disparity of effort by those who practice it, it is the purpose of this inquiry, first, to address certain issues which arise in a 20th century context and, secondly, to allow Maritain to address those issues as he unfolds his theory of art. The question of social function is quickly addressed; attention is then given to three representative themes of Maritain's outlook: 1) art as a virtue of the practical intellect, 2) the roots of the creative act in the preconscious life of the intellect, and 3) the inescapable role of intellect in artistic production. In addressing these themes, it will become evident that the question of social utility in appraising the fine arts is ill-placed.

A philosopher's attitude toward art is of necessity deeply influenced by his theory of knowledge, and it can tell us almost as much about the philosopher as a well-wrought intellectual biography. To use an example from 20th century American philosophy, John Dewey's reduction of science to a kind of art form or to technology is a consequence of a long philosophical journey which led him from a youthful Hegelianism to the naturalism of *Experience and Nature* and *Art as Experience*.[3] In Dewey's analysis, art exists not for its own sake but as a problem-solving technique. As technique, it has a large and important function in society. Citing August Comte, Dewey refers frequently to the role of art in promoting social goals; he speaks of the moral office and human function of art. As he reads cultural history, the first stirrings of dissatisfaction and the first intimations of a better future are always found in the works of art. Art is *the* incomparable organ of instruction, the paradigm of knowledge, perfectly combining knowing and doing. Science itself is best understood as art. Like Karl Marx, Dewey subordinates art to the collective. Just as the ultimate criteria of science is its utility, so, too, art is ultimately to be judged by the role it plays in society.

Sometimes the instruction is oblique. Consulting the writings of certain artists themselves, we find the painters Kandinsky and Mondrian, deliberately and for ideological reasons, setting out to destroy natural forms, traditional symbolism, and what they called "superficial imagery" in order to liberate the spirit.[4] Their aim was not to paint something different, but to paint something which resembled as little as possible the objects of ordinary experience.

Concerning the end of art, Maritain not only differs with Dewey but, as shall momentarily be shown, with Ortega and Tolstoy as well. All three authors, Dewey, Ortega and Tolstoy, concentrate on the practical or social aspect of art. There are profound reasons for this. The insistence on the utility of art is the result of a functional interpretation of intelligence. In the words of Ortega, "A man thinks in order to maintain himself among things."[5] Even Maritain's mentor, Henri Bergson, defined man as *homo faber*, not *homo sapiens*; man is made to fabricate.[6] Leo Tolstoy links art to communication and judges it in terms of its effectiveness in facilitating intercourse between man and man.[7] To define art, says the author of *War and Peace*, we must conceptually divorce it from beauty, or from that which pleases us, and consider it as one of the conditions of human life. Art is the transmission of feelings we have judged to be important. The emphasis is on transmission. By contrast, Maritain writes, "Art by itself tends to the good of the works not to the good of the man. The first responsibility of the artist is toward his work."[8] Its transcendent end is beauty.

What are we to make of these seemingly contradictory views on the nature of art? It is perhaps a truism to say the "philosophers are not so much wrong in what they affirm as they are in what they deny." A simple distinction, second nature to Maritain, but one apparently neglected by Tolstoy and Ortega, would help set the matter straight. I have in mind the distinction between servile and fine art which acknowledges the instrumental character of much artistic production while leaving the way open for art which serves no other purpose than to please. That which pleases can at the same time communicate. The pleasure it gives may be due in part to the nobility of the subject matter it portrays or to the sentiment it conveys. But if edification or the communication of a message is made paramount, the artifact is apt to fail and to take on the character of a mere instrument.

Maritain can appreciate art for its own sake primarily because he has a classical notion of intellect. As the Greeks respected natural forms and enjoyed their beauty, so too, they respected disinterested inquiry for its own sake. Knowledge does not have to end in making or doing to be worthwhile; knowledge is its own end. Maritain is Greek in this respect. Just as the aim of science is understanding, not power or technology, so, too, the fine arts have as their primary end the disclosure of being under the aspect of beauty. Science may issue in technology, the fine arts themselves may serve, but both exist primarily to satisfy the mind's appetite for knowledge and beauty.

Significantly, in defending the instrumental or practical character of knowledge, John Dewey denies the reality of science understood as a quest for intelligibility in the light of causes and principles. Science for Dewey is description and prediction. Its aim is the manipulation of material in the light of agreed-upon ends. Interesting, too, is the moralism that runs through much of Dewey's philosophy, a moralism that is absent in Maritain although he wrote a book called *The Responsibility of the Artist*.[9] In that book Maritain condemns "art for the social group." What is called *l'art engagé*, enlisted art, or drafted art, he believes is inevitably propaganda art, either for moral or antimoral, social, political, religious or anti-religious purposes. "Art, like knowledge, is appendant to values which are independent of the interest, even the noblest interests, of human life, for they are the values of the intellectual order." Maritain is neither moralist nor reformer. He is the philosopher utilizing the categories of being in order to understand. His is the legacy of Aristotle and Aquinas.

The essays which first brought him attention were published in French in 1920 under the title *Art et Scholastique* (the English translation appeared ten years later in 1930). His continued reflections on art eventually gained for him an invitation to deliver the inaugural series of the Andrew W. Mellon Lectures at the National Gallery of Art in Washington, soon to become the most prestigious series in North America. (Gilson was later to give the fourth set of lectures in that annual series.)

The Mellon lectures were published as *Creative Intuition in Art and Poetry*. In them Maritain, using poetry as the primary example, attempts to analyze the preconscious life of the intellect in the creative act. His analysis presupposes an Aristotelian theory of the virtues and a Thomistic epistemology. In the process of employing those instruments in an area he knows well, Maritain succeeded in sharpening his theory of knowledge itself. In *Creative Intuition in Art and Poetry* Maritain recognizes many modern enemies, among them, subjectivism, irrationalism and instrumentalism. He emerges from battle where we might expect him to be, faithful to the classical tradition as represented by Aristotle and Aquinas.

II

To examine some of the principal themes of *Creative Intuition in Art and Poetry* is to discover not only a philosophy of art but an epistemology and a metaphysics. Critics have remarked that the book is not an easy one, and that judgment is to some extent true. But in spite of its philosophical abstruseness there is a certain freshness and elegance to it.

Maritain's fundamental perceptions are derivative. He inherits from Aristotle and the scholastics a theory of knowledge and a theory of the virtues, but Maritain makes this advance. By reflecting primarily on poetry, he is positioned to examine in microscopic detail the intellect as it creates. His choice of poetry as the exemplary form of art is in part attributable to his wife, Raissa, herself a poet. Within their circle of friends, there were not only poets but painters, sculptors and musicians of rank. From those friends Maritain was to gain valuable insights into the creative process. His problem was to understand that process as a philosopher.

Two things are required of one who would follow Maritain's analysis of intelligence and the creative process: 1) acquaintance with the Thomistic theory of knowledge, and 2) the experience of having written a poem. For Aquinas, two intellectual powers can be identified: the "abstracting" or "agent intellect," and the "passive" or "understanding intellect." The agent intellect, which Thomas thought is the faculty by which man most resembles God Himself, is a power that is constantly in act. Like a never-ceasing beam of light the agent intellect illuminates objects presented to it by means of the senses. Intellectual knowing is contingent on sense experience, but is not reducible to sense experience. The intellect is able to discern in the empirically-given data elements which the senses themselves are formally not able to appreciate. That same intellect is not only able to abstract from the singular to the universal, but is able to *express* what it knows in an act called "understanding." Before the mind even forms a concept there is a pre-conscious mingling or merging of sensory with intellectual materials. The vagaries of mingling, grouping and insight depend upon an individual's intellectual history, the habits acquired over a lifetime. You and I, confronted with the same pastoral landscape, may comprehend in a similar manner, but only to a point. What we make of that landscape depends upon previous experience and the habits of learning which each of us has acquired. We are sometimes furious with a friend who "cannot see the woods for the trees," but then we realize that he or she hasn't been prepared to "see." Not everyone is capable of the same degree of abstract thought or even of the same degree of appreciation of natural forms. As conceptual ability varies, so, too, does artistic ability and the ability to appreciate. To avoid racing ahead to Maritain's conclusion, however, it is necessary to allow his argument to unfold as he himself presents it.

The speculative intellect, Maritain maintains, knows only for the sake of knowledge. It longs to "see," and only to "see." Truth, or the grasping of that which is, is its only goal and its only life.[10] The practical intellect, on the other hand, knows for the sake of action. "From the very start its object is not *being* to be grasped, but human activity to be guided and human tasks to be achieved."[11] Practical intellect is immersed in creativity. Its very life is to mold intellectually that which will be brought into being, to judge about ends and means, and to direct and even to command our powers of execution."[12] Two kinds of practical activity must be distinguished. Moral judgment or prudence is to be differentiated from artistic judgment, though both are concerned with means to ends.

The difference between prudence and art is this: prudence is the intellectual determination of actions to be done; art, by contrast, is the intellectual determination of works to be made. With respect to works made, a further distinction is to be drawn, namely, that between the useful and the fine arts. The former satisfy a specific need and are governed by the exigencies of that end or need. The fine arts are motivated, on the other hand, not by a particular need, but by the demand of the will to release the pure creativity of the spirit in its longing for beauty. The will tends to this end according to rules discovered by the intellect. The end is beauty, and not a particular need to be satisfied. In art, as in contemplation, intellectuality goes beyond concepts and discursive reasoning, and is achieved through a "congeniality" or "co-naturality" with the object, which love alone can bring about. To produce in beauty, says Maritain, the artist must be in love with beauty.[13]

The distinction between the useful and fine arts is not to be understood in too absolute a manner. The Greeks were aware that in the humblest work the craftsman or the artisan is also properly concerned with beauty. Maritain prefers to distinguish between the two using the terms "subservient" and "self-sufficient." The fine arts, because of their immediate relation to beauty and to the creativity of the spirit are free; they belong to the world of liberal arts. Intuitive or non-discursive reasoning will in a large measure determine their character.

Nevertheless, the fine arts, from the very fact that they belong in the generic realm of art, participate in the law of useful arts. Thus the conceptual, discursive, logical reason, or better, the working reason, plays a necessary, though secondary, part in the fine arts. This part is only instrumental because it relates to the particular ways of making an object. If it gets the upper hand, it destroys the work of fine art.[14]

The normal climate of art is intelligence and learning. The intellect is reflective by nature; even the practical virtues cannot develop in their own sphere without a more or less simultaneous development of reflectivity. And the name of reflective intelligence in the domain of art is critical reason. An artist cannot be guided by instinct alone.[15]

How, then, explain certain seemingly irrational tendencies in modern art? In Maritain's judgment modern art endeavors to free itself from nature and the forms of nature. It seeks liberation from the conventions of language and form and is consequently marked by a tendency to be obscure. In 20th century art there is a decided movement away from conceptual, logical and discursive reasoning. Though modern art may at times display a suicidal attitude of contempt for reason, it is by no means, in its essence, a process of liberation from reason itself. Reason possesses a life both deeper and less conscious than its articulate logical life, for prior to logical reason there is intuitive reason.[16]

Maritain distinguishes between a conscious and a pre-conscious life of intellect. The pre-conscious life of the intellect he identifies with the initial activity of the agent intellect, the first stage in the birth of a concept. Part of his break with Bergson was the result of Maritain's conviction that the Thomistic doctrine of agent intellect better allowed him to understand the pre-conscious wellsprings of creativity.

In spite of these distinctions, Maritain is careful to present man as a single entity; man is neither intellect nor body, neither spirit nor sense. The imagination proceeds or flows from the essence of the soul through the intellect; the external senses proceed from the essence of the soul through the imagination, for they exist in man to serve the imagination.[17] Concepts and images can belong to the preconscious. The common root of all the powers of the soul is the spiritual unconscious. In this root activity, the intellect and the imagination, as well as the powers of desire, love and emotion, are engaged in common. The powers of the soul envelop one another, the universe of sense perception is in the universe of imagination, which is in the universe of intelligence.[18] All powers within the intellect are stirred and activated by the light of the illuminating intellect. According to the order of the ends and demands of nature, the imagination and the senses are raised in man to a state genuinely human where they somehow participate in intelligence, and their exercise is, as it were, permeated with intelligence. Thus Maritain can say, "poetry is the fruit neither of the imagination nor of the intellect alone... It proceeds from the totality of man, sense, imagination, intellect, love, desire, instinct, blood and spirit, together."[19]

Maritain characterized poetic knowledge as "affective," as "knowledge through inclination," as "a conaturality or congeniality" in which the intellect is at play, not alone, but together with the affective inclinations and dispositions of the will, and as guided and shaped by them. Poetic knowledge is not rational knowledge, knowledge through the conceptual, logical and discursive exercise of reason, but it is, nevertheless, genuine knowledge, although it is obscure and perhaps incapable of giving an account of itself. Poetic knowledge is born in the unconsciousness of the spirit. It is essentially creative and tends to express itself in a work.[20]

"Poetic intuition is not directed toward essences," says Maritain, "for essences are disengaged from concrete reality in a concept, a universal idea, and scrutinized by means of reasoning."[21] Essences are an object of speculation; they are not the thing grasped by poetic intuition. "Poetic intuition is directed toward concrete existence as conatural to the soul pierced by a given emotion."[22] But poetic intuition does not stop at a given existent, a given particular, but transcends it, in the manner of a sign that stands for something more. Things are not only what they are, they refer beyond themselves, suggesting more than they actually possess. Poetic intuition can neither be learned nor improved by exercise and discipline, for it depends on a certain natural function, natural freedom of the soul and the imaginative faculties, and on the natural strength of the intellect. Though poetic activity is by nature subjective, it is still disinterested. It engages the human "self" in its deepest recesses, but in no way for the sake of the ego. Self-revelation is always for the sake of the art work.

Continuing his analysis of poetry, Maritain finds himself in a position to say something about beauty. He accepts Aquinas's analysis which recognizes in the thing called beautiful three essential characteristics: integrity, proportion, and clarity (*splendor formae*).[23] While beauty is a transcendental in the Thomistic sense, and everything which exists, to the extent that it exists, may be called beautiful, aesthetic beauty, says Maritain, is the beauty most naturally proportioned to the human mind. Aesthetic beauty may be regarded as a particular determination of transcendental beauty. It is transcendental beauty as confronting not simply the intellect, but the intellect and sense activity together. Beauty, Maritain suggests, is not the object, but the "end beyond the end" of poetry. In the case of plastic and visual art, the cognitive function of the intellect is entirely subordinated to its creative function. The intellect knows in order to create. Poetry, by contrast, is essentially free. There is nothing that may exercise command or mastery over it. In poetry there is only the urge to give expression to that knowledge which is poetic intuition, and in which both the subjectivity of the poet and the realities of the world awake obscurely in a single awakening. In a certain sense, poetry has no object; it creates its own object. Poetry tends toward beauty, but not toward beauty as an object to be known or to be made. A better way to put it is to say that poetry, in effecting its proper end, engenders beauty. Like other fine arts it tends more intimately to produce a good work than to produce a beautiful work. The fine arts cannot make beauty their end. To the extent to which they make beauty an object, their object, and in tending toward beauty, forget that beauty is more than an operational end -- being the end beyond the end -- they recede from beauty. Beauty is achieved almost accidentally, as a by-product of the work produced.

III

Maritain utilizes his analysis of poetry in an attempt to give a sympathetic reading to much 20th century painting.[24] Non-representative painting, he recognizes, breaks away from nature; it turns away from things and the grasping of things, and renounces seeing into the inner depths of nature. In breaking away from the existential world of nature, non-representative art condemns itself to fall short of its own dearest purposes and the very ends for the sake of which it came into being. Cut off from the poetic grasp of things, non-representative art will attain only the most limited form of beauty, namely, the mute beauty of the best balanced objects produced by the mechanical arts. There is no exercise of the free creativity of the spirit without poetic intuition. The crucial mistake of abstract art has been -- unwittingly -- to reject poetic intuition and, therefore, to reject systematically the existential world of things. All in all, abstract art, taken as a system, is in the same predicament as idealist philosophy; both are walled in.[25]

As an exercise or experiment, non-representative painting has value, but primarily as technique. It is Maritain's opinion that non-representative art reflects a period of stagnation or regression, rather than to advancement or progress in the history of art. Its great mistake has been to put the instrumental and the secondary before the principal and the primary. Another mistake has been to conceive of forward movement only in terms of a flight from natural forms. The mistake has been to look for freedom from something, at first from a servile imitation or copying of natural appearances, but eventually from the existential world of nature itself. Instead of looking for freedom to achieve in one's work a more and more genuine revelation both of things and the self, it has denied any referent against which it can be measured. Contemporary painting will get out of its predicament when it understands that the only way to effective transposition, deformation, recasting, or transfiguration of natural appearances is through the insight provided by poetic intuition. Poetic intuition does as it pleases with natural appearances, not by any technical trick, but by virtue of its inner pressure.[26]

IV

Given its twentieth century course, it is Maritain's judgment that poetry has never been in greater need of reason, of genuine human wisdom.[27] Wisdom presupposes a realm of knowledge, which pertains to the poet not as a poet, but as a man, and on which depends the universe of thought presupposed by his activity as a poet. The allurements of magic must be counterbalanced by the judgmental character of rational knowledge. Poetry may be the heaven of working reason, a divination of the spiritual things of sense. Poetry may be truly spiritual nourishment, but it does not satiate, it only makes a man hungrier. That hunger has to be fed by sources other than poetry, though poetry in a peculiar way is proximate to those sources. In a certain sense, poetry is akin to mystical experience, for both poetic and mystic insight are born near one another in the center of the soul. In another sense, poetry is not unlike metaphysics. "Metaphysics snatches at the spiritual in an idea through the most abstract intellection; poetry reaches it in a flash by the very point of the sense sharpened through intelligence."[28] Poetic knowledge analogically participates in the contemplative character of philosophy, for it is knowledge of the very interiority of things. Thus, because it is, in its own way, spiritual communion with being, poetry transcends those arts, which are entirely encompassed in and committed to practical knowledge in the strict sense of the word, knowledge only to make. It is because of this transcendence that poetry enjoys a universal dominion over all the arts which have to do with beauty.

Poetic experience is, for the most part, a transient and fleeting experience. This experience is, to a large extent, hidden in the preconscious. Thus when we look for some verbal expression bearing witness to the inner experience of composers and painters, we are often obliged to satisfy ourselves with the external and indirect.[29]

"The poetic sense, in the work, corresponds to the poetic experience in the poet."[30] The poetic sense is to the poem what the soul is to man. "It is the poetic intuition itself communicated to the work in its native, pure and immediate efficacy."[31] It might be said that the poetic sense is the inner melody of the poem. The logical or intelligible sense is only one of the elements or components of the poetic sense. "The poetic sense is an immanent meaning made up of meanings: the intelligible meanings of the words...the imaginal meanings of the words...the musical relations between the words, and between the meaningful contents with which the words are laden. Thus the intelligible sense, through which the poem utters ideas, is entirely subordinate to the poetic sense."[32] It is with respect to the intelligible sense that a poem is clear or obscure. "A poem may be obscure or it may be clear," says Maritain, "what matters is only the poetic sense."[33] The law of intelligibility imposed by tradition has been the occasion for innumerable mediocre poems, where the logical sense was made to prevail over the poetic sense. But modern poetry swarming with obscure poems, good and bad, has effected full recognition of the necessary primacy of the poetic sense.

No poem can be completely obscure, "for no poem can completely get rid of the intelligible sense."[34] A poem cannot be without poetic sense and intelligible meaning, subordinate though it may be. "Conversely, no poem can be absolutely clear, since no poem can receive its being from the intelligible or sense uniquely."[35] Some poems, it may be noted, are only seemingly obscure, others are obscure in essence.

The very first effect and sign of poetic knowledge and poetic intuition, as soon as they exist in the soul, "is a kind of musical stir, and unformulated song, with no words, no sounds, absolutely inaudible to the ear, audible only to the heart."[36] How account for this fact? On the one hand there is an actual flash of knowing, born through spiritualized emotion. On the other hand, there is "a spiritual milieu -- a kind of fluid and moving world, activated by the diffuse light of the Illuminating Intellect, and seemingly asleep but secretly tense and vigilant -- which is the preconscious life of the intellect, and of imagination and of emotion, empty of any actual concept or idea, but full of images and full of emotional movements, and in which all the past experiences and treasures of memory acquired by the soul are present in a state of virtuality. It is within this fluid and moving milieu that poetic experience and poetic intuition exist, not virtually, but as an act or actuation definitely formed."[37]

Maritain continues, "The expansion of the poetic intuition in its vital milieu develops, and at the same time, the intuitive pulsions also expand and become more and more distinct; explicit images awaken, more distinct emotions resound in the fundamental emotion. Then there is in the soul of the poet an enlarged musical stir, a music no longer almost imperceptible, but more and more cogent, in which the soundless rhythmic and harmonic relations between intuitive pulsions, together with their soundless melody emerge into consciousness. This enlarged musical stirring is the spontaneous start of operative exercise. With it the process of expression begins, in a first transient and tendential stage."[38] It tends to verbal expression. But the actual verbal expression of this musical stirring constitutes a second and distinct stage. There are, therefore, two distinct musics, two essentially distinct stages in poetic expression: the music of intuitive pulsions within the soul, and the music of words which will pass outside of the soul.

Poetry cannot do without music. The primary role of music in poetry is not the music of words but the internal music of the intuitive pulsions. There has been a reversion of introversion, from an externalization to an internalization of music. Without modern poetry we may never have become fully aware of the importance of this inaudible, wordless and soundless music. It is easy to verify such observations if we read modern poets exercising at the same time our power of introspection, and paying attention not only to the words but to what they produce within ourselves. "A poem is an engine to make us pass through or beyond things."[39] The classical poem aims to express and signify the trans-reality caught by creative intuition, but in order to do so it must use the instrumentality of definite things which stand as objects of thought, and are signified by logically organized concepts. The modern poem signifies only the trans-reality caught by poetic intuition, without being bound first to signify a definite set of things standing as objects of thought. It has, thus, one single significance which has to do with poetic intelligence, not with rationalized and socialized communicability. "The music of words in modern poetry, still necessary as it may be, yields the foremost place to another, more internal music. Music is pushed back inwardly. What matters essentially now is the music of intuitive pulsions, which passes into the work of words freely -- without being repressed or obliterated by the exigencies of the logos -- and to which the reader in his turn is finally taken by this work of words."[40] Modern poetry, as the immediate expression of this internal music, is thus given intelligibility in terms of its source and attainment.

Finally, three aspects or levels of poetry, Maritain calls them "epipharies of creative intuition," are identified: the first and most basic intentional value in the poem, he says, is the poetic sense.[41] It is followed by the action and the theme which are complements or objective reflections of the poetic sense. The third may be called "number" or "harmonic expansion." Through the latter the poetic sense and the action are complemented or externally reflected, in the same way, analogically speaking, as natural substances are extended by quantity. The number or harmonic expansion of the poem is the vital concurrence of the multiple, or the vital order, bringing to complex orchestral unity parts struggling to assert their own individual claims. It is through harmonic expansion that the work is possessed of a kind of external music. For the extent to which it has number, its visible or sonorous qualities, its impact on the senses and power of delighting them, its own charge of sensitivity and sensuousness are penetrated with the secret measure of reason and logic. Harmonic expansion becomes the vital order.

Put another way, the three stages of creative intuition may be identified as: first, the pre-conscious, nonconceptual life of the intellect, and this is the state of the poetic sense from which the poem receives its essence; secondly, the state of nascent logos where the work exists as thought and is given its action and theme; and thirdly, the state of formed logos or the work in making in which the poetic intuition passes into the poem through the instrumentality of the number or harmonic expansion. These are the three epiphanies of poetic intuition or creative emotion. Relating this analysis to the three aspects of the beautiful previously noted Maritain writes: "Radiance or clarity, which is the absolutely primary property of beauty, and matters first of all, appears principally (I do not say uniquely) in the poetic sense or inner melody of the work; integrity, in the action and the theme; and consonance, in the number or harmonic structure."[42]

V

With this account of the creative process behind us, the questions we raised at the beginning of this lecture seem almost naive. Whether or not our personal experience is deep enough to verify every aspect of Maritain's reflections on art and the creative process, he clearly shows that for anyone who would be fully human, artistic production is a necessity. Just as all men are called to a life of contemplation so all are called to a life of creativity, a creativity that has no end other than the delight it produces.

This is not to say that fine art cannot serve. Art in the service of the temple is a case in point, but Maritain's genius is this: he has graphically shown how intimately associated with human nature is the disposition to create. To be fully human is to bring into being works which stand apart from the self, but which nevertheless reflect the innermost aspects of the artist's being. That revelatory act is not self-centered nor subjective but is instead directed toward disclosing the real which is the object of both artist and viewer. The vocation of an artist is an aspect of the human vocation, namely, self-perfection. Not all who attempt to create will emerge among the ranks of the immortals, but all are called.

Gabriel Marcel once remarked that the spirit of our age is basically "ontophobic." Maritain by contrast consciously grounds his theory of art in a metaphysics of nature and human nature and in doing so achieves a certain power which others such as Dewey do not possess. Maritain is open to a transcendent dimension of experience, both little "t" and big "T." He is open to the perennial or the time-transcendent, and to Transcendent Being Itself. Because Maritain understands the relevance of the past, appreciating the role of the inherited, he better understands making. He is also in a position to judge outcomes. By a law of human nature, the now-directed is incapable of evaluating even the now.

On this point Ortega and Maritain would be in complete agreement. Ortega writes, "Only in proportion as we are desirous of living more do we really live ....Obstinately to insist on carrying on within the same familiar horizon betrays weakness and a decline in vital energies." But "To excel the past we must not allow ourselves to lose contact with it; on the contrary, we must feel it under our feet because we have raised ourselves upon it." How different is the outlook of Dewey, for whom "custom," "habit," and the "inherited" veil the eye's ability to perceive. For the now-directed Dewey, the only problem is the mechanical one at hand. For Maritain, artistic production reflects a time-transcending intellectual awareness, an awareness grounded, not only in the immediate but also in the experience of previous generations as disclosed through history, but above all in insights gleaned from theology and philosophy.

The artist is not simply a technician; for in creating, the artist discloses the possibilities of being. He is not, as Tolstoy would make him, merely a communicator of his own subjective feeling. The artist more than any other human being participates in the divine creative act, bringing into being an object which at once satisfies intellect under the aspect of "truth," the will under the aspect of "good" and the whole man under the aspect of "beauty." To my knowledge, no one has rendered more attractive the high vocation of artist than Maritain. One puts down *Creative Intuition in Art and Poetry* wondering if the book, in fact, is not one love song to his wife, Raissa.

Notes

1 *Art and Scholasticism*, trans. J.F. Scanlan. (New York: Sheed and Ward, 1930); The A.W. Mellon Lectures, published as *Creative Intuition in Art and Poetry*. (New York: Pantheon, 1953).

2 cf. Leo N. Tolstoy, *What is Art*? (New York: Bobbs Merrill, 1960); *Experience and Nature*, John Dewey (New York: MacMillan, 1948) and *Art as Experience*, (New York: Minton Balch and Company, 1934). Ortega y Gasset, *The Dehumanization of Art* (Princeton, New Jersey: Princeton U. Press, 1968).

3 Dewey's theory of art is contained within his philosophy of science and is regarded by some as the key to his entire philosophy, since he reduced science to art or technique.

4 For an interesting discussion of modern art see Ortega y Gasset, op. cit., p. 21 ff. cf. Maritain, *Creative Intuition in Art and Poetry* pp. 215-21. Maritain's sympathetic, yet critical reflections will be discussed later.

5 Op. Cit., p. 196.

6 *The Two Sources of Religion and Morality*. (New York: Holt, 1935).

7 Op. Cit., p. 49.

8 (New York: Charles Scribner's Sons, 1960), p. 24.

9 Ibid.

10 p. 49.

11 Ibid.

12 Ibid.

13 p. 58.

14 p. 63.

15 p. 65.

16 p. 73ff.

17 p. 107.

18 p. 110.

19 p. 111.

20 pp. 117-118.

21 pp. 125-26.

22 p. 126.

23 Chap. V, p. 160ff.

24 Chap. VI, p. 209ff.

25 p. 220.

26 pp. 223-226.

27 p. 234.

28 p. 235.

29 pp. 250-251.

30 p. 257.

31 p. 258.

32 p. 259.

33 Ibid.

34 Ibid.

35 p. 261.

36 p. 301.

37 Ibid.

38 pp. 302-303.

39 p. 318.

40 p. 321.

41 Chap. IX, pp. 354-405.

42 p. 370.

Simeon the Righteous

Louis Finkelstein

In the later centuries of the First Commonwealth of Judea and the Second Commonwealth the population consisted essentially of two groups. There was the aristocratic patrician group consisting of the priests, most of whom were well-to-do landowners (see *Sifre Deut.* 352, p. 409), the lay owners of large provincial estates who lived in Jerusalem, and the rustic population. The second class consisted of the traders and workers of the marketplace of Jerusalem and the surrounding villages. In my book on *The Pharisees* (3rd ed., 1962, pp. 101 ff.) I endeavored to show that the differences in the interpretation of the law between the Sadducees and the Pharisees can be traced to the differences in outlook between these two groups.

However, it must be noted that while there was about a score of differences between the Sadducees and the Pharisees, the *Mishna* and kindred works record hundreds of controversies within Pharisaism. Many of these controversies are recorded as dividing the Pharisees into two groups or, as they are called, "houses," the Shammaites and the Hillelites.[1] Curiously enough, these differences too can be explained by the differences in social background. Thus, it turns out that many of the landed aristocracy and priesthood whom one would normally expect to follow the Sadducean teaching were Pharisees of the Shammaitic persuasion, while the merchants and artisans followed the Hillelite tradition.

The question arises, how did it happen that some of the landed aristocracy were Sadducees while others were Shammaitic Pharisees? The answer must be sought in the genius of Simeon the Righteous, the greatest of the post-biblical high priests and one of the foremost leaders of Pharisaism. In *Mishna Abot* 1.2 we are told that Simeon the Righteous was one of the last members of the Great Synagogue, the legislative body of the Pharisees. This can only mean that Simeon the High Priest associated himself with the Pharisees instead of with the Sadducees. His maxim was "The world stands on three pillars: on Torah, the ritual of the Temple, and deeds of kindness."[2]

It is remarkable that a high priest should place the study of Torah before the Temple worship. What could have moved the high priest to become a member of the Pharisaic Great Synagogue? The answer to this must be that the occasion was the proclamation by Antiochus III that Jewish law was the law of the land, so far as Jews are concerned.[3] It was necessary in view of this proclamation to define Jewish law. Apparently Simeon the Righteous and his followers agreed with the Pharisaic teachers on a formula which enabled them to present Jewish law as a unit. They did this by accepting a compromise which both the Pharisees and many Saducean families were willing to adopt. The Pharisees agreed that the Court of the Chamber of Hewn Stones, whose members were drawn from their aristocratic lay and priestly families, was to be the supreme tribunal in a number of areas of Jewish law.[4] On the other hand, in order to prevent the Court from rendering decisions which the Pharisees could not accept it was agreed that the Court should always include at least one or two Pharisaic teachers and that only a unanimous decision by the Court was valid.[5] The Saducean families who followed Simeon the Righteous further agreed to accept Pharisaic teaching as their own in about a score of issues. These included such issues as the date of the festival of Shabuot,[6] permission to use light on the Sabbath eve,[7] the water pouring ritual on Sukkot,[8] the Pharisaic rule for the ritual of the high priest on the Day of Atonement,[9] and others which are enumerated in my book on the Pharisees.[10] On the hundreds of other issues, the Saducean families preserved their own customs. One of the families which followed the leadership of Simeon the Righteous was none other than the Maccabees,[11] who had large estates in Modin and became Pharisaic leaders.

As Pharisaism was now divided between the proto-Shammaites and proto-Hillelites, we find that beginning with Jose b. Joezer and Jose b. Johanan there were in each generation two Pharisaic leaders, presumably one representing the proto-Shammaites and one representing the proto-Hillelites. When the Talmud reports that until the time of Jose b. Joezer there was no controversy concerning Jewish law,[12] what it means is that there was no controversy among Pharisees. But after the time of Simeon the Righteous, with the introduction into

Pharisaism of a large and influential group of former Sadducees, there necessarily arose two parties within Pharisaism. These continued for five generations, during which the Pharisees were led by two scholars, one chosen from the neo-Pharisees, the other from the old Pharisees. Thus, to have devised this compromise, enabling both groups to live together and be united, was undoubtedly an achievement of historical proportions and ultimately enabled Judaism to resist Hellenization.

Among the doctrines which the neo-Pharisees agreed to accept was the belief in the Resurrection of the dead. Ben Sira, who praises Simeon the Righteous in a moving poem,[13] refused to accept this doctrine,[14] but this dogma was vital to Pharisaic thinking, and the members of the Great Synagogue introduced a paragraph in the *Amidah* proclaiming their belief in the Resurrection. This meant that no Sadducee could lead a Pharisaic congregation in prayer. On the other hand, Antigonus, the disciple and probably the successor of Simeon the Righteous as Pharisaic leader, taught "Be not like servants who serve their Master with the expectation of reward; be rather like servants who serve their Master without expectation of reward." He did not deny the Resurrection but tried to persuade his fellow Pharisees not to insist that belief in the Resurrection was essential to their faith.

The question arises, what kept the two groups of Pharisees with such different customs and interpretations of the law together? After all, among these differences were problems of marriage. Some marriages which the proto-Hillelites considered forbidden were considered mandatory by the proto-Shammaites. The children of those marriages would be illegitimate according to the Hillelites but legitimate according to the Shammaites. Some foods which were permitted by the Hillelites were prohibited by the Shammaites. The answer is that there existed a Pharisaic association constructed after the manner of the Phoenician and Greek trade associations. A member of this association was called a *haber*, that is, member. These members could trust one another to be kept informed about any matters which from the point of view of any particular member would be a violation of the law. The existence of this association itself points to an outstanding figure as its creator. No personality less than the high priest, and indeed a rare high priest, could have accomplished the task of inventing this association. In other words, the existence of the Pharisaic association points to Simeon the Righteous as its author.

Notes

1. Many additional controversies between these groups are recorded as being between individuals. Thus differences of opinion between R. Eliezer and R. Joshua or R. Eliezer and R. Akiba reflect differences between the "houses".

2. *Mishna Abot* 1.2.

3. The Jews under the leadership of Simeon the Righteous had assisted Antiochus III in his battle against the Egyptians. He was very grateful to them and as a result issued the proclamation giving Jewish law the force of imperial law so far as Jews were concerned.

4. *Sifre Deuteronomy* 152, p. 235.

5. *Mishna Horayot* 1.4, and see *Tosefta Horayot* 1.3, p. 474.

6. The date of the other festivals was always fixed by their time in the calendar and it was agreed that the Court of the Chamber of Hewn Stones was the ultimate authority in setting the date of the new moon and thus fixing the date of the holiday. The decision of this Court regarding the calendar was valid even if it turned out to be mistaken or deliberately wrong (*Sifra Emor*, perek 10.2-3). However, the date of Shabuot was fixed by counting the days after the reaping of the first barley harvest (*Lev.* 23.15). The Sadducees held that the barley harvest should begin on the night after the Sabbath of the Passover week. The Pharisees held that the counting should begin on the second night of Passover.

7. The Sadducees forbade the use of fire on the Sabbath even if it was kindled on Friday before dark. The Pharisees not only permitted it but held that the lighting of the candles before the Sabbath was imperative.

8. The Pharisees held that Sukkot was the season of judgment concerning the rains and therefore introduced a number of customs which were considered necessary to bring plentiful rain. Among these was the elaborate ceremony of water pouring described in *Mishna Sukkah*, Ch. 5.

9. The Sadducees held, on the basis of *Lev.* 16.2, that the Deity appeared in the Holy of Holies and therefore the high priest offering the incense on the Day of Atonement should prepare it before entering the Holy of Holies so that he will not see the Deity and die. The Pharisees denied that the Deity could be seen and insisted that the incense should be put on the fire in the Holy of Holies itself.

10. *The Pharisees*, pp. 101 ff.

11. Judah the Maccabee considered it necessary to obtain forgiveness for the soldiers who had died and were found wearing pagan emblems. This can only mean that he believed in the Resurrection of the dead and that the soldiers needed forgiveness for this transgression even after death. This was a Shammaitic doctrine (Second Maccabees, Ch. 12.42).

12. *B. Tamurah* 15b.

13. *Ben Sira* 50.1 ff.

14. *Mishna Yebamot* 1.1.

Education by Example: A Motif in Joseph and Maccabee Literature of the Second Temple Period

Lawrence E. Frizzell

Introduction
In Jewish tradition the five books of Moses hold the place of honor in Israel's sacred writings as the *Torah* or "instruction" of God. Some people, even in ancient times, seemed to emphasize the legislative teachings or commandments, so the Greek translators chose the word *"Nomos"* or "Law" to render *Torah*. Indeed, laws provide the practical norms whereby people guide their lives and teach their offspring. However, in most cultures legislation has its complement in inspiring narratives. Heroes and heroines of times long past are presented as worthy of imitation. They exemplify the ideal that offers a synthesis about the meaning of life. Jews recognize that commandments offer a basis for *halakhah*, the way to go in life, which is completed by *haggadah*, a set of narratives presenting insights regarding imitation of God in the ambiguities of human life.

My study of edifying narratives will be divided into two parts: 1.) developments of the Joseph narrative from the Book of Genesis and 2.) the accounts of martyrdom in the Second and Fourth Books of Maccabees.

I. Joseph the Patriarch
In the patriarchal narratives of Genesis, the story of Joseph contains a number of profound lessons, couched within a drama that has inspired writers from the Second Temple period down to Thomas Mann.

Family jealousies are shown in the rivalry between spouses of Jacob and a reaction to the favoritism shown toward Joseph, the lad whose dreams provoked his half-brothers to threats of violence and a quick sale which reduced him to slavery in Egypt. Although God seemed to be silent, Joseph's faith and moral sensitivity were rewarded. He tested and then forgave his brothers: "The evil you planned to do against me has, by God's design, been turned to good that he might bring about, as indeed he has, the deliverance of a numerous people" (*Gen.* 50:20; see 45:5-8).

1. Joseph and Asenath[1]

The book of Genesis records with tantalizing brevity that the Pharaoh gave Joseph a wife named Asenath, daughter of Potiphera, priest of On (41:45). They had two sons, Manasseh and Ephraim (41:50-52).

Jewish readers during the Second Temple period would wonder about the example set by the patriarch. Did he marry a Gentile? The novel about Joseph and Asenath (dated the period between 100 B.C.E. to 100 C.E.) resolves this problem by telling of her dramatic conversion.

The author portrays Joseph, now Pharaoh's favored servant, not only as a wise and righteous young man, but also as one who observes even the dietary laws of the Torah. When the Pharaoh's chosen representative Joseph meets the 18 year old Asenath, her father suggests that she treat him like a brother. As she goes up to kiss Joseph, he stops her: "It is not fitting for a man who worships God ...to kiss a strange woman who will bless with her mouth dead and dumb idols..." (8:5). Then, noticing her distress, Joseph asks God to bless her, to renew her spirit and number her among his people. This example of stern adherence to principles followed by a gesture of mercy was the beginning of her conversion. Not only does she reject the idolatry of her father, but she becomes a "city of refuge" for all converts to Judaism.

Pharaoh's son loves Asenath, but the Pharaoh wants to arrange marriage with a foreign princess. The jealous prince planned to kill Joseph so that he can marry Asenath. Simeon and Levi reject his offer of riches for murdering Joseph by explaining: "We are men who worship God and it does not befit us to repay evil for evil" (23:9). He then lies to the four sons of Leah's and Rachel's handmaidens: "I heard Joseph your brother saying to Pharaoh my father... 'Children of my father's maid-servants are Dan and Gad, Naphtali and Asher, and they are not my brothers. I will wait for my father's death and I will blot them out from the earth...'" (24:8-9).

Their ambush of Asenath's chariot is foiled by Benjamin. The wicked brothers beg Asenath for mercy and she saves them from the wrath of Simeon and Levi. She exhorts them: "Do not do evil for evil to your neighbor. To the Lord will you give (the right) to punish the insult done by them" (28:14).

Thus Asenath shows that she has learned the lesson of forgiveness from Joseph at a more profound level than the sons of Jacob, who are beneficiaries of Joseph's kindness.

The Testament of Joseph[2]

On his death bed the patriarch Jacob calls his sons around him for a final message. This begins a tradition followed by Moses (Deut.33), Tobit (4:2-21) and others. During the Second Temple period (perhaps in the second century B.C.E.) literature purporting to be the Testaments of the Twelve Patriarchs appears. Each develops an exhortation to virtue around the strengths or failings of the sons of Jacob.

The Testament of Joseph begins with a poetic review of the tragedies and triumphs of his life (1:2-7).

The Book of Genesis tells how Joseph is sold to an Egyptian officer in Pharaoh's service. This man's wife tries to tempt him to commit adultery. When he spurns her advances, she frames him and he is imprisoned.

The Testament of Joseph focuses on this temptation and expands the account of the woman's wiles. The temptations continue for seven years and take a variety of forms: threats and enticements followed by a request for instruction in God's Word (4:1-8).

She later says that she would kill her husband, so that Joseph could marry her, but Joseph threatens to reveal the crime. Next she spikes food with drugs, but God warns Joseph against them. She threatens suicide unless Joseph would acquiesce. He prays and replies: "Why, wretched woman, are you troubled and disturbed, blinded by sin?

Remember that if you kill yourself, Astheta, your husband's concubine, who is jealous of you, will beat your children..." (7:5).

Then the author refers to the story, recorded in Genesis 39:6-23, that she snatches his garment and claims that he had tried to rape her. A brief account of Joseph's imprisonment tells of his intense prayer. Joseph concludes this narrative by exhorting his listeners:

"So you see, my children, how great are the things that patience and prayer with fasting accomplish. If you, too, pursue self-control and purity with patience and prayer with fasting in humility of heart, the Lord will dwell among you, because He loves self-control" (10:1-2).

The virtues presented for imitation are patience in afflictions and purity. Self-control that is exercised in fasting, accompanied by constant prayer provide the two-fold basis for Joseph's rejection of temptation. The Jewish man during the Second Temple period, especially if he lived in the Diaspora, might find either attraction or enticement among foreign women. This was a great concern of Jewish teachers from the time of Ezra in the fourth century B.C.E. and onwards.

The second part of this Testament reflects on Joseph's virtue of piety and fraternal love. When he is sold by his brothers to the Ishmaelite traders, the youth claims to be a slave of their household so that he would not disgrace them (11:3). After recounting further details of his sufferings, Joseph concludes:

"So you see, my children, how many things I endured in order not to bring my brothers to disgrace. You, therefore, must love one another and in patient endurance conceal one another's failings. God is delighted by harmony among brothers and by the intention of a kind heart that takes pleasure in goodness" (17:1-3).

The Testament goes on to speak of Joseph's love and care of his brothers and their families, even after the death of the patriarch Jacob. "I did not exalt myself above them arrogantly because of my worldly position of glory, but I was among them as one of the least" (17:8).

This leads to another exhortation: "If you live in accord with the Lord's commands, God will exalt you with good things forever. And if anyone wishes to do you harm, you should pray for him, along with doing good, and you will be rescued by the Lord from every evil" (18:1-2).

The Testament of Benjamin continues the reflection on Joseph. "Now, my children, love the Lord God of heaven and earth; keep his commandments; *Pattern your life after the good and pious man Joseph*... Fear the Lord and love your neighbor. Even if the spirits of Beliar seek to derange you with all sorts of wicked oppression, they will not dominate you, any more than they dominated Joseph, my brother. How many men wanted to destroy him, yet God looked out for him!... Joseph also urged our father to pray for his brothers, that the Lord would not hold them accountable for their sin which they so wickedly committed against him" (3:1-6).

A number of times in these documents the ways in which Joseph forgives his older brothers is stressed. Forgiveness, that most difficult of virtues, is an aspect of love, and should reflect the divine forgiveness that is needed by all. The challenge to imitate God is presented in many ways throughout the Torah. "Be holy, for I the Lord your God am holy" (Lev. 19:2) is a direct command. Elsewhere the example of God is placed before the people of Israel, especially through the experience of Moses the second time he ascended Mount Sinai. The sacred Name revealed to Moses at the burning bush (Exod. 3:14) is interpreted to mean the God who is "merciful and gracious, slow to anger, and abounding in lovingkindness and faithfulness...*forgiving iniquity and transgression and sin*..." (*Exod.* 34:6-7). The story of Joseph presents this pattern of forgiveness in the drama of human existence.

II. The Martyrs during the Persecution of Antiochus IV

The drama of Israelite and Jewish history includes many periods of excruciating tests followed by vindication. One of these is celebrated each year in late November or December, the feast of Hanukkah. In an effort to unify the Seleucid empire, the emperor Antiochus IV Epiphanes tried to impose the benefits of the Greek culture upon minorities within his domain. He reasoned that these peoples should speak Greek, enjoy a Greek education and worship in the Greek manner. He placed a statue of Zeus in the Temple of Jerusalem and demanded that Jews show allegiance first, by refraining from their own religious practices (such as circumcision) and secondly, by offering sacrifice to Greek deities. This demand was unacceptable to many Jews on both counts.

The Hasmonean family of Mattathias and his five sons led the revolt which was eventually successful. The Temple was restored to proper worship in the winter of 164 B.C.E.

The motif of teaching by example occurs in the Second and Fourth Books of Maccabees. Here spiritual resistance to persecution is given pride of place over the physical prowess and military genius of Judas Maccabeus and his followers.

The author of 2 Maccabees calls his work a condensation of a five-volume history by Jason of Cyrene (2:23). The work is structured after the Deuteronomic theology of history which divides Israel's story into a pattern of five stages:[3]

1. A time of divine blessing, during which the people are at peace (3:1-40).

2. A sin which introduces alienation and chaos into Israel (4:1-5:10).

3. Punishment by God, often using a foreign power as an instrument (5:11-6:17).

4. A turning point which involves divine forgiveness and Israel's conversion (6:18-8:4).

5. Judgment against Israel's enemies and salvation for the repentant people (8:5-15:36).

Thus, Second Maccabees shows that the Jews in the Land enjoyed peace during the reign of the good high priest, Onias. The great sin came when the usurpers of priestly leadership, Jason and then Menelaus, accepted Antiochus' program of Hellenization. After this, Antiochus sacked the Temple, which was understood as God's punishment for the priestly sin. The turning point in the drama was the death of martyrs, whose witness to God's commandments constituted vicarious atonement for the people's sins. Only then did Judas Maccabees begin the military revolt, that brought liberation for the Jewish people (8:3-4).

The author's theological interpretation is explicit just before he presents the witness of Eleazar and the mother with her seven sons. ..."These punishments were designed not to destroy but to discipline our people...(The Lord) never withdraws his mercy from us. Though he disciplines us with calamities, he does not forsake his own people" (6:12-17).

The first martyr is a ninety year old scribe named Eleazar. He is forced to submit to those carrying out Antiochus' orders. Greeks sacrificed pigs and the test of obedience was to eat this meat. Eleazar spat out the unclean flesh and went willingly to the rack of torture. The men offer to free him so that later he could bring his own meat and merely pretend to share in the sacrificial meal. He rejects simulation, "lest many of the young should suppose that Eleazar in his ninetieth year has gone over to an alien religion...for the sake of living a brief moment longer, they should be led astray because of me, while I defile and disgrace my old age" (2 Macc. 6:24-25).

Eleazar first considers the onus which his age and role as teacher place upon him. Personal or selfish concerns should never take precedence over one's duty to the community and especially to the younger generation.

He continues by contrasting fear of men and awe before God. "For even if for the present I should avoid the punishment of men, yet whether I live or die I shall not escape the hands of the Almighty" (6:26). All that happens through good or evil use of free will comes under divine scrutiny and judgment. The persecutors should recall this as well.

Finally, Eleazar declares that his death will "leave to the young a noble example of how to die a good death willingly and nobly for the revered and holy laws" (6:27). Courage should be contagious, so his proof of fidelity under duress will uplift others facing the same or similar ordeals. Eleazar died with a profession of faith and acceptance (6:30). The author concludes the narrative with the remark that his death was "an example of nobility and a precedent of valor to be remembered not only by the young but by the multitudes of his nation" (6:31).

2 Maccabees chapter 7 narrates the trials and execution of a woman and her seven sons.[4] There is no allusion to the witness of Eleazar in this account. From the testimony of these martyrs there is

great emphasis on their faith in the resurrection of the body. The second brother addresses King Antiochus: "You accursed wretch, you dismiss us from this present life, but the King of the universe will raise us up to an everlasting renewal of life, because we have died for his laws" (7:9).

As in the Book of Daniel, this faith responds to the dilemma of persecution. The Torah was given so that the people could *live* by keeping its ordinances (Lev. 18:5). Here those faithful to God's law *die* while apostates are rewarded by the King. The prophets and Psalmists of ancient Israel insisted that life is defined as communion with the living God; this life, they reasoned, cannot be interrupted even by the death of one's body. By the Second Temple period, some Jews in the Holy Land professed faith in the resurrection, while those in the Greek-speaking countries stressed immortality of the soul. In both cases they emphasized that a righteous life is essential to a meaningful doctrine of immortality and resurrection. This point is expressed by the fourth brother. "One cannot but choose to die at the hands of men and to cherish the hope that God gives of being raised again by him. But for you there will be no resurrection to *life*!" (7:14). Because God will judge everyone according to his or her deeds, the king is told: "Do not think that you will go unpunished for having tried to fight against God!" (7:19, see 7:34-38).

The first evidence of the great influence of these "Acts of the Martyrs" comes in the first century C.E. when a long discourse is dedicated to Eleazar, here designated as a priest, and the woman with seven sons. It has been called the Fourth Book of Maccabees, but is a philosophical rather than historical document.[5] The author wants to prove that reason should control human passions and foster the four cardinal virtues, prudence, temperance, fortitude and justice (1:2-7, 18; 5:23). "By far the best example I could furnish is the heroism of those who died for virtue's sake, namely Eleazar and the seven brothers with their mother" (1:8). Throughout this work the link between Eleazar and the others is clear, whereas Second Maccabees presents two distinct episodes.

The speeches placed on Eleazar's lips are eloquent expressions of Jewish piety (5:14-38). The speech concerning good example (6:16-23) does not add any new points to that of Second Maccabees.

The dialogue of the brothers with the King points to the conduct of Eleazar. "You seek to terrify us with your threat of death by torture as if you had learned nothing from Eleazar but a short while ago. But if, for the sake of their religion and enduring through torments, old men of the Hebrews have remained faithful to the end, it is even more appropriate that we who are young should die in disregard of the tortures you impose on us, the very tortures our aged teacher triumphed over..." (9:5-6).

Thus Eleazar's fidelity has borne fruit, and this challenge to imitate him extends to the younger generation. In this account the first brother does not lose his tongue to the torturers. He cries out: "Imitate me, my brothers; do not become deserters in my trial nor forswear our brotherhood in nobility..." (9:23).

The surviving brothers "formed a holy choir of piety as they encouraged each other with the words: 'Let us die like brothers all, brothers, for the sake of the Law. Let us follow the example of the three youths in Assyria, who despised the same trial by ordeal in the furnace'" (13:9, see 16:3).

The author repeats the teaching of Second Maccabees (8:3) that the consecration of these martyrs led to the defeat of Israel's enemies and the purification of the Land, "since they became, as it were, a ransom for the sin of our nation..." (4 Macc. 17:21-22).

We are still too close to the tragic events of the Nazi period in Europe to discern the full implications of those acts of martyrdom for the Jewish people and the Land of Israel today; however, both the example and prayers of the patriarchs and the martyrs resonate down through the centuries.

Notes

1. See the translation by C. Burchard in *The Old Testament Pseudepigrapha*, ed. J.H. Charlesworth (Garden City: Doubleday, 1985) volume II pp. 177-247. Quotations are from this version.

2. See the translation of H.C. Kee in *The Old Testament Pseudepigrapha* (1983) volume I pp. 819-828. Quotations are from this version.
Studies on the Testament of Joseph, ed. George W.E. Nickelsburg, Jr., (Scholars Press, 1975) includes the essay of Walter Harrelson, "Patient love in the Testament of Joseph," pp. 27-35. The most complete investigation is by Harm W. Hollander, *Joseph as an Ethical Model in the Testaments of the Twelve Patriarchs*. (Leiden: E.J. Brill, 1981).

3. George W.E. Nickelsburg, Jr., *Jewish Literature between the Bible and the Mishnah*. (Philadelphia: Fortress, 1981) p. 118.
The most complete commentary is Jonathan Goldstein's *II Maccabees* (Anchor Bible). Garden City: Doubleday, 1983. The Revised Standard Version of the Apocrypha is used for quotations.

4. See Robert Doran, "The martyr: A synoptic view of the mother and her seven sons," *Ideal Figures in Ancient Judaism: Profiles and Paradigms* ed. John J. Collins and George W.E. Nickelsburg (Atlanta: Scholars Press, 1980) for talmudic and midrashic developments of this story. The reflections of the Alexandrian Jewish scholar have been studied by Thomas H. Tobin, "Tradition and interpretation in Philo's portrait of the Patriarch Joseph," *Seminar Papers*: Society of Bibical Literature Annual Meeting 1986 (Atlanta: Scholars Press, 1986) pp. 271-277.

5. The translation of H. Anderson in *The Old Testament Pseudepigrapha* volume II pp. 531-564 is used here.

Augustine's Manichaean Turn: The Physical World in the New Creation

Robert A. Herrera

The theme of the coming end and future transformation of the world runs through the New Testament. The early Christian community appropriated key themes from Jewish apocalyptic, incorporating and modifying them. In contrast to prophetic thought, in which the hope of a coming kingdom is usually related to the restoration of the Davidic line, in apocalyptic eschatology the future hope becomes supra-celestial and transcendent. The rivals are spiritual forces, not earthly powers. Paul's theology agrees with Jewish apocalyptic in its eschatological dualism. The final judgment will complete both the evil of the evildoers and the righteousness of the just ones.

Following the path of the Jewish apocalyptic writers of the intertestamental period, who believed that the promised redemption would include not only mankind but the whole creation[1], this notion, that the physical world shares in the redemptive process, is found in Paul and *Revelation*. Among the most forceful passages are *Romans* 8,19-24, *Colossians* 1,15-20, and *Revelation* 21,1-3. Whether the redemption will occur by means of gradual transformation, cataclysm, or periodic renewal, it will resemble the lost, paradisical world. The end will, in some way, correspond to and recapitulate the beginning.

Although the Christian Church of both East and West accepted this belief in its broad strokes, the Eastern Church has historically received it with greater enthusiasm and has been characterized by what Vladimir Lossky called "cosmic consciousness"[2]. God has decreed that the created universe - implenitude and non-being further weakened by original sin - will acquire the fullness it lacks by means of a process which reverses the depredations of original sin. Created wills, by means of their fidelity to the uncreated will of God, will generate a force which will impel all creatures towards their ultimate goal of perfect union with God[3]. In this enterprise, the small but precious physical world, often compared by the Eastern Fathers to the lost sheep in the parable of the Good Shepherd, will enjoy a privileged role.

This teaching, basically that of Maximus, reached the West, somewhat modified, in John the Scot's *De divisione naturae*, and was received by the theological community with confusion, suspicion, and alarm. Several centuries before, Irenaeus, an emigré from the East, had received a different welcome. In any case, while the cosmic aspects of redemption have been muted in the West, finding an echo only in marginal areas such as alchemy, it is still of substantive importance to the Eastern Church. The theme is familiar in Russian literature of the past century: Bulgakov insists that Christ's resurrection permeates the whole of nature, that the life of the world to come is the making eternal of everything in this age worthy of such transformation.[4]

Augustine seems to mark a watershed in the development of this theme as, from the fifth century on, speculation in the West on the cosmic aspect of redemption assumes a decidedly minor role. Moreover, the conception of paradise underwent a laborious transformation from geographical place to the spiritual disposition of the individual soul. Today, it strikes us as decidedly odd that the denial of a material paradise was considered theologically suspect until the sixteenth century. In the end, paradise becomes a type of the mystical life, "une participation intime à la vie paradisiaque première"[5]. Can Augustine be faulted for this tilt away from the cosmic towards the personal and spiritual?

It cannot be denied that in many passages Augustine luxuriates in the attributes of redeemed matter, though most are centered on the human body and not the physical world. This is evidenced in many of his works but is especially prominent in *De civitate Dei* where he considers the status of the resurrected body. He suggests that it will be youthful, that it will possess sexual distinctions, but that it will be transformed into a new incorruptibility and immortality, without any trace of age.[6] The New Jerusalem will establish a harmony between the resurrected bodies and the renewed physical world, in which the immortal spiritual bodies will be able to see the physical bodies of the New Heaven and the New Earth, enjoying God's presence radiating throughout his creation.[7] Although his descriptions are frankly utopian, Augustine's delighted emphasis on human redemption can only dim the lustre of the physical bodies of the redeemed cosmos.

Despite his rhetorical flourishes, Augustine could hardly be fully at ease with beliefs which were strongly opposed by his philosophical mentors, the NeoPlatonists. He was aware that the "Platonists" opposed the belief in the resurrection of the body and that Porphyry thought the ultimate transformation of the world to be ludicrous.[8] That Augustine held both beliefs, is a tribute to his faith. How he held them is a matter for investigation.

A clue to the question under consideration is found in an early commentary on *Romans*. Discussing *Romans* 8,19-23, Augustine warns that the text should not be understood as attributing affects to "trees, grass, stone, and the like."[9] This is a Manicaean error. It denies that all creatures are recapitulated in man. The classic Pauline statement that "the created universe awaits with eager expectation for God's sons to be revealed" is restricted to that which, in man, is sick and subject to corruption. Again, commenting on *Ephesians* 1,10, Augustine identifies "heavenly things" with angels and "earthly things" with man, in effect bracketing the physical world.[10] Although he dwells at length on the distinctions between the corruptible human body and the glorified body, he fails to discuss substantially the parallel distinction which suggests itself, that between the present world and the glorified world.

It stands to reason that Augustine's nine-year career as a Manichaean Auditor, his defection from the sect and conversion to Christianity, must be taken into account, as must his polemical works and later writings, which contain references and backward glances to those years. If he was successful against the Manichee-without, perhaps the victory was not as overwhelming against the Manichee-within. Augustine was accused of Manichaean sympathies both at the beginning and end of his episcopal tenure. His accusers, Megalius of Calama and Julian of Eclanum were also Bishops, the latter perhaps the most brilliant of his many adversaries. Although the Manichaean polemic dominated his episcopate up to about 405 A.D., he kept Mani's *Letter of the Foundation* at hand in Hippo during his later years, making critical notes on its margins.[11]

The many works written during the Manichaean polemic include treatises, letters, and minutes of debates. They range from the scholarly to the popular, the profound to the trivial, in which insightful argument is matched by abusive hectoring. From *De moribus ecclesiae catholicae et de moribus Manichaeorum* [388] to the *Contra Faustum* [397] in thirty-three books, the polemic included works of the stature of *De libero arbitrio* [391] and *De utilitate credendi* [391], a sort of prolegomena for the later, more extensive, *Contra Faustum*.

Augustine's attack against the Manichees was directed against three prime targets: (1) their dualism; (2) their objections to the Old Testament; (3) their accusation that the Catholic Church was hostile to reason. He had experienced their attraction and acknowledged being influenced by the latter even after the strength of the first two had waned. In any case, the three were intertwined with their cosmology at the center, a colorful and persuasive depiction of their major beliefs. The cosmic drama, played out in the struggle between the Kingdom of Light and the Kingdom of Darkness, was reproduced in man's inner life.[12]

Manichaean dualism was anchored in the problem of evil. If it was impossible for evil to come from a good God, it resulted from the invasion of the Kingdom of Light by an opposing force, the Kingdom of Darkness. In man also, an external, evil force attacks and attempts to overpower the passive, internal good. The Creator God of the Old Testament was replaced by the Father of Light, a passive non-creator, while the Manichaean religion endeavored, above all, to insure that man's good part would remain unaffected by the evil substance and that the light-particles imbedded in matter would be liberated.

Matter was the obsession of the Manicheans. They attempted to walk the tightrope between defilement, through contact with matter, and sacrilege, by offering violence to the light imprisoned within matter. They were prohibited from eating meat, drinking wine, owning property and tilling the soil. That the implementation of their regulations usually extended only to the Perfect and not the Auditors, allowed for a certain leeway in practice.

To complicate matters, the Manichees were basically a Christian enthusiast sect, the "Church of the Holy Spirit." From the orthodox point of view, they were blatantly heretical, rejecting the Old Testament, the Creator God, the Incarnation, the Resurrection, and were particularly scandalized by the Christian eucharist, as it reversed their aspiration of liberating light-particles from matter. Their "good news" was, in the apposite words of Peter Brown, that the visible world was a "gigantic pharmacy," in which light would be distilled from the matter that imprisons them.[13] In this way, every physical process became part of the drama of salvation. The universe itself was the result of this mixture of light and darkness, good and evil. They believed that light, the divine element, was especially present in the vegetable kingdom, seeing in the fruit of trees a symbol of "*Jesus Patibilis*," the suffering Jesus, a revamped version of the gnostic messenger.[14]

The problem of evil was an effective lure for the Manichees. Once human malice and general evil is accepted - both Augustine and the Manichees believed both to be clearly verified by experience - then what should be thought of God? The ploy was a superb opening towards their beliefs, which Augustine insists, are attacks against both God and his creation. It enfeebles God, infecting him with evil, and destroys the integrity of creation. He urges, that as all which exists is good insofar as it exists, evil cannot be a substance and God cannot be harmed. He connects their metaphysical errors with their moral aberrations. In a lengthy critique of the "three seals" of Manichaean ethics, he touches on several of their more bizarre beliefs, making the nice point that their credo leads them into the position of having more compassion for cucumbers than for human beings.[15]

The final section of *De Genesi contra Manichaeos* has a brief but useful summary of contrasting Manichaean and Christian views. Augustine indicates that the Manichaeans believe that part of God's substance is vitiated by evil, that evil is a substance, that God forgives himself, is mutable, and substantially affected by human sin. Christians believe that God is immutable, evil is not a substance, all substances are good, God forgives sins, and no one is substantially affected by the sins of others.[16] If Augustine warns repeatedly of the frenetic charlatanism of the Manichees, he is hardly lethargic in his criticism of them: they teach false doctrines, indulge in outlandish speculation, and lead their followers into moral turpitude. To counter the extravagances which he details in the *Confessions*,[17] Augustine insists, to the point of satiety, that the whole of nature is created, and monotonously makes comparisons between Creator and creation to illustrate his thesis.

Several years later, during the anti-Pelagian struggle, he turns a critical eye on the Manichaeans, again accusing them of denying God's creative omnipotence. At this time [cir. 420 a.d.] he begins to give serious consideration to the rather wild accounts of their moral depravity which would seem to follow from their denial of personal responsibility for sin. Man is overpowered by an evil force to which he does not consent. Augustine, though he moves closer to the "Platonists," does not move to the opposite pole. Even while still engaged in the Manichaean polemic, he denies that the soul could enjoy perfect beatitude before the resurrection of the body. The soul, he indicates, has a natural inclination to govern a body, and this must be satisfied before the person, in his entirety, is constituted. This position he does not change even when his NeoPlatonic readings help him to break loose from a chilling incapacity to conceive of God as immaterial, which he duly blames on the Manichees. Only when the body *"per futuram commutationem"* receives a spiritual form and is reunited with its soul, will the person be able to enjoy perfect vision.[18] In this way, both the materialism of the Manichees and the immaterialism of the NeoPlatonists are avoided and orthodoxy maintained.

Perhaps what irritated Augustine most was the confused mixture of good and evil, light and darkness, which constituted their world. In a lengthy letter to Jerome, he indicates that *De libero arbitrio* was written against the Manichees with the purpose of detaching the inviolable nature of God from the flawed nature of creatures.[19] The mixture of good and evil, which pervades every cranny of the universe, must be denied, and clear distinctions must be drawn. Augustine had earlier noted that the primal light, water and fruit - which constitute a theological bridge stretching from *Genesis* to *Revelation* - should not be identified with physical elements because of the danger of falling into the practice of worshipping things as do the Manichaeans.[20]

It may be conjectured that a justification of the Creator God led Augustine to place a lower value on material creation and consequently to mute the cosmic implications of the eschaton. The move, in any case, corresponds to his priorities of God and the soul. He believes that the very expertise of the philosophers in Physics [Natural Philosophy] leads to their errors concerning both God and the soul. While the philosophers wondered at the changeableness of things within the sublunary region of the world, Augustine wonders at the intrinsic non-being of the cosmos. While creation is an outrage to the philosophical mind and eternalism congenial, Augustine rejects eternalism and its twin, the cyclical theory, in favor of creation and a linear unfolding of time. For Augustine, if the truth will make you free, it will, first of all, liberate you from the *mundus* and its strictures.

Augustine's muting of the redemption of the physical world should be considered a stage in the Jewish-Christian demythologizing of the cosmos. It dovetails nicely with his goal of recapitulating creation in man, man in Christ, and Christ in God, so that ultimately there will be one Christ, loving himself.[21] Presently, however, creation is a hierarchy, with rational creatures at the summit and physical nature at the bottom. Augustine, while urging the unity of creation, strengthens the boundaries which separate God from man, and man from lower creation.

Although he was very much aware of the bonds which link man to the animal kingdom, Augustine thought that there was no substantial relation between them.[22] Animals do not have rational souls. He adumbrates Descartes' surgical detachment of rational beings and non-rational beings, without the inconvenience of converting animals into automata. It was Augustine's reaction against the doctrines of the Manichees, their moral hubris and intellectual slovenliness, which blasphemed God and blurred the contours of reality, which provided the point of departure for his considerations on the status of the physical world, its place in the new creation, and consequently, set the course of these speculations for some time to come.

Notes

1. D.S. Russell, *The Method and Message of Jewish Apocalyptic* (Philadelphia: Westminster, 1976), pp.267ff., 280ff.

2. *The Mystical Theology of the Eastern Church*, trans. Fellowship of St. Alban and St. Sergius (Cambridge: James Clarke, 1968), pp. 110-113.

3. *Ibid.*, p. 105, note 2.

4. Sergei Bulgakov, "Meditations on the Joy of Resurrection". *Ultimate Questions*, edited by A. Schmemann (New York: Holt, Rinehart and Winston, 1965), pp 301-302.

5. Dom Anselme Stolz, *Théologie de la Mystique* (Chevetogne: Editions des Benedictins D'Amay, 1947), pp. 18-30, esp. p. 27.

6. *De civ.* Dei 22, 21. Refer to Henri I. Marrou, *The Resurrection and St. Augustine's Theory of Human Values*, trans. M. Maria Consolata (Villanova: Villanova Univ. Press, 1966).

7. *De civ. Dei* 20, 16.

8. *Ibid.*, 22, 11, 1.

9. *Expositio quarundam Propositionum ex Epistola ad Romanos*, No. 35.

10. *Enchiridion* 62, 16.

11. *Retract.* 2, 28.

12. The best account of Manichaean theory and practice is still Henri Charles Puech, *Le Manichéisme: son fondateur, sa doctrine* (Paris: S.A.E.P., 1949). Also helpful is Gerald Bonner, *St. Augustine of Hippo: Life and Controversies* (Norwich: The Canterbury Press, 1986), pp. 157-236.

13. *Augustine of Hippo* (Berkeley: Univ. of California Press, 1969), p. 56ff.

14. For the Gnostic background refer to Hans Jonas, *The Gnostic Religion* (Boston: Beacon Press, 1963).

15. *De moribus* 2, 17, 53.

16. *Ibid.* 2, 29, 43.

17. 3, 10; 7, 2 et al. For Augustine's evaluation refer to *Conf.* 13, 30, 45; *Contra Faustum* 20, 15; *Enarr.in Ps.* 141, 18, et al.

18. *Contra duas Ep. Pelagianorum* 2, 2, 2-3.

19. *Ep.* 146, 7.

20. *De Genesi contra Manichaeos* 1, 3, 6; 1, 5, 8; 2, 25, 38.

21. *In Ep. Ioannis ad Parthos* 10, 3.

22. *De moribus* 2, 17, 59.

On the Role of Modality in Aristotle's Metaphysics[1]

Jaakko Hintikka

PRE-INDEX

PERSONS
   Aristotle
   Megarians

SUBJECTS
   Change (*kinesis*)
   dynamis vs. *energeia*
   energeia vs. *dynamis*
   entelecheia
   Existence
   Form
   Kinesis
   Matter
   Megarianism
   Modality
   Motion (*kinesis*)
   Modality
   Potency (potentiality)
      active vs. passive
   Substance
      unity of substance

1. Substance as a union of matter and form

One of the most crucial and at the same time most puzzling questions concerning the central books Z-θ of Aristotle's *Metaphysics* concerns the structure of his overall argument. What are his problems, and how does he propose to approach them? For instance, what is the relation of Aristotle's discussion of modality in *Met. θ* to his discussion of substance in *Met.* Z-H? Aristotle's writings are in general characterizeld by a remarkable tenacity in pursuing his main line of thought, obscure though his detailed remarks often be. If so, how is he led by his argument concerning the nature of substance in *Met.* Z-H to his analysis of potentiality in *Met. θ*? My aim in this paper is to suggest an answer to these questions.

In so doing, we obviously have to start from Aristotle's main business, which is his concern with the notion of substance. Now one of the most crucial problems concerning substance which Aristotle discusses in *Metaphysics* Z-H is the unity of substance.

> The substratum is substance, and this is in one sense matter... and in another sense the formula or shape (that which being a 'this' can be separately formulated), and thirdly the complex of these two, which alone is generated and destroyed, and is, without qualification, capable of separate being. (*Met.* H 1, 1042 a 25-32.)

Aristotle apparently assimilates matter and potentiality to each other, and likewise form and actuality:

> by matter I mean that which, not being a 'this' actually, is potentially a 'this.' (*Ibid.* a 27-28.)

But how do the two components, matter and form, manage to be combined into *one* entity, substance in the third (and most proper) sense? What constitutes the *unity* of a substance? Aristotle discusses this question at length in *Met.* H. His answer is stated at the end of that book:

> But, as has been said, the proximate matter and the form are the same, the one potentially, and the other actually. Therefore to ask the cause of their unity is like asking the cause of unity in general, for each thing is a unity, and the potential and the actual are in a way one. Thus there is no cause other than whatever initiates the change from potentiality to actuality. (*Met.* H 6, 1045 b 17-22.)

The kind of potency which characterizes matter is clearly the kind of potentiality that is sometimes known as the passive potency. It is distinguished from active potencies by Aristotle. Aristotle explains the distinction in *Met.* Δ 12:

> 'Potency' then means the source, in general, of change or movement in another thing or in the same thing *qua* other, but also [ii] the source of a thing being moved by another thing or by itself *qua* other. (1019 a 18-21.)

These two kinds of potencies, which we may call the active and the passive potency, are reciprocal. The one is the active source of the same change or movement which the other one is the passive capacity of undergoing. Clearly it is this correlative connection that Aristotle is appealing to at the end of *Met.* H to explain the unity of matter and form in a substance. The two kinds of partial potencies are but two sides of the same coin or, more literally, of the same total potentialities. The one can only be defined by reference to the other. Hence no further explanation is needed to account for their unity -- or so Aristotle's idea goes.

Admittedly, the unity of passive potency and the correlated active potency is not the same as the contrast between a passive potency and the correlated actuality. However, for Aristotle's purposes the two contrasts can be treated as equivalent in that for him actuality and an active potentiality are closely related. Hence we can say that the unity of substance is according to Aristotle based on a correlation of active and passive potentialities which makes them pairwise one in the sense which Aristotle needs. Matter *is* the passive potentiality needed for the being of substance, and the form constitutes the actuality which serves as the active potency. Their correlative identity is supposed to explain the unity of substance.

2. Aristotle explains too much

Why isn't this all that Aristotle had to say? Why couldn't he rest on his ontological laurels and stop the metaphysical inquiry which he had conducted in *Met* Z-H right there? An answer to this question touches the heart of the role of modal notions like potentiality in Aristotle's metaphysics. It shows what the hidden problems are which beset Aristotle's metaphysics of modality and which forced him to continue the inquiry he had conducted in *Met.* Z-H and carry it to the treacherous territory of modality in *Met. θ*. It shows in brief, the *raison d'être of Met. θ*.

If what has been said so far were the whole story, Aristotle would indeed be in trouble. Why? The gist of his reconciliation of matter and form into one happy unity in *Met.* H is the idea that the *unity* of a substance is *completely* explained by these two factors. Unfortunately for Aristotle, this explains too much. It will also explain the automatic *being* (existence) of a substance as soon as the two factors (active and passive potency) are present. For Aristotle consistently emphasizes that unity (being one) and simple being (being as existence) go together. For instance, in *Met.* Γ 2 we read:

> ... being and unity are the same and are one thing in the sense that they are implied in one another as principle and cause are ... 'one man' and 'man' are the same thing, and so are 'existent man' and 'man.' (1003b 23-27.)

Hence Aristotle's explanation of the unity of substance works only if the presence of the correlated active and passive potencies explains completely the being of a substance. The substance must come to be as soon as these two potencies are present together.

That this was Aristotle's general idea is seen from what he says in *Met.* H -- the idea, that is to say, that the simultaneous presence of correlated active and passive potencies, rightly understood, must lead to actualization.

An active and a passive potentiality are *partial* potentialities. Aristotle presupposes in *Met.* H, first, that these two together constitute a *total* potentiality which does not need further components to be a potentiality in the fullest possible sense. Second, he is assuming that such a total potentiality is immediately and automatically realized as soon as all its components are present. For otherwise some further explanatory factor would be needed to account for the realization, and Aristotle's explanation of the unity of substances would not be viable. In *Met. θ* 5, 1048 a 1-15 Aristotle accordingly first explains that in the case of what he calls rational potencies a desire or will is needed for their realization, for they have two different alternative outcomes:

> Since that which is potential is potentially something at some time and in some way (and with all the other qualifications which must be present in the defini-

tion), and since some things can produce change according to a rational formula and their potencies involve such a formula, ... as regards [such potencies], when the agent and the patient meet in the way appropriate to the potency in question, the one *must* [emphasis added] act and the other be acted on... Therefore everything which has a rational potency, when it desires that for which it has a potency and in the circumstances in which it has the potency, *must* do this [emphasis added].

Aristotle's further explanations show nicely the co-operation of active and passive partial potentialities in a complete potentiality, which he has just asserted to be realized as soon as it is present:

And it has the potency in question when the passive object is present and is in a certain state ... To add the qualification 'if nothing external prevents it' is no longer necessary; for it has the potency on the terms on which this is a potency of acting, and it is this not in all circumstances but on certain conditions, among which will be the exclusion of external hindrances; for these are barred by some of the positive qualifications. (1048 a 15-22; cf. also *Met. θ* 7, 1049 a 5-7.)

But this seems to lead to a paradoxical and untenable result. For the purpose of explaining the unity of substance, Aristotle had to assume that once the correlated active and passive potencies are present in the case of a substance, they must be realized; the substance must actually be there. Otherwise further ingredients will be needed to bring about a substance, and Aristotle's neat explanation of the unity of substance as a combination of two correlated factors will be insufficient. In the quoted passage, Aristotle seems to generalize this to all potencies. Indeed, it is hard to see how he could justify his treatment of the unity substances unless he could treat it as a special case of his general theory of potentiality. But the general principle Aristotle seems to be appealing has the catastrophical consequence of driving him to a Megarian position. Every pair of full-fledged active and passive potentialities *must* be automatically realized. There is no room for unrealized potentialities, unless there are merely partial potentialities, for instance, passive potentialities without their active complement, or *vice versa*, or otherwise lower-grade potentialities. I have argued in the monograph referred to in note 1 that there were strong forces in Aristotle's thinking that pushed him toward this untenable position. We have now found an additional temptation for Aristotle to adopt the Megarian view, and say that only what is actual is, in the most full-fledged sense of the word, really potential.

3. Aristotle's way out

Of course, Aristotle does not want to accept the Megarian conclusion. In *Aristotle on Modality and Determinism* we explored several of his attempted way out, such as his famous discussion of future contingents in *De Int*.9.[2] Here it suffices to concentrate on his definitive solution of this self-inflicted problem.

Where could Aristotle find a satisfactory solution? First, how could Aristotle disentangle himself from the Megarian implications of his own position? What this question means in most general terms is: Where could Aristotle find full-fledged potentialities that are unmistakably present but have not yet been realized?[3]

An answer is suggested by the idea of *dynamis* as a power or tendency. How can such a power be manifested? A *dynamis* must be a potentiality of something in the sense of having this something as its characteristic end or outcome. Now it lies close at hand to say that a *dynamis* can be 'seen' in two different ways: either from the fact that its end (i.e., what it is a potentiality of) in fact comes about or else from the fact that a change or movement toward that end is taking place. In the first case, potentiality has already been realized, and no wedge has been driven between possibility and actuality (and necessity). However the second case is what Aristotle can use. Indeed, it is his only opening here. In such a case, a *dynamis*, that is, a power or potentiality, is unmistakably present, for how else could there be a change in the right direction? Nevertheless in such a case the potentiality has not yet been realized, for the outcome has not come about. In such cases, and in such cases only, can Aristotle find room for unactualized possibilities and hence escape the menace of determinism. The Megarian arguments, or at least some of them, can be accommodated in this account by saying that in the second type of case a change or movement is necessarily initiated as soon as the potentiality is present. From this it does not follow, however, that the potentiality itself is instantaneously actualized in the sense that the outcome is immediately realized. This, then, is the way -- the only way -- in which a genuine potentiality can exist unfulfilled according to Aristotle.

From this vantage point, several pieces of our puzzle at once fall into their places. If the only way in which potentiality can exist unfulfilled is in the form of a change towards its fulfillment, such a change or *kinesis* is the only form of actual existence which a potentiality can enjoy is so far as it is only a potentiality (i.e., in so far as it is still unfulfilled). But to say this is to assent *verbatim* to Aristotle's famous definition of *kinesis*:

> The actuality (*entelecheia*) of what exists potentially, in so far as it exists potentially, is *kinesis*. (*Phys.* III 1, 201 a 10-11; the same formula is given at 201 a 27-29 and at 201 b 4-5).[4]

Now we can see what is meant by 'the actuality of what is potential' by Aristotle. Surprisingly or not, it means precisely what it says. The only way in which a potentiality can exist (be actual) as *potentiality*, that is without already having given rise to whatever it is a potentiality of, according to Aristotle as a change (movement) toward that which is potentiality of.

4. Kineseis vs. energeiai

More generally, we can see how Aristotle's distinction between *kinesis* and *energeia* not only forms a natural complement to his theory of modality but also serves as a missing link which serves to free him from the clutches of determinism. What gives the distinction a special flavor is that *kineseis* and *energeiai* are considered by Aristotle in more than one capacity.

(i) In a sense, they are for him different kinds of *goals* or *ends* of potentialities, namely, in the sense that one kind of potentiality is (completely) realized when it has given rise, not just to an ongoing *kinesis*, but to a *completed kinesis*, another kind when it has given rise to an *energeia* -- which cannot help being complete.

(ii) In another sense, *kinesis* and *energeiai* are different *ways in which a potentiality can manifest itself*, either incompletely (as an incomplete *kinesis*) or completely (as an *energeia*). Moreover, in a sense a *kinesis* is never the outcome or end of a potentiality (i.e., is never what the potentiality is a potentiality of), for when a potentiality is manifested as a *kinesis* we have a (potential) product or end separate from the activity in the form of which a potentiality is manifested.

This explains -- among other things -- the apparent inconsistency Aristotle exhibits in using the notion of *energeia* in *Met.* θ 6. This makes no sense unless the *dynamis-energeia* contrast has a dual role in Aristotle. It must mark, not just the potentiality-actuality polarity, but also a distinction between two different kinds of potentiality as well.

The important thing to realize is thus the dual role of the *kinesis-energeia* contrast as being at one and the same time a distinction between two kinds of potentiality *and* a distinction between potentiality and actuality.

5. The unity of substances

What we have found also shows what the intended link is between the concept of substance and the distinction between the two kinds of potentiality. It is that the kind of potentiality we are dealing with in the case of substances is the *energeia* type. Indeed in *Met. θ* 8, 1050 b 2-3 Aristotle says in so many words that 'evidently, therefore, substance or form is *energeia*'. The force of Aristotle's words is missed far too easily, We tend to take Aristotle as saying that a substance is an actual entity in contradistinction of merely potential ones. But, even though this is true, it misses Aristotle's precise point, which is captured better by saying that Aristotle is telling us *what kind of potentiality* it is that a substance can possess and that leads to the existence of a substance. He is saying that it is of an *energeia* type potentiality (and hence a potentiality that cannot be disentangled from the corresponding actuality). For this reason, it is inevitably realized as soon as it exists as a full-fledged (first-order) potentiality. It is for this reason, and in this sense, that a substance is an actuality for Aristotle. Otherwise, he would face the awkward question: why cannot a substance, too, exist merely potentially? Surely the potential-actual distinction must be capable of applying also to substance! How can Aristotle deny the possibility of a substance's existing possibly but not yet actually? The answer is that a substance can exist potentially, but since this existence, it was found above, is of the *energeia* type, it guarantees for Aristotle automatic being of the substance in question and by the same token guarantees for Aristotle an equally automatic unity.

Thus Aristotle's ultimate solution for the problem of the unity of substances is to be sought in *Met. θ*, as is indeed seen from what he says there:

> Clearly, then, in one sense the potentiality for acting and being acted on is the same..., and in another sense it is not; for it is partly in the patient (for it because

it contains a certain principle, and because even matter is a kind of principle, that the patient is acted upon), and partly in the agent. (*Met. θ* 1, 1046 a 19-27.)

It is the distinction and clarification of these two senses that Aristotle is undertaking in *Met. θ*.

The answer to the problem of the two kinds of potentiality that emerges from *Met. θ* is the one briefly outlined above. Since a substance is an *energeia*, it is automatically realized as soon as the two component potentialities are present. Because of their mutually complementary character, a substance is also automatically and intrinsically one. The reason why this does not lead to a Megarian position is that *energeia*-type potentialities are not only the ones. There are also those potentialities which manifest themselves as *kinesis* and whose mode of existence is as a *kinesis*.

Thus Aristotle avoids the threat of being pushed into a Megarian position, for he can now happily acknowledge all sorts of unrealized potentialities of the other, *kinesis*, type. However, the line of thought which threatened to push him towards a Megarian position still applies to substance and indeed leads Aristotle to a number of interesting conclusions. Among them there is, as was noted, the thesis that substance is (is *only*) an actuality.

6. The primacy of actuality - the primacy of substance

Now we can also see a further purpose which is served by Aristotle's discussion of the priority of *energeia* in *Met. θ* 8-9. Because this is the type of potentiality-cum-actuality exhibited by substances, Aristotle's argument in effect is an attempted proof of the primacy of substances. As such, it may be thought of as fulfilling the promise Aristotle in effect made in *Met. Γ*, viz. to try to show that substance is primary with respect to the other categories.

Indeed, Aristotle's purpose of showing the primacy of substances in *Met. θ* 8-9 is shown by his own words.

Earlier, I ventured to identify the active element in potentiality with the form. What evidence is there for any such identification? The answer is that what Aristotle does in *Met. Z* 7-8 can be viewed as an argument for this very conclusion. In *Met. Z* 7, 1032 b 11-15 Aristotle concludes that things artificially generated always come from another instance of the same form, which is the *arkhe* of its coming-to-be.

> Therefore it follows in a sense that health comes from health and house from a house; that which has matter from that which has not (for the art of medicine or of building is the form of health or the house).

Hence it is the form which is, in terms of Aristotle's own formulation in *Met.* Δ 12, 1019a 15-16, 'the *arkhe* of motion or change which is in something other than the thing changed'.

Moreover, the same is true of things naturally generated, according to Aristotle:

> ... by which they are generated is their formal nature, which has the same form as the thing generated (although it is in something else); for man begets man.

Hence the tentative identification I relied on can be justified. Moreover, as a by-product of this justification we can now see the place of *Met.* Z 7-8 in Aristotle's overall line of thought.

7. Potency vs. passive potency

An interesting correction to popular ways of reading Aristotle is beginning to emerge here. We can now see that Aristotle was not formulating his last and final view when he identified the form-matter contrast with the actuality-potentiality contrast. Since a substance is an *energeia*, matter cannot be a potential substance, for such a potentiality must at once be realized. Rather, Aristotle's point is that form and matter together constitute an *energeia*-type potentiality which is interchangeable with the corresponding actuality in the sense that it is *ipso facto* realized. In fact Aristotle needs, as was noted in the beginning of this paper, this automatic realization of a potential substance in order to explain the unity of form and matter in a substance. This unity is not one of potentiality and actuality, but of passive and active potentiality.

Another way of putting the same -- or closely related -- point is to say that what happens in *Met.* θ is that the matter-form contrast is transformed from a contrast between potentiality and actuality into a contrast between two kinds of potentiality, the *dynamis* type of potentiality and the *energeia* type potentiality. The former is the passive potentiality, the latter is the active one. The latter is always actual in some matter or other, but its realization in some specific medium may be as it were slowed down by the nature of the corresponding passive potentiality which turns the realization into a process of *kinesis*.

It follows from this that Aristotle's argument in *Met. θ* for the priority of the actuality is in effect an argument for the priority of form in the characterization of substances. There is thus a great deal to be said for those interpreters who argue that Aristotle really identified a substance and its form.

In an earlier work, I have shown that throughout his works Aristotle consistently made the same distinction between two different types of potentiality of possibility.[5] This is the same distinction as the *kinesis-energeia* contrast, when it is taken to pertain to kinds of potentiality. One corollary to this result is that Aristotle had nothing remotely like the concept of purely logical possibility. For clearly neither an *energeia* type potentiality nor a *kinesis* type potentiality is a pure logical possibility.

Notes

1. This article overlaps with the monograph, Jaakko Hintikka et al., *Aristotle on Modality and Determinism (Acta Philosophica Fennica*, 29:1, Helsinki, 1977) and is calculated to bring the central results of that monograph to bear on Aristotle's treatment of the unity of substance.

2. See Jaakko Hintikka, *Time and Necessity* (Oxford: Clarendon Press, 1973), chapter 8; and *Aristotle on Modality and Determinism* (note 1 above), chapter 3, sec. 17, which I am following here.

3. I am following here *Aristotle on Modality and Determinism* (note 1 above), chapter 4, sections 21-26.

4. See W.D. Ross, *Aristotle's Physics: A Revised Text With Introduction and Commentary* (Oxford: Clarendon Press, 1936). Ross's mistaken reading of *entelecheia* as 'actualization' rather than 'actuality' is all the stranger as he is fully aware that this word in Aristotle normally means 'actuality' or 'complete reality' in a rather strong sense (cf. e.g., Met. θ, 4, 1047 b 1-2). See W.D. Ross, *Aristotle's Metaphysics: A Revised Text with Introduction and Commentary* I-II (Oxford: Claredon Press, 1924).

5. See *Aristotle on Modality and Determinism* (note 1 above).

Compensation for the Study of Torah in Medieval Rabbinic Thought

Professor Ephraim Kanarfogel

As an inheritor of the legacy of the Geonim, whose academies developed extensive systems of support and fundraising, Andalusian Jewry was predisposed to providing financial support for its scholars.[1] Jewish communities in Spain continued to do so throughout the Middle Ages, despite Maimonides' well-known position that Torah scholars who decided not to work, but to live on the salaries provided by willing benefactors, were profaning the name of God. Indeed, Maimonides notes that his position is against the dominant [Sefardic] communal practice of his day.[2] R. Shmuel *ha-Nagid* (d. 1056) had already endorsed the very practice that Maimonides condemns when he proclaimed that he would support and maintain any scholar who wished to make Torah study his profession (*lihyot torato ummanuto*).[3] R. Avraham ibn Daud refers to important scholars who were supported by patrons and to scholars and judges who received salaries from their communities.[4] R. Yehudah b. Barzilai (c. 1100) provided Talmudic justification for these practices. Moreover, R. Yehudah maintained that communal support for judges and scholars is both prevalent and obligatory.[5]

In several recent studies, B. Septimus has argued that Maimonides' position condemning professionalized scholarship was accepted and endorsed by major Spanish halakhists of the thirteenth century, such as R. Meir ha-Levi (Ramah) and R. Yonah of Gerona. According to R. Yonah, a scholar must derive his sustenance from secular pursuits. Thus, R. Yonah cites Rambam's famous diatribe against subsidized scholarship in his own commentary to *Avot* 4:7.[6]

Careful comparison of Rambam's comment to Rabbenu Yonah's reveals that R. Yonah's citation is suggestively selective.[7] R. Yonah omits Maimonides' praises for Tannaim and Amoraim such as Hillel

135

and Rav Yosef, among others, who held various menial jobs rather than supporting themselves from the study of Torah. Also absent is the claim, made several times by Rambam, that people were prepared to support these scholars, but were never asked to do so, no matter how great the scholars' needs. Maimonides gives a non-economic interpretation to the Talmudic dictum that "[a scholar] who wishes to benefit [because of his Torah study] should do so like Elisha" (Berakhot 10b). All that Elisha ever received was the honor extended by his hosts, which included hospitality and lodging. Rambam emphatically rejects the possibility, suggested by others, that Elisha accepted any monetary gifts. R. Yonah, on the other hand, acknowledges that this Talmudic passage does endorse a means of providing economic assistance for scholars.[8] In addition, R. Yonah notes the Talmudic statement of approbation for one who gives gifts to a scholar (Ketubot 105b), which was also derived from the career of Elisha, with the modification that such gifts may be accepted only if they were of the type that would normally have been given to an important non-scholar as well. Maimonides does not refer to this Talmudic passage at all.

Although R. Yonah writes that a person who is healthy enough to work should not benefit from Torah (*le-hanot be-kavod Torah*), it appears from the opening section, and from the tone throughout, that R. Yonah's comment was intended mainly to prevent a scholar from abusing his position and privileges. Septimus admits that no thirteenth-century Spanish halakhist openly attempted to suppress subsidies, salaries or contributions.[9]

Indeed, R. Yonah elsewhere provides ample justification for the compensation and support of scholars who were dedicated to their studies. In a comment to Proverbs 14:4, R. Yonah explains that the farmer must tolerate the slovenly habits of the ox and allow the animal to fulfill its needs because the ox is so productive for the farmer. So too, scholars should be tolerant of the masses. Such tolerance will enhance respect for scholars and facilitate the acceptance of religious instruction and admonition, but it also fulfills a somewhat more temporal purpose. The masses should be treated well, "in order that the people carry the burden [of the scholars] so that they can be free to study day and night..."[10] Just as one suffers the slovenliness of the ox because of its productivity, the scholar must tolerate the burdens which are placed upon him by various people, because they can be helpful to him in his scholarly endeavors.

In his *Iggeret ha-Teshuvah*, R. Yonah recommends that one who wishes to further the study of Torah should "come to the aid of *rabbanim* and *talmidim* who study for the sake of heaven. He should contribute towards the support of scholars so that they will remain in his city and study Torah because of him."[11] In his *Commentary to Proverbs*,[12] R. Yonah writes that the purpose of the righteous man in striving to acquire wealth is to be able to devote himself to the support of sacred causes and to assist those who fear God and make His name known.[13] Perhaps, R. Yonah's position is that scholars should not pursue the support of communities or patrons, but they may accept needed support if it is offered.[14] The sources of R. Yonah which Septimus cites are directed to the scholar. A scholar must not devalue Torah scholarship by seeking to make it the major source of his livelihood and by becoming financially dependent upon others. At the same time, the community is obligated to reach out and support those scholars who need help in order to continue to study seriously.

Prof. Septimus suggests that according to Ramah as well, there is to be no tangible reward in this world for Torah study. Therefore, like Rambam, he considers professionalized scholarship to be unacceptable. The claim of H. Schirmann that Ramah earned his living as a teacher of Talmud must be rejected, on the grounds that to do so would have violated Ramah's principles.[15]

In fact, however, Ramah discusses in detail the payment of teachers in a community and is receptive to the idea of communal support for education.[16] It appears that Ramah opposed, at most, the supporting of scholars whose sole pursuit was study. On the other hand, scholars who were involved in the teaching of Torah, and who received payment in the form of *sekhar battalah*, as compensation for their abstention from other work, would elicit no objection from Ramah even though Rambam, as noted by Septimus, explicitly rejects the notion of *sekhar battalah* as an acceptable method of payment.[17] Indeed, both R. Yonah and Rambam who, in Septimus' view, agreed with Rambam's position that professional scholarship per se ought to be eliminated, nonetheless saw nothing wrong with allowing teachers of Talmud to be compensated by means of *sekhar battalah*.[18]

It should be noted that all of the aforementioned Sefardic halakhists, including Maimonides, approved the granting of tax exemptions to qualified scholars.[19] Ramah and R. Asher b. Yeḥiel (in a responsum addressed to a Spanish Jewish community) even granted tax exemptions to one who had a profession but devoted as much time as he could to his studies. According to Ramah, the scholar is exempt "not because of his poverty but because of his Torah."[20] There were some Spanish communities which would not grant an exemption to a scholar who did not devote himself exclusively to study.[21] The fact remains, however, that some form of tax-exemption for scholars was the norm in Sefardic communal and intellectual life.

Only among Tosafists do we find contemporaries of Maimonides who also rejected the utilization of any form of *sekhar battalah* and contended that in practice, a scholar should study without compensation and must earn his livelihood in a profession other than teaching. The author of a twelfth-century Ashkenazic commentary to *Avot*, perhaps Rashbam, interprets the phrase in *Avot* 1:6, "and despise rabbinic position," to mean that one must "lower himself in order to secure employment," and not receive payment for rabbinic functions, including teaching.[22] Elsewhere in his commentary, the author states that Torah must be taught to others neither for self-aggrandizement nor for compensation. The author explicitly rejects the practice of paying a teacher *sekhar battalah*, although he notes that there are those who accepted payment by relying on this concept.[23] R. Eliezer of Metz praised Rabiah as one who "ran away from honor in order not to appear haughty and in order not to receive compensation on account of [his knowledge of] Torah."[24] Several texts reveal the non-teaching occupations of important Tosafists, including Rashbam.[25] Many Tosafists, who taught students, did not earn their livelihoods from teaching. Indeed, it was common practice in Ashkenazic society for scholars to work at some kind of profession in order to earn their livelihoods and devote any remaining time to their studies.[26]

Interestingly, the twelfth century saw a change in the attitude of Christian scholars toward the receiving of payment for teaching God's word. The masters in the new urban schools, which were opened in numerous cathedrals in the twelfth century, received payment for their teaching. These teachers were paid for their instruction in the form of salaries from public authorities, ecclesiastical prebends or, most often, monies paid by the students themselves. This was, of course, not the practice in the monasteries. Opposition to the practice of paying a master was neutralized by the claim that the teacher's payment was the result of the labor and time expended in the service of his students rather than payment for his knowledge. While some twelfth-century thinkers still clung to the notion that to live a scholarly life meant to live a life of poverty, others lived quite comfortably.[27]

Ashkenazic Jewry had to deal with the obvious tension between the need to provide teachers and scholars with a livelihood and the halakhic problems inherent in receiving payment for teaching Talmud. Unnamed Tosafists concluded from their analysis of relevant passages in the Babylonian Talmud that it was permissible for one to receive compensation for teaching Talmud if he had no other means of support. Moreover, even if a teacher had the ability to do other work, he was entitled because of the importance of his chosen vocation to *sekhar battalah*, provided that he did not receive compensation from any other position.[28]

R. Isaac of Corbeil maintained that any teacher whose students do not comprehend immediately but require the teacher to expend effort (*toraḥ*) to insure that they grasp the material being taught, may also receive payment. On the other hand, teachers of students who grasp the lessons as they are being taught should not be compensated.[29] R. Isaac does not identify further the students who are included in this last group. His formulation implies that Talmudic scholars, who lectured to learned students in an academy, were not permitted to receive payment for their teaching.

Undoubtedly, there were teachers of Talmud in Ashkenaz who did rely on the various justifications and received payment for their teaching.[30] To be sure, the teacher who accepted compensation could have done so in order to spend additional time in the study of Talmud, and so these arrangements might be perceived as a form of professionalized scholarship. The payment of *sekhar battalah*, nevertheless, was made only to someone who taught and thus provided a service to others, not to one who was engaged solely in study.[31] There is no evidence, in the period prior to 1348, of any salaries or stipends paid to scholars so that they could make Torah study their profession.[32] Even if the formulations which sought to curb the payment of *sekhar battalah* were not always heeded, they reflect a strong desire within Ashkenazic society to withhold compensation from those who were engaged in Torah study.

Although no salaries or subsidies were offered to scholars, it was deemed appropriate to aid scholars to earn a livelihood with less effort. R. Gershom was asked a question concerning a scholar who taught Talmud to a group of older students. He had no salaried or official position and did not receive compensation for his lessons. He earned his livelihood from business dealing with Gentiles who were his clients exclusively. R. Gershom ruled that the monopolistic business relationship that the scholar had developed must be protected by the community, even though this community was not accustomed to allowing its members to retain monopolies.[33] "The community is mandated by Talmudic law to protect and aid this scholar, whose work is the work of heaven (*melekhet shamayim*)[34] and who teaches Torah without compensation, in order that he not be distracted from his studies."[35] Some limited forms of assistance could not be withheld for practical reasons. The ideal, that a scholar should not earn a livelihood from his studies, retained its prominence. Indeed, its influence was felt with regard to other aspects of a scholar's livelihood, such as tax exemptions, in which the scholar's privileges were curtailed.

There is almost no discussion in Ashkenazic rabbinic literature about providing tax exemptions for scholars. *Sefer Ḥasidim*, one of the few sources in medieval Ashkenaz to refer to this issue, maintains that tax exemptions for scholars, which were mandated by Talmudic law, were reserved for those scholars who earned no livelihood and spent all of their time engaged in study (*toratan ummanutan*).[36] Since the practice in Ashkenaz was that all scholars, who needed to earn a livelihood and were capable of doing so, had to work at an occupation of some type, none of these scholars qualified for a tax exemption. Only a scholar who was independently wealthy or was completely impoverished could qualify for a tax exemption. Thus, the absence of discussion concerning the granting of tax exemptions for scholars in Ashkenazic rabbinic literature may be explained by the fact that in practice, Ashkenazic communities did not grant tax exemptions to scholars.[37] A. Grossman and D. Berger have argued that the small size of the pre-Crusade Ashkenazic communities, the high percentage of scholars in the communities even as they grew larger numerically, and the leadership roles which many scholars took in these communities rendered the granting of tax exemptions to scholars almost impossible.[38] I. Ta-Shema has shown that a more lenient Ashkenazic position developed post-1348, but that even then, there was still stiff opposition to exemptions for scholars.[39] R. Ḥayyim Paltiel (a younger contemporary of R. Meir of Rothenburg)[40] writes that the greatest scholars of his day paid taxes.[41]

In the conflict between the benefits of professional scholarship and the demands of spirituality, spirituality largely triumphed in Ashkenaz.[42] Salaries,[43] stipends, and even tax exemptions were not available to scholars.[44] The Tosafists, no less than Maimonides, wished to foster a religious economy in which *talmud Torah* and *derekh ereṣ* would remain two separate and distinct values. Maimonides' community did not succeed in enforcing the ideal; to a significant degree, the society of the Tosafists transformed vision into reality.[45]

Notes

1. See B. Septimus, "Kings, Angels or Beggars: Tax Law and Spirituality in a Hispano-Jewish Responsum," *Studies in Medieval Jewish History and Literature*, v.2, ed. I. Twersky (Cambridge, 1984) [hereafter cited as Septimus, "Tax Law"], pp. 317-19. See also H.H. Ben-Sasson in *Zion* 41 (1976): 35-36, and below, n. 13.

2. See Maimonides' *Perush ha-Mishnayot* to *Avot* 4:7, ed. J. Kafaḥ, pp. 441-46; *MT Talmud Torah* 3:9-11; and *Iggerot ha-Rambam*, ed. J. Kafaḥ, p. 134. Cf. I. Twersky, *Introduction to the Code of Maimonides* (New Haven, 1980), p. 5, n. 6, and pp. 81-83. According to Prof. Twersky, Rambam is denouncing the "managerial methods" of the Geonim, which created an "institutionalized and professionalized class of scholars supported by public and often high-pressured philanthropy..."

3. See *Sefer ha-Qabbalah*, tr. G.D. Cohen, pp. 74-77.

4. *Sefer ha-Qabbalah*, pp. 66, 70-71, 77, 80, 83. See also M. Steinschneider in *He-Ḥaluts* 2 (1853): 61, and A.A. Neuman, *The Jews of Spain* (Philadelphia, 1942), v.2, pp. 64-65.

5. See R. Jacob b. Asher, *Arba'ah Turim, Ḥoshen Mishpat*, #9. See also R. Yehudah's *Sefer ha-Shetarot*, ed. S.Z.H. Halberstam (Berlin, 1898), pp. 131-32; *Sefer ha-Qabbalah*, p. 141 (note to line 408); and below, n. 43.

6. Septimus, "Tax Law," pp. 316, 321, and "Piety and Power in Thirteenth Century Catalonia," *Studies in Medieval Jewish History and Literature*, v. 1, ed. I. Twersky (Cambridge, 1979), pp. 218-20. Septimus bases his analysis principally upon passages from the commentaries of R. Yonah to Proverbs and *Avot*. These passages are found in *Perushei Rabbenu Yonah 'al Massekhet Avot*, ed. M.M. Kasher and Y. Blacherowitz (Jerusalem, 1966), pp. 62f., 20f., and 41f; *Perush Rabbenu Yonah 'al Mishlei* 10:15 (correct "Piety and Power," p. 230, n. 161), and related comments on Proverbs 24:3, 14:24, 11:11. For Ramah, see below, n. 15.

7. See the analysis of R. Yonah's comment to *Avot* 4:7 and comparison to the comment of Maimonides in R. Yeruḥam b. Meshullam, *Sefer Toledot Adam ve-Ḥavvah*, 1:2 (Venice, 1753), fol. 17a.

8. The assistance referred to, according to R. Yonah, is *mattil melai le-kis shel talmid ḥakham*. Rashi, *Pesaḥim* 53b s.v. *mattil*, explains this practice, which is viewed favorably by the Talmud, to mean that one ought to provide a scholar with merchandise so that he can sell it and thereby profit. Rambam, later in his comment to *Avot* 4:7 and in a responsum, approves of the investment or man-

agement of a scholar's capital by others based on the formulation in *Pesaḥim*. See "Tax Law," p. 328, n. 63. It is significant, however, that Rambam chose not to use this concept to explain away the Elisha passage. The Elisha passage appears to approve generally the notion of benefitting scholars. Maimonides perhaps did not wish to link this passage to any form of economic assistance, lest the broadly permissive tone of the ruling be construed as a justification for expanded monetary support. R. Yonah apparently did not share this concern.

9. "Tax Law," p. 321.

10. *Perush R. Yonah Gerondi 'al Mishlei* (repr. Tel Aviv, 1963), 14:4 (p. 69). Septimus mentions neither this source, nor the one in the following note. Cf. A. Shrock, *R. Jonah b. Abraham of Gerona* (New York, 1948), p. 137.

11. *Iggeret ha-Teshuvah*, ed. B. Zilber (Bnei Brak, 1968), pp. 22-23. *Sefer Orḥot Ḥayyim*, v.1, *Hilkhot Talmud Torah*, section 10, quotes this passage in the name of R. Yonah as legal precedent.

12. *Perush 'al Mishlei*, 10:15 (p. 41). This comment is cited by Septimus; see above, n. 6. He regards it as one of several sources reflecting the view of R. Yonah that all devout Jews, including scholars, should strive to earn their livelihoods from some secular pursuit. In Septimus' paraphrase: "...the righteous will seek wealth for the sake of Heaven and use it to noble purpose." It should be noted, however, that scholars are not specifically included in this comment among those who ought to seek wealth. On the other hand, the "noble purpose" for which righteous men should seek wealth includes, in R. Yonah's words, the following: "*ve-ya'azor lineso yir'ei ha-Shem ule-hagbir yedei modi'ei Shemo...*"

13. See the so-called *Perush R. Yonah 'al ha-Torah*, ed. S. Yerushalmi (Jerusalem, 1980), pp. 106, 207-08, 216. The author notes that devoted scholars received support to enable them to continue their studies without recourse to any other profession "from the days of the Geonim." See also the treatise *Dinei Melammed* attributed to R. Yonah, ed. B. Zilber (published with his edition of *Iggeret ha-Teshuvah*), pp. 11-12.

14. Cf. *Yerushalmi Ḥagigah* 1:7.

15. Septimus, *Hispano-Jewish Culture in Transition* (Cambridge, 1982), pp. 12, 112, 124, n. 76; "Tax Law," pp. 315-16.

16. See *Yad Ramah to Bava Batra* 21a (2:58) and Ramah's collection of responsa, *Or Ṣaddiqim* #241.

17. See Septimus, "Tax Law," p. 316, n. 27.

18. See Ramban in *Shittah Mequbbeṣet* to *Bava Batra* 8a s.v. *ha-kol* (end), and R. Yonah, as cited by R. Yeruḥam b. Meshullam, above, n. 7. See also the commentary of R. Asher b. Yeḥiel to Bekhorot 4:5, and Ritba to *Nedarim* 37a.

19. Septimus, "Tax Law," p. 327.

20. See Septimus, pp. 322-23; I. Ta-Shema, "Al Petur Talmidei Ḥakhamim me-Missim Bimei ha-Benayim," *Iyyunim be-Sifrut Ḥazal, ba-Miqra, uve-Toledot Yisrel*, ed. Y.D. Gilat et al. (Ramat Gan, 1982), pp. 313-14; and E.E. Urbach, "She'elot u-Teshuvot ha-Rosh be-Kitvei Yad uvi-Defusim," *Shenaton ha-Mishpat ha-Ivri* 2 (1975): 141-42. Cf. A. Shrock, *Jonah b. Abraham of Gerona*, pp. 139-40.

21. See the case addressed by Ramah in Septimus, pp. 309-13, and see Ta-Shema, pp. 315-16. Note that Ri Migash (Rif) and perhaps Ramban also favored more restrictive requirements for exemption. See Septimus, pp. 314, 323, n. 48, and Ta-Shema, p. 313.

22. *Maḥzor Vitry*, ed. S. Hurwitz, pp. 471-72. On the identity of the author of this commentary, see I. Ta-Shema in *Qiryat Sefer* 42 (1977): 507-08.

23. *Maḥzor Vitry*, p. 524.

24. *Sefer Rabiah*, ed. V. Aptowitzer, I:452 and V. Aptowitzer, *Mavo la-Rabiah*, pp. 15-16. See also *Piyyutei R. Simeon bar Isaac*, ed. A. Habermann (Jerusalem, 1938), p. 186: "*osei melakhah u-mit' abbeqim ba-afarah ve-ein nehenin bi-khevodah ve-lo ya'asuhah qardom velo attarah...*," and R. Eleazar Roqeaḥ, *Perush 'al ha-Torah (Devarim)*, ed. S. Kanevsky (Bnei Brak, 1981), p. 171.

25. See H.H. Ben-Sasson, *Toledot 'Am Yisrael*, v.2, (Tel-Aviv, 1969), pp. 79-80; M. Breuer, *Rabbanut Ashkenaz Bimei ha-Benayim* (Jerusalem, 1976), p. 19; Aptowitzer, *Mavo la-Rabiah*, p. 338; and M. Frank, *Qehillot Ashkenaz u-Vatei Dinehen*, pp. 22-25. On Rashbam, see Urbach, v.1, p. 46. On R. Tam, see E.E. Urbach, *Ba'alei ha-Tosafot*, v.1, p. 62. Cf. H. Soloveitchik, "Can Halakhic Texts Talk History?" *AJSreview* 3 (1978): 172, n. 54; *Sefer ha-Yashar* (Responsa), ed. S. Rosenthal, p. 31; and I.A. Agus, *R. Meir of Rothenburg* (New York, 1947), v.1, p. 25.

26. See *Tosafot Berakhot* 11b s.v. *she-kevar niftar* and *Tosafot R. Yehudah Sir Leon*, ed. N. Zaks (Jerusalem, 1969), ad loc. See also *Tosafot Yeshanim* to *Yoma* 85b, s.v. *teshuvah*, and *Maḥzor Vitry*, pp. 494-95. Cf. *Sefer Tashbeṣ* #193, and *Siddur Ḥasidei Ashkenaz*, ed. M. Hershler (Jerusalem, 1975), pp. 32, 54, 151. As Ben-Sasson, ibid., noted, moneylending is an occupation that readily lends itself to this goal. R. Yosef b. Moshe, a student of R. Yisrael Isserlein, attributes the great achievements of Ashkenazic scholars in the earlier period to the fact that Jews at that time could lend money at interest to Gentiles much more easily than they could in his own day. These transactions were not time consuming, and rabbinic scholars consequently had abundant free time for their studies. See his *Leqet Yosher* (Berlin, 1903), pp. 118-19, and M. Breuer, *Rabbanut Ashkenaz*, p.. 19. Cf. *Sefer Ḥasidim*, ed. J. Wistinetski, #765.

27. See G. Pare, A. Brunet, P. Tremblay, *La Renaissance du XII siècle: Les Ecoles et l'Enseignement*, pp. 75-82; G. Post, K. Giocarinis, R. Kay, "The Medieval Heritage of a Humanistic Ideal: 'Scientia donum dei est, unde vendi non potest'," *Traditio* 11 (1955): 197-210; J. LeGoff, *Time, Work and Culture in the Middle Ages*, (Chicago, 1980), pp. 64, 120; J.W. Baldwin, *Masters, Princes and Merchants* (Princeton, 1970), v.1, pp. 117-120, 125-30, and "Masters of Paris from 1179 to 1215," *Renaissance and Renewal in the Twelfth Century*, ed. R.L. Benson and G. Constable (Cambridge, Mass., 1982), pp. 158-65; L.K. Little, *Religious Poverty and the Profit Economy in Medieval Europe* (Ithaca, 1978), pp. 33, 173, 176-78; N. Orme, *English Schools in the Middle Ages* (London, 1973), pp. 118-19, 157-58; and A. Murray, *Reason and Society in the Middle Ages* (Oxford, 1978), pp. 228-30. The Christian ideal of poverty, an ideal which was absent from or at least far less prominent within Judaism, obviously played a role in this issue. See Little, *Religious Poverty*, pp. 78-81, 101, 111, 121-22, 148-50.

28. *Tosafot Bekhorot* 29a, s.v. *mah ani be-ḥinnam*. R. Asher b. Yeḥiel, in his commmentary to *Nedarim* 37a, attributes these rulings to Ri. See also R. Yeruḥam b. Meshullam (above, n.7), and E.E. Urbach, *Ba'alei ha-Tosafot*, v.2, pp. 667-69. Cf. Rashi, *Qiddushin* 58b s.v. *bi-sekhar*; *Tosafot ad loc.*; and *Sefer Ḥasidim* #1496.

29. *Sefer Mizvot Qatan* #106. R. Isaac bases his ruling on the position of Rav (*Nedarim* 37a) that the teacher of young children can be compensated, because he is watching them (*sekhar shimmur*). R. Isaac assumes that any teacher who has to work hard to insure that his students learn and progress is performing a kind of *shimmur* and thus may receive compensation. Cf. *Shir ha-Shirim Rabbah* to the phrase in ch. 8, verse 12, "*ha-elef lekha Shelomoh*." See also Y. Lange, "Pisqei R. Yizḥaq mi-Corbeil," *Ha-Ma'ayan* 16 (1976): 99-100; R. Samson b. Ẓadoq, *Sefer Tashbeṣ* (Warsaw, 1865), #525; and *Dinei Melammed* (above, n. 13), p. 11.

30. Note that the source cited above (n.24) concerning Rabiah indicates that someone wished to pay him for his teaching.

31. The views of Ri and R. Tam, *Tosafot Ketubot* 105a, s.v. *dayyanei gezerot*, concerning communal payment for judges through *sekhar battalah* and the like were formulated to solve problems of Talmudic intepretation and do not appear to reflect actual practices in medieval Ashkenaz. Cf. R. Joel Sirkes, *Bayit Ḥadash* to *Tur Ḥoshen Mishpat* 9, s.v. *ve-katav*.

32. The responsum of R. Meir of Rothenburg (*Responsa* [Prague, 1895] #942) that according to Y.Y. Yuval (*Rabbanim ve-Rabbanut be-Germanyah, 1350-1500*, [Ph.D. dissertation, Hebrew University, 1985], p. 13, n. 16) deals with an early example of an academic salary probably refers to the salary of a member of the nascent professional rabbinate in Ashkenaz; see below, n. 43. *Sefer ha-Gan*, which, as correctly interpreted by Yuval, does refer to an academic salary or stipend, is a fifteenth century Austrian work by a certain R. Isaac b. Eliezer. More organized charitable contributions and communal support for students

and scholars became quite common in the post-1348 period. See M. Breuer, *Ha-Yeshivah ha-Ashkenazit be-Shilhei Yemei ha-Benayim*, (Ph.D. dissertation, Hebrew University, 1967), pp. 13-16, and J. Katz, *Massoret u-Mashber* (Jerusalem, 1958), pp. 224-25, 229, 266-67.

33. *Responsa of R. Gershom*, ed. S. Eidelberg (New York, 1955), #68. Cf. A. Grossman, *Ḥakhmei Ashkenaz ha-Rishonim* (Jerusalem, 1981) p. 411, and above, n. 8. In responsum #73, R. Gershom describes an incident in which he was hired to teach several students and became ill. It is possible and perhaps likely that R. Gershom taught these students Talmud. Grossman, p. 116, suggests that R. Gershom supported himself in this manner while he was a young man, prior to his emergence as a leading scholar.

34. On the use of *melekhet shamayim* in this context, see *Sefer Ḥuqqei ha-Torah* in N. Golb, *Toledot ha-Yehudim be-Ir Rouen Bimei ha-Benayim* (Jerusalem, 1976), pp. 181-82; *Tosafot R. Pereṣ* to *Bava Meṣi'a* 77a, s.v. *savar lah*; I. Twersky, *Rabad of Posquières*, pp. xx-xxi; and idem, *Introduction to the Code of Maimonides*, pp. 170-75.

35. See the ruling attributed to R. Isaac Or Zarua' by later Ashkenazic sources (*Responsa of R. Jacob Weil*, #151; *Terumat ha-Deshen* #342; and see also *Haggahot Asheri* to *Bava Batra* 2:12), as well as *Sefer Or Zarua'*, *Hilkhot Ṣedaqah*, #26. Yuval (above, n. 32, pp. 12-13), plausibly assumes that R. Isaac is reflecting relevant Talmudic texts or paraphrasing Rashi's interpretations of them rather than describing the realia of his own day. See also Rashi to *Shabbat* 114a, s.v. *le-mitraḥ be-rifteh*, and M. Breuer, *Rabbanut Ashkenaz*, p. 19.

36. See *Sefer Ḥasidim* #807, 1493.

37. I. Ta-Shema, "Al Petur" (above, n. 20), pp. 316-19.

38. See A. Grossman, *Ḥakhmei Ashkenaz ha-Rishonim*, pp. 411-14, and D. Berger's review, "Ḥeqer Rabbanut Ashkenaz ha-Qedumah," *Tarbiz* 53 (1984): 482.

39. See above, n. 37. See also Y. Dinari, *Ḥakhmei Ashkenaz be-Shilhei Yemei ha-Benayim* (Jerusalem, 1983), pp. 25-26. Breuer, *Ha-Yeshivah ha-Ashkenazit*, p. 11, claims that granting of tax exemptions to scholars in fifteenth-century Ashkenaz was done in order to provide an additional financial benefit for heads of academies. See above, n. 32.

40. On the identity of R. Ḥayyim Paltiel, see Y. Lange in *'Alei Sefer* 8 (1980): 140-45.

41. See *Responsa of R. Meir of Rothenburg* (Lemberg, 1860), #424. There are two additional sources which indicate that leading scholars paid taxes in thirteenth century Ashkenaz; see Ta-Shema, "Al Petur," p. 318.

42. On the connotations of the term *toratan ummanutan* in Ashkenaz, see *Terumat ha-Deshen* #342; Dinari (above, n. 39), p. 26; and cf. Judah ibn Tibbon's introduction to his translation of *Hovot ha-Levavot* (repr. Jerusalem, 1969), p. 6.

43. The only salaried religious functionary in mainstream Ashkenaz was the cantor; see *Responsa of R. Meir of Rothenburg* (Berlin, 1891), #234; *Sefer Ḥasidim* #1599, 1601; I. Agus, *Teshuvot Ba'alei ha-Tosafot* #91; *Teshuvot Maimuniyyot, Qinyan #27*; Sefer *Or Zarua'*, v.1, responsum #113, p. 40; and L. Landman, *The Cantor: An Historic Perspective* (New York, 1972), pp. 21-27. Payment and communal appointment of rabbis did not begin until the late fourteenth or early fifteenth century. See Agus, *Teshuvot Ba'alei ha-Tosafot*, pp. 18-31; E.E. Urbach's review of Agus in *Qiryat Sefer* 30 (1955): 204-05, and Agus' rejoinder in *Jewish Quarterly Review* 49 (1958-59): 219-20; M. Breuer, *Rabbanut Ashkenaz*, pp. 9-22; S. Schwarzfuchs, *Etudes sur l'Origine et le Développement du Rabbinat au Moyen Age* (Paris, 1957), pp. 24-27; and Y.Y. Yuval, *Rabbanim ve-Rabbanut be-Germanyah*, pp. 9-16. The development of a salaried, professionalized rabbinate (whose appointments were approved by the communities) occurs much earlier in Spain. See A.A. Neuman, *The Jews in Spain* v.2, pp. 86-91; S. Albeck, "Yesodot Mishtar ha-Qehillot bi-Sefarad 'ad ha-Ramah (1180-1244)," Zion 25 (1960): 114-21; J. Katz, "Rabbinic Authority and Authorization," *Studies in Medieval Jewish History and Literature*, ed. I. Twersky, v.1 (Cambridge, 1979), p. 49.

44. Two other related formal privileges were also unavailable in Ashkenaz. Spanish scholars were entitled to place a person who shamed them under a ban. See *Responsa of Ribash*, #202, citing rulings of Rif and Rambam. Yuval, pp. 377-78, has determined that the earliest use of this privilege in Ashkenaz was in the late thirteenth century. (To Yuval, p. 378, n. 202 add: Y. Lange [above, n. 29], p. 95.) They could also collect fines (often referred to as "*litra zahav*") from those who embarrassed them. In Ashkenaz, there is no evidence for the exercise of this privilege until the late fourteenth century; see Yuval, pp. 392-93. Breuer, *Ha-Yeshivah ha-Ashkenazit*, p. 16, maintains that monies collected from these fines were a source of revenue for academy heads in the late medieval period (post-1348). Cf. Dinari (above, n. 39), pp. 22-25.

45. For additional comparative analysis and bibliography, see my forthcoming *Jewish Education and Society in the High Middle Ages* (Wayne State University Press).

Perspectives on Health in the Judaic and Islamic Traditions - An Essay Prepared in Honor of Professor Arthur Hyman

Jacob Jay Lindenthal

Introduction

The increased emphasis on technology within modern medicine has radically altered many of the ways in which health care is delivered. Of the many consequences of this transformation, the problem of resolving the subsequent challenge to deeply ingrained Western values regarding health and life repeatedly surfaces. Both clinicians and administrators increasingly find themselves in anomic situations resulting from the conflict between them, due to reasons of conscience and training, offering state of the art benefits to their patients and, in deference to cost-conscious government and other third party payors, curtailing such benefits. As a result, many physicians, health care planners and large segments of the public are growing concerned that such a compromising situation may result in injury to the basic processes of the doctor-patient relationship due to compliance on the part of both the patient and the doctor[1] and clinical efficacy.[2]

Traditionally, in the United States, such standard ethical concerns over decision-making and the balance of power in the modern medical relationship between the doctor, patient and government arise from conflicts between modern medical technology and "Western" values. Despite their familiarity to the majority of the American population, these values are not representative of all ethical traditions. Consequently, the dynamics of the relationship between values and medicine also differ within such traditions. A case in point can be found in an examination of the ethical traditions within Judaism and Islam and their contribution to and perspective of medicine.

There are an estimated 5,860,000 Jews[3] and between 2 and 5 million Moslems[4] in this country. Jewish and Islamic professionals play important roles in health care delivery and it is essential that both the laity and the professional worlds increase their awareness of the value substrate of these religious faiths. This paper seeks to adduce some of the religious principles of Judaism and Islam as they relate to medical and health care. The discussion begins with historical and philosophical perspectives in each religious system. Specific reference will be paid to prevention as well as to divine intervention and the role of prevention. Finally, we will focus on a current matter of great concern, namely criteria of death.

Historical Perspectives

Jews share with Muslims an enormous role in the translation of early Greek treatises into Arabic Syriac and Hebrew. Contributions of both faiths include their own medical treatises as well as extensive clinical work at the courts of nobility. Health and medical care in both faiths is inextricably bound up with the minutiae of daily activities. For the Jew, as for the Moslem, proper ethical and moral behavior in daily life serves as the foundation for both the preservation of health and the prevention of illness. Jews believe in the wholeness of the human person and in the inherent value of life as stated by Moses: "Behold, I have set before you this day life and good, death and evil. Therefore choose life...".[5] In both Judaism and Islam, there is a great deal of stress placed on the value and goodness of life from which an all-encompassing preoccupation with health is derived.

Rabbinic scholars were well versed in anatomy, gynecology, pathology, physiology, fertility and sterility.[6] Many prominent ones were also physicians as exemplified by Chanina, Shmuel, Ami, Yehuda Halevi, the Rambam, and his son Abraham, Nachmanides, Moshe Ibn Tibon and Yosef Albo. Muslim philosophers/physicians were also highly knowledgeable and made important contributions to the fields of anatomy, physiology, infectious diseases, pediatrics, anesthesiology, bacteriology, opthalmology, and pharmacology, medicine, surgery and gynecology.[7] Mention of great Moslem physicians must include Abu Bakr Muhammed Ibn Zakariya Al-Razi otherwise known as Rhazes (841-926 A.D.). Rhazes was also one of the most prolific physicians of all time having written over 100 medical treatises. His major compendum entitled *Al-Hawai*, "Continent of Medicine" consisted of 20 volumes. Another distinguished medical personality was known as Abu Ali Al-Husin Ibn-Sina otherwise known as Avicenna (980-1037 A.D.) whose works profoundly influenced the world's medical literature. Moslems played homage to his work by referring to him as *Shaikh al-Ra'is* or *Mu'allim-i-Thani*, or the second teacher after Aristotle.

Evident in books and manuscripts outlining the recorded experience of clinicians, is that Jews, like Muslims, played important roles in the field of medicine during the Dark Ages when other potential contributing civilizations lay dormant. Members of both faiths shared a concern for both the personal and public dimensions of hygiene as well as an acute interest in the bodily changes which take place as a consequence of disease.

Fundamental Health Values

The study of medicine or *Tibb* in Islam is second in importance only to religious knowledge, otherwise known as *'umm al-ulum'* of the mother of knowledge. Islamic tradition places enormous emphasis on health as reflected by a quote in the *Sahih Tirmidhi* from King David, who is considered a Prophet in Islam, on its importance, "Health is a secret treasury. One hour's sorrow ages a man by one year. Health is the diadem of the health man, and can be seen by the sick only. Health is an invisible pleasure and comfort."[8] Perfection of morals or ethics is conducive to health in this life, and tranquility in the afterlife. Knowledge of both the body and soul is a *sine qua non* in a process of perfection of morals. The body houses the soul and both are intimiately bound up with one another in a divinely mysterious manner. Numerous acts are prescribed for the health of the body, many of which have been incorporated into the *shari'ah* (jurisprudence). Disease is the end state of a continuous process of disharmony between the spirit and the body which can be reversed through *tawhid* or unity of thought and sentiments of peace and good. There is an all encompassing emphasis placed in Islam upon the preventive aspects of disease in contrast to the curative.

Judaism teaches that the value of human life is supreme and takes precedence over virtually all other considerations. This attitude is most eloquently summed up in a talmudic passage regarding the creation of Adam:

> Therefore only a single human being was created in the world, to teach that if any person has caused a single soul of Israel to perish, scripture regards him as if he has caused an entire world to perish; and if any human being saves a single soul of Israel, scripture regards him as if he had saved an entire world.[9]

Compare this with the Islam version, "Whoesoever killeth a human being for other than manslaughter or corruption in the earth it shall be as if he killed all mankind and whoesoever saveth the life of one, it shall be as if he had saved the life of all mankind."[10] Human life in Judaism is not a good to be preserved as a condition of other values, but is an absolute, basic, and precious good in its own right. While the obligation to preserve life is commensurately all-encompassing, the Islamic view, as we shall learn, is somewhat tempered.

The Greeks created the field of medicine as a whole and the Jews created *preventive* medicine. Franz Boas addressed this point when he wrote that "It corresponds to the reality, in both the actual and chronological point of view, to consider the Jews as the creators of the science of public hygiene."[11] One reason for this is found in the subjective aspects of one dominant theme running through the Jewish contribution to medicine. While the Greeks were concerned with symptomatology, the Jews had a predilection for causation and hence a heightened dwelling on preventive medicine. Jews were primarily predisposed to the question "why" rather than "what"; an outlook conducive to strategies of prevention. Proper health for the Jew meant proper living. A contribution unique to the Jew in this vein is the Sabbath, the salutory aspects of which are unquestionable in the prevention of disease and the promotion of health.

A fundamental contribution of Islam to medicine was also in its preventive aspects. Some of Mohammad's direct words on this issue include, "If you hear about plague in a land, do not go to it, but if you were in that land, do not run away".[12] Others include, "No son of

Adam would fill a container worse than his stomach"[13]; "The stomach is the home of illness and dieting the head of a treatment".[14] Inherent in preventive medicine is that of cleanliness and one finds, "And thy garments keep free from stain"[15]; and, "O ye who believe when ye prepare for prayer, wash your faces and your hands to the elbows, rub your heads (with water) and wash you feet to the ankles".[16] The Koran also entreats its followers with regard to proper foods as follows:

> ...forbidden you (for food) are: dead meat, blood, the flesh of swine, and that on which hath been invoked the name of other than Allah; That which hath been killed by strangling, or by violent blow, or by a head long fall, or by being gored to death; that which hath been (partly) eaten by a wild animal: unless he are able to slaughter it (in due form); That which is sacrificed on stone (alters); (Forbidden) also is the division (of meat) by raffling with arrows; that is impiety.[17]

Islamic jurisprudence placed heavy emphasis on hygiene with the human environment. The Muhtasive was a legal enforcement agent and responsible for the application of Islamic rulings including those involved with cleanliness and hygiene.[18] Islamic principles of hygiene include the modern principles of isolation, substitution, shielding, treatment, and prevention, notions which are basic to the trade of the modern public health practitioner.[19]

Moslem physicians are urged to care for their own health, so as to set an example for the community, "And make not your own hands throw you into destruction"[20]

Human Intervention

There have always been those who have argued from a theological basis that medical intervention implies an interference with a divinely inspired course of events. This view was rejected by both Judaism and Islam. Rabbinic teaching reognized that intervention for the purpose of thwarting the natural course of the disease could be sanctioned only on the basis of specific Divine dispensation. Such license is found, in at least two places within talmudic exegesis. The first is in the scriptural passage dealing with compensation for personal injury, "And if other men quarrel with one another and one smites the other with a stone or with the first and he die not but has to keep in bed...he must pay the loss entailed by absence from work and he shall cause him to be thoroughly healed".[21] Another is derived from Nachmanides who also finds the obligation of the physician to heal is inherent in the commandment, "And you shall love your neighbor as yourself".[22] As a specific instance of the general obligation to manifest love and concern for one's neighbor, the obligation to heal encompasses not only situations posing a threat to life, limb or the restoration of impaired health, but also situations of lesser gravity warranting medical attention for relief of pain and promotion of well-being.

An eloquent midrashic narrative reflects both recognition of man's inherent lack of authority to tamper with physiological processes, since, prima facie, such intervention could be construed as a violation of the natural order, as well as awareness that permission to practice the medical arts is a matter of specific divine dispensation: It occurred that R. Ishmael and R. Akiva were strolling in the streets of Jerusalem accompanied by another person. They were met by a sick person. He said to them, "My masters, tell me by what means I may be cured". They told him, "Do thus and so until you are cured". The sick man asked them, "And who afflicted me?" They replied, "The Holy One, blessed be He." The sick man responded, "You have entered into a matter which does not pertain to you. [God] has afflicted and you seek to cure! Are you not transgressing his will? R. Akiva and R. Ishmael asked him, "What is your occupation? The sick man answered, "I am a tiller of the soil and here is the sickle in my hand". They asked him, "Who created the vineyard?" He answered, "The Holy One, blessed be He". R. Ishmael said to him, "And you enter into a matter which does not pertain to you! [God] created [the vineyard] and you cut his fruits from it". He said to them, "Do you not see the sickle in my hand? If I did not plow, sow, fertilize, and weed, nothing would sprout". R. Akiva and R. Ishmael said to him:

> "Foolish Man! Have you never in your life heard that it is written, "...as for man, his days are as grass; as a flower of the field, so he flourished"[23]; Just as if one does not weed, fertilize, and plow, the trees will not produce [fruit], and if fruit is produced, but is not watered or fertilized, it will not live but die, so with regard to the body. Drugs and medicaments are the fertilizer and the physician is the tiller of the soil.[24]

The Moslem approach to human intervention and the role of the physician has very similar parallels to those of Judaism. The Jewish physician is required to view his work as an instrument of God's limitless power of healing and to accept the fact that the Almightly can furnish cures of which he might not be aware.[25] Among Moslems, Allah is considered the "Shafee" or the "Healer", and the physician is an instrument of divine action. It is considered appropriate for Moslem physicians to acknowledge this fact both before beginning examining a patient by reciting "Bismillahirrahmanirrahim" in the name of G-d and afterward with "Alhamduulillah" - praise be Allah. Belief in Allah, not the work, physician or action of drugs, is considered the sufficient agent. In the words of the Koran 20, "When I am ill, it is He who cures".

Moslem philosophy with regard to ethical practices of the physician are inseparable from the ethics and morality of the clinician's personal life. A physician lacking personal moral values in life, cannot practice medicine. The derivation of such thinking resides in the words of Allah, "Allah has never put two hearts within one body".[26] Personal morals and ethics supersede knowledge and skill. The reasoning is that if one has lacunae in his knowledge or skills, a sense of truthfulness will impel the individual to admit his failings.

The relationship between a physician and his/her patient differ in Islam and Judaism from Western values as found in American law. The legal system of our country is firmly rooted in Anglo-Saxon common law. Under that legal system, the relationship between a physician and his patient is a contractual one. Therefore, legally, a physician has the absolute right to refuse to treat a patient who is not yet under his care. In effect, he may refuse to enter into a contract with the would-be patient. This attitude is reflected in the code of ethics of the American Medical Association which declares, "A physician may choose whom he will serve". Judaism, to the contrary, regards the physician not simply as acting on behalf of the patient, but as acting in the service of God. He/she is, in effect, God's messenger and dares not shirk the responsibility thrust upon him.

An examination of the Oath of Maimonides[27] and a recently written "Oath of Muslim Physician"[28], reveal that both Judaism and Islam require testimony of belief in the role of one God as a Creator and the need to be subservient to Him. Both faiths also request succor in dealing with patients. Contemporary secular codes, including that of the American College of Surgeons,[29] the International College of Surgeons,[30] and the Geneva Declaration of Medical Ethics,[31] make no mention of such a Higher Being. The Moslem code is understandably taken in the name of the Creator of all the heavens and earth and a promise to follow the dictates of the relevations of Mohammad. Both the Moslem and Maimonidean codes eliminated injunctions implying sexual restrictions.

The Definition of Death

Islam acknowledges the inevitability of death in the following Koranic passages, "Every soul shall have a taste of death"[32]; "Truly thou wilt die One day, and truly they too will one day"[33]; "Nor can a soul die except by God's leave, the term being fixed as by writing"[34]; "Allah takes away the souls upon their death; and those who do not die during their sleep, those on whom He has passed the decree of death, He keeps with Him and the rest he restores for a term ordained. Verily in this are signs for those who reflect.[35] Islam also acknowledges the sanctity of life, "And do not with your own hands cast yourselves into destruction"[36]; "Nor kill (or destroy) yourselves: For verily God hath been to you most merciful."[37]; "And slay not your children for fear of want. We shall provide for them and for you. Lo! Their slaying is a great sin."[38]

Muslim physicians are permitted to transgress the dictates of the Koran in order to preserve human life:

> I find nothing in what has been revealed to me that forbids people to eat any food except carrion, running blood, and swine flesh for they are unclean - and any flesh that has been profanely consecrated to deities other than Allah, but whosoever is complete to eat any of these, neither intending to sin, nor to transgress, will find Allah forgiving and merciful.[39]

If there were the slightest possibility that life could be extended for a mere fraction of a second, all laws in Jewish life, with the exception of the following three, adultery, idolatry and incest, are suspended.[40]

Heroic means are not encouraged by Islam, particularly if it is scientifically certain that life cannot be restored. Accordingly, it is not incumbent upon the Muslim physician to keep an individual alive by heroic means if that individual is likely to remain in a vegetative state. This view is contrary to the Jewish law which mandates the suspension of biblical restrictions regardless of how remote the likelihood of saving a person may be.[41] Thus, while Islam insists on the use of ordinary means, Judaism demands that extraordinary measures also be taken. This latter outlook does not factor in physical pain, expense, repugnance, danger or cost into the equation.

There is at least one exceptional circumstance in Judaism, which may preclude treatment and this is exemplified by the moribund individual whom, in the judgment of medical authorities, will not survive more than seventy-two hours. The obligation to heal terminates only at that point when all known medical means have been exhausted. Once a person is moribund, there is no obligation to heal and the, "...removal of anything which constitutes a hindrance to the departure of the soul, such as a clattering noise or salt upon the tongue, since such acts involve not hastening of death but only removal of the impediment..."[42]

Islam does not clearly identify the exact moment at which death occurs. This fact is derived form the Koranic Sura 23:100 in which three stages of life are portrayed: 1. Life in this world; 2. The moment of death during which the body and soul are separated and includes the time when the body is returned to the earth and the soul is in a state Barzakh awaiting the judgement day; The third period involves the day of resurrection and the final stage of life. It is thought that the vagueness of the definition of death deliberately allows for a redefinition thereof as dictated by technology. The use of Qiyas and IJMA HADITH serve as the basis for dealing with this issue in view of the fact that the definition of death is not clearly addressed either in the Koran or the Hadith.

Maadh - ibn-i-Jabal The Governor designate for YEMEN paid a visit to Prophet to take his leave before departure. The following conversation took place:
Prophet - On what basis shalt thou decide and judge cases?
Maadh - Accroding to the Book of God (Koran).
Prophet - And if thou dost not find any provision there in?

> Maadh - Well, then, I shall make every effort with my own opinion. The Prophet was so delighted at this reply that he exclaimed, "Praise be to God who hath guided the envoy of His envoy to what pleaseth the envoy of God."

Islam accepts brain death as a criterion for death. This is predicated on the notion that a person is composed of 3 parts, NAFS, the self, ROOH, the spirit, and QUALB, the spiritual hear or mind. Since the above mentioned components of the individuals reside in the brain alone, the death of this organ is coterminous under Islamic Jurisprudence with death. The Hadith, "...suggests that while the exact defintion of death has been kept deliberately vague, permission is granted redefine death with advances in technology".[43]

Moslem law denies the physician the right to terminate human life and this includes an unborn baby. The only circumstance under which an unborn child may be aborted is if it represents a threat to the life of the mother, a view similar to that in Judaism.[44] Islam accords a number of rights to the fetus, including those of inheritance if a fetus is born alive and subsequently expires the inheritance of its legal heirs. A woman sentences to death has that execution postponed until she delivers and nurses that child, even if the pregnancy is illegitimate.

The total cessation of brain function, including that of the brain stem, is equated with death in Orthodox Judaism. Any destruction of the medulla, in Jewish law, can be regarded as analogous to decapitation. Thus, Judaism[45] and Islam[46] are in agreement with an approach agreed upon by the Ad Hoc Committee of the Harvard Medical School to Examine the Definition of Death.[47]

The Harvard criteria stress that there be no suspicion of drug influence which can stimluate brain death, no movement, responsiveness to light, or to noxious stimuli, or corneal reflexes, unresponsive coma and body temperature as low or lower than 95 Fahrenheit.

We have tried to highlight some of the salient Judaic and Islamic principles guiding health care practice and in the process have learned many of the similarities and differences. I choose to honor Professor Arthur Hyman by ending this paper with a quote from one of his colleagues, the distinguished Harry Austryn Savitz, who concluded a seminal paper on the contributions of various cultures to the evolution of medicine by reworking well-known words from Isaiah as follows, "And it shall come to pass in the last days that all the surgeons will break their instruments into playthings and their scalpels into toys. No surgeon will need to use his knife, for the whole world will be filled with knowledge as water covers the sea, and disease will be wiped off the earth".[48]

Notes

1. Marshall H. Becker, "Sociobehavioral Determinants of Compliance", *Compliance with Therapeutic Regiment*, eds. David L. Sackett and R. Brian Haynes (City: Johns Hopkins University Press, 1976) 40-50.

2. Barbara Starfield, Christine Wray, Kelliann Hess, Richard Gross, Peter S. Birk and Burton C. D'Lugoff, "The Influence of Patient-Practitioner Agreement on Outcome of Care", *American Journal of Public Health* 71.2 (1981): 127-131.

3. *American Jewish Yearbook* 80 (1980): 159.

4. Martin E. Marty, foreword, *Health and Medicine in the Islamic Tradition*, by Rahman Fazlur (New York: Crossroad Publishing Company, 1987) xi.

5. *Deuteronomy* 30:19

6. *Kuzari*, Discussion 4, Chap. 31.

7. Hakim Mohammed Said, *Al-Tibb Islami* (Karachi, Pakistan: Hamdard National Foundation, 1976) 23-27.

8. ibid 38.

9. *Sanhedrin* 37a.

10. Koran 5:35.

11. Harry Austryn Savits, "National Traits in Medicine with Special Reference to the Jew", *Medical Journal Record* 127: 16-18, 70-72.

12. Sahih al-Bukkarr, *Book of Medicine*, Division 71, Chapter 30, Volume 7 418.624.

13. Sunan al-Tirmidhi, *Bab al-Zuhd*, ed. al-Maktabah al-Salaftiyah, 2nd ed. (Saudi Arabia: Medina, 1974) Chapter 47, "Abd al-Wahab 'Abd al-Lutif".

14. Ibn Majah, *Book of Medicine*, ed. Muhammed Fu'ad 'Abdul Baqui, 2nd ed. (Cairo: Isa al-Babi al-Halabi Publishing Co., 1974) Chapter 3.

15. Koran 74:4.

16. ibid 5:7.

17. ibid 5:4.

18. Tarik M. Al-Soliman, "Environmental Purity and Cleanliness: Applications and Practices in Early Muslim Society", *Journal of Islamic Medical Association* 20 (1988) 57-62.

19. John M. Last, *Public Health and Preventive Medicine*, 11th ed. (New York: Appleton-Century-Crofts, 1980).

20. Koran 2:195.

21. *Exodus* 21:19-20.

22. *Leviticus* 19:18.

23. Psalms 103:15.

24. *Midrash Temurah* found in *Otzer Midrashim*, ed. Y.D. Eisenstein, (New York: Reznick, Menschel and Company, Inc., 1915), Chelek Aleph 106, Yalkut Horaim 48.

25. *Jewish Medical Law* compiled and edited from Eliezer Yehuda Waldenberg. Avraham Steinberg, *Tzitz Eliezer*, trans. David B. Simons (Jerusalem/California: Gefen Publishing, 1980) 23.

26. Koran 33:4.

27. "Oath of Maimonides", *Collection of Codes of Ethics*, Museum of International College of Surgeons, Chicago, IL.

28. Wahaj D. Ahmad, El-Kade, Ahmed El-Kadi, and Bashir A. Zikria, "Oath of a Muslim Physician", *Journal of the Islamic Medical Association* 20 (1988) 11-14.

29. "Fellowship Pledge of the American College of Surgeons", *Collection of Codes of Ethics*, Museum of the International College of Surgeons, Chicago, IL.

30. "Pledge of the International College of Surgeons", *Collection of Codes of Ethics*, Museum of the International College of Surgeons, Chicago, IL.

31. "Geneva Declaration of Medical Ethics", *Collection of Codes of Ethics*", Museum of the International College of Surgeons, Chicago, IL.

32. Koran 3:185.

33. ibid 39:30.

34. ibid 3:14.

35. ibid 39:42.

36. ibid 2:195.

37. ibid 4:29.

38. ibid 17:31.

39. ibid 6:145.

40. *Shulchan Arukh, Orach Chaim* 329:3.

41. ibid 392:3.

42. *Talmud, Yoreh De'ah* 339:1.

43. Faroque A. Khan, "The Definition of Death in Islam: Can Brain Death Be Used As A Criteria of Death in Islam?", *Journal of the Islamic Medical Association* 18 Jan.-June (1986) 18-21.

44. Y.L. Untermann, "The Law of Pikkuah Nefesh and Its Definition", *HaTorah V'HaM'dinah* 4(1952) 22-29.

45. F.J. Veith, J.M. Fein, Tendler M.D., "Brain Death I: A Status Report of Medical and Ethical Considerations", *Journal of the American Medical Association* 238 (1977) 1651-1655.

46. Ahmed Sharet, "Modern Medical Procedures in the Light of Islamic Jurisprudence", *Islamic Medicine*, ed. I. El Sayeed, Kuwait Ministry of Public Health, January (1981) 400.

47. Ad Hoc Committee of the Harvard Medical School to Examine the Definition of Brain Death, "A Definition of Irreversible Coma", *Journal of the American Medical Association* 205 (1968) 337-340.

48. Savitz, 72.

Platonic and Christian: The Case of the Divine Ideas

Professor Bernard McGinn

Neither philosophical systems nor religious beliefs are abstract a-temporal entities. Both are developing traditions based upon concrete communities of interpretation. Philosophical texts exist within hermeneutical contexts similar to those in which sacred texts are continuously re-interpreted to meet changing situations and new demands. Platonism, perhaps more than any other of the major Greek systems of thought, has a history of extraordinary diversity. Each age in the history of Western thought has had to confront the paradox of Plato the master of true scientific knowledge (*episteme*) versus Plato the elusive dialogist and maker of myths.

Some of the most fascinating chapters in the history of Platonism have had to do with the interaction between this long philosophical tradition and the monotheistic faiths of Judaism, Christianity and Islam. The encounter between Platonism and Christianity has been particularly rich. What is most interesting to the student of the history of philosophy and most profitable to the historian of theology is the study of the process of mutual adaptation and correlation that took place when Platonism was used for the theoretical and systematic expression of Christian belief. A full study of the interplay between Platonism and Christianity would be the work of many volumes, but it may be possible to give a brief and necessarily incomplete sketch of one example of a major theme by way of illustration. The example I have chosen is the intradeical interpretation of the Platonic Forms or Ideas, that is, the teaching that the Ideas are Ideas in the divine mind.

It is a difficult question to determine exactly where Plato thought the Ideas or Forms to be. There were, of course, passages in the dialogues that later Platonists used to support their intradeical readings;

but the close affinity of the Ideas and the Mathematicals, the texts that suggest that the Ideas are outside the First Principle or produced by it (e.g., *Timaeus* 28A, 29A; *Philebus* 15B; *Republic* 597BD), and the very vagueness and fundamentally non-personalistic way in which Plato uses the term "god" and its cognates, make the extradeical interpretation the likely one. It is important to note, however, that for Plato the Ideas, by definition, are multiple, since the concept of an Idea is something that is identical with itself and therefore distinct from every other Idea.[1] Because of this multiplicity, the Ideas were to create difficulties in systems of thought and belief where the transcendental realm must, by definition, be a unity. A second difficulty connected with the Ideas went even deeper. In attempting to guarantee the objective truth of human knowledge by making our world of experience subject to a higher realm composed of abstractive objects like those produced by the human mind, Plato subordinated reality to intellect in such a way that subsequent thinkers were bound to inquire where the reality of the concrete objects we experience really comes from.[2] At the risk of drastically over-simplifying the history of Greek thought, we can suggest that two broad solutions to this *aporia* can be discerned. One immanentized the reality of the Ideas into the essences of concrete substances, as Aristotle did; the other transcendentalized the kind of mind required to think the Ideas so that they became more than mere projections of human abstractive thought.[3] The history of the latter enterprise constitutes our story.

Aristotle's trenchant criticism of the theory of Ideas from his immanentist position (e.g., *Met.* I 978b-991b) as well as his insistence that in the divine thought "the thinking will be one with the object of thought" (see *Met.* 1074b-1075a), doubtless played an important part in the evolution of the intradeical interpretation. This is true negatively in the sense that the Stagirite's attack created insurmountable problems for the causative activity of a separate realm of Ideas. The positive side, one which Aristotle did not see because of his emphasis on "Self-Thinking Thought" as a final cause alone, was in the emphasis given to the intellectual nature of the First Principle.

Given the fragmentary nature of our sources for the early history of the Platonic tradition, we do not know exactly who was the first to affirm in clear fashion that the Forms or Ideas are to be found in some way *in* the First Divine Principle. Perhaps this took place as early as

Xenocrates in the fourth century B.C.E.: more likely Antiochus of Ascalon in the first century disseminated the idea to the philosophical world.[4] The gradual melding of the Platonic Demiurge and the Stoic Logos in the philosophy of the last century before the Christian era was a potent force in the emerging conviction that the Platonic Ideas are in some way the Ideas of God.[5] By the time of Seneca (*Ep.* 65.7) the position is clear even in Latin sources.

A number of important essays have been devoted to the history of the intradeical interpretation of the Platonic Ideas, especially by H.A. Wolfson and W. Norris Clarke.[6] Without adopting Wolfson's pan-Philonian view of the evolution of Western thought, we must still start with Philo, the first thinker to give us a full, if not always clear, picture of one way of effecting this marriage between monotheistic faith in a personal God and Platonizing thought.

For Philo the Ideas are creations of God, that is, they are generated. Taken together, they form the intelligible world (*kosmos noetos*) that is the model for our visible one. The Alexandrian's chief contribution lies in his thoughts on the location of the ideas: "As, then, the city which was fashioned beforehand in the mind of the architect held no place in the outer world, but had been engraved in the soul of the artificer as by a seal; even so the universe that consisted of ideas would have no other location than the Divine Reason (*ton theion logon*), which was the author of this ordered frame."[7] Two things are important to note about Philo's views. First, the Logos, after the manner of Aristotle's "Self-Thinking Thought," seems to be identical with the intelligible world and hence with the Ideas themselves. Therefore the Ideas form a unity in diversity. Second, the Logos is both divine and not divine, the perfect Platonic mediator between the extremes of reality. "To his Word, his chief messenger, highest in age and honor, the Father of all has given the special prerogative, to stand on the border and separate the creature from the Creator."[8] The exact relation of the Ideas to the creator is not always clear in Philo. In a sense the Ideas are both *intradeical* in that they pre-exist virtually in God and *extradeical* insofar as the Logos is the real mediator between God and the visible world, as Wolfson avers.[9]

The author of the Prologue of John's Gospel does not, of course, mention the Ideas themselves; but in claiming that the Logos was not only with God in the beginning but "was God" (John 1:1) and that "all things were made through him" (1:2), he provided the fundamental New Testament warrant for all Christian speculation on the intradeical interpretation of the Ideas. Subsequent Christian intradeical readings, however, continued to be influenced by Later Platonic developments, especially those found in Neoplatonism.

Plotinus, the Father Of Neoplatonism, identifies the second hypostasis (pointedly always called *Nous* and not *Logos*) with the intelligible world of the Ideas (e.g., *Enn.* V.5.1-3, and V.9.9). The relationship of Nous to the Ideas is complex and has produced considerable misunderstanding. All the Ideas are united in Nous--"each individual idea is not something other than Nous, but is Nous. Nous as a whole is all the Forms and each individual Form is an individual Nous" (*Enn.* V.9.6). Thus the Ideas are both one in Nous and also potentially manifold as well, so that Nous is a unity-in-diversity, a paradoxical "One-Manyness."[10] This unity in diversity is also characteristic of what we might call the Aristotelian side of Nous, that is, its nature as a Self-Thinking Thought that is coterminous with Being itself, "Intellect making Being exist in thinking it, and Being giving Intellect thinking and existence by being thought" as he puts it in *Enn.* V.1.4. Because of this duality, Being and the Ideas must be excluded from the absolute simplicity to be found in the One, the first hypostasis and source of all. Are there Ideas in God? Yes and no, because both the One and the Nous are spoken of as "god," though in varying ways. What is clear, however, is that the Ideas are quite distinct from the First Principle, and if being within the First principle is the real definition of intradeical interpretations of the Ideas, then Plotinus does not belong in this camp.

The gap between Plotinus and Augustine in this regard is striking. As Etienne Gilson has pointed out,[11] not matter how much he was influenced by the Neoplatonists, Augustine refused to put his deeply personal God beyond the level of Being or existence. He was also adamant, especially in his classic treatment of the Ideas in the *De diversis quaestionibus* 83, q.46, that Intelligible Being, that is, the unity of the Ideas, is intradeical, that is, it is to be found in God's Mind (*in mente divina*) as the co-eternal Logos or Word. The Word contains the exemplars (*rationes aeternae*) of all created things and through them has direct knowledge of all particulars.[12]

Augustine established the classic Western understanding of the location and role of the Platonic ideas, but was this doctrine really a coherent one? Norris Clarke claims that Augustine "did not see clearly the difficulty of the ideas as real multiplicity in God."[13] If the Ideas are the "really real," as they must be in any Platonic system, then they must be multiple, and to introduce any non-relational (that is, non-trinitarian) multiplicity into God is to compromise Christian monotheism. Plotinus protected his highest God, the One, from the slightest whiff of such multiplicity; Augustine did not. I will take up this criticism of Augustine and other Christian Platonists below.

The next major original treatment of the divine Ideas in Latin Christian thought is that of the ninth-century Irish thinker, John the Scot. John put the Ideas, or primordial causes as he preferred to call them, in the second division of *natura*, the realm of that which is created and creates. As produced by the Father in the Word, he claims that "our reason for saying that the primordial causes of things are coeternal with God is that they always subsist in God without any beginning in time, and our reason for saying that they are not in all respects coeternal with God is that they receive the beginning of their being not from themselves but from their creator."[14] The primordial causes are not only the "really real" for John, they are also completely one and thus no threat to divine unity. "The primordial causes when seen by the intellect to be substantially existing in the Beginning of all things, that is, in the only begotten Word of God, are a simple and indivisible One, but when they proceed into their effects that are multiplied in infinity they acquire their numerable and ordered plurality."[15]

Eriugena's view of the one-manyness of the Ideas has so puzzled the critics that it has been attacked from opposite viewpoints. Etienne Gilson viewed it as a Platonic invasion of good Augustinian exemplarism and used it to create the dubious axiom: "...in any doctrine in which there is the slightest gap between the Christian God and the divine Ideas, the breadth of that gap is exactly in proportion to the ontological Platonism of the doctrine."[16] Norris Clarke, on the other hand, accused John of "being a better Christian than a Neoplatonist" because he transfers the absolute simplicity that should belong to the One to the level of Logos or Nous.[17] The implication of John's doctrine is that the very Being of the primordial causes, and therefore of all things in their created unfolding, is their being thought by God, a solution that Clarke finds "something like the Hegelian mode of idealism,"[18] but that might more justly be seen as a prime example of the kind of adjustment that makes Christian Platonists different from their pagan ancestors.

The subsequent history of the intradeical interpretation of the Ideas does not show any significant developments before the thirteenth century, despite some interesting variations in what we might call an Eriugenean mode among the thinkers of the "Chartrian" tradition in the twelfth century. In the age of High Scholasticism, however, there was considerable original thought devoted to the Divine Ideas. Bonaventure and Meister Eckhart, good Platonists that they were, put the Ideas and their exemplary function at the center of their thought, though in rather different ways.[19] Thomas Aquinas, though less a Platonist, maintained a central role for the Ideas too.[20] Henry of Ghent, Duns Scotus, Petrus Thomae and others, under the influence of Avicenna, strove to re-introduce a gap between God and the Ideas by ascribing to them, apart from their identity with God, some form of being, an *esse diminutum* or *esse intentionale*.[21] In the fourteenth century, William of Occam and his followers, claiming that if the Divine Ideas are real this would imply multiplicity in God, denied them outright despite the authority of Augustine and the tradition.[22]

Given this long and controversial history, we may well ask why the Divine Ideas were so important to Christian thinkers. I would suggest that the fundamental importance of placing the Ideas in the Word or Logos was to maintain an intelligible bond between the incomprehensible divine reality and our own world. Indeed, one might say that the more unknowable and apophatic God became, the more necessary a role the Ideas as exemplars played in giving philosophical and theological significance to the knowledge possible to our intellects and in guaranteeing some analogy between divine and human intellection. Occam and the nominalists, of course, felt no such need for intelligible harmony between the divine and created realms. For them the Divine Will choosing by *potentia ordinata* a likely order and arrangement for this world was all that was needed. By *potentia absoluta* God had the ability to contradict and subvert whatever intelligibility, metaphysical and moral, makes up this cosmos. The Christian Platonists, on the other hand, were convinced that the intelligiblity found in this universe was not merely an ordained act of the divine will, but also had a real relation to an intelligible order in God. This was not an attempt to measure the immeasurable God by a human yardstick; it was an argument that the human mind's hunger for truth was divine in both origin and goal, that the human precisely as intellectual being was really the image of God. The intradeical interpretation of the Platonic Ideas may not be the only way to explain this important conviction of Christian belief, but it was one of the most effective for centuries.

We can also say that the intradeical interpretation of the Ideas reinforced the personalist conception of God found in Christianity, Judaism and Islam. Though it would be a mistake to exclude all later pagan Neoplatonists from something like a personal relation with the First Principle, it is obvious that the three monotheistic faiths needed a God who in some way is a thinker as well as a doer--a subject in a transcendental sense.

Despite these good intentions, some students of the history of philosophy have seen the intradeical interpretation of the Ideas as deeply flawed in two ways. First, the Platonic Ideas are necessarily real and necessarily multiple, something that is inconsistent with the simplicity of the Christian God. According to A.C. Pegis, Thomas Aquinas alone overcame this problem by recognizing that an intelligible order is not necessarily linked to a real multiplicity. Norris Clarke, with rather more justice, recognized that John the Scot also affirmed "the existential identity of all the divine ideas, however distinct in their intelligibility or *esse intentionale*, with the simple act of the divine mind thinking them."[23] The same is also true of such thirteenth-century Platonists as Bonaventure and Eckhart.

A second criticism directed against the intradeical interpretation of the Divine Ideas has been the claim that if the "really real" is identified with the Ideas, the value of material reality is either denigrated or eviscerated. As Norris Clarke puts it, such a position is inconsistent "with the value given to created existence as the gift of God's love and the decisive value given to human salvation freely worked out in contingent history through the Incarnation of the Son of God and the free moral response of historical man."[24] A full answer to this criticism cannot be given here, but it should be noted that assigning material reality a crucial, if secondary, reality within a harmonious hierarchy of values is not necessarily either to denigrate or eviscerate it. However different their respective interpretations, Platonists like Augustine, John the Scot, Bonaventure and Eckhart agreed with Aquinas on the fundamental premises of the intradeical interpretation of the Platonic Divine Ideas: (1) that existence in the Ideas is a higher form of existence than material existence; (2) that created material reality is both good and necessary to the perfection of the universe; and (3) that material existence cannot be understood apart from the Divine Ideas, the source of all intelligibility.

Notes

1. See A.C. Pegis, "The Dilemma of Being and Unity. A Platonic Incident in Christian Thought," in R. Brennan, ed., *Essays in Thomism* (New York: Sheed and Ward, 1942), pp. 156-58.

2. See A.C. Pegis, "Cosmogony and Knowledge I. St. Thomas and Plato," *Thought* 18 (1943), pp. 649, 653, 658, 660, 663.

3. See Pegis, *ibid.*, pp. 645-46, on this.

4. The doctrine is hinted at in Antiochus's pupil Cicero. See Stephen Gersh, *Middle Platonism and Neoplatonism: The Latin Tradition* (Notre Dame: University of Notre Dame, 1986), Vol. 1, pp. 145-54.

5. For some studies of the early stages, see Roger Jones, "The Ideas as the Thoughts of God," *Classical Philology* 21 (1926), pp. 317-26; Audrey Rich, "The Platonic Ideas as the Thoughts of God," *Mnemosyne*, Series IV. 7 (1954), pp. 123-33.

6. H.A. Wolfson, "Extradeical and Intradeical Interpretations of Platonic Ideas," in *Religious Philosophy. A Group of Essays* (Cambridge: Belknap Press, 1961), pp.27-68. W. Norris Clarke, "The Problem of the Reality and Multiplicity of the Divine Ideas in Christian Neoplatonism," *Neoplatonism in Christian Thought*, ed. Dominic O'Meara (Albany: SUNY Press, 1982), pp. 109-27. See also L. de Rijk, "Quaestio de Ideis," in *Kephalaion. Studies offered to Professor C.J. de Vogel*, ed. by J. Mansfeld and L.M. de Rijk (Assen: Van Gorcum, 1975), pp. 204-13.

7. Philo, *De opificio mundi* V. 20 (Loeb ed., Vol. I, p. 17).

8. Philo, *Quis rerum divinarum heres sit* 205 (Loeb ed., Vol. IV, p. 385).

9. Wolfson, *art. cit.*, pp. 37-38, sees the intradeical and extradeical stages as successive; but it has been argued by David Winston in *Philo of Alexandria* (New York: Paulist Press, 1981), pp. 10-16, that Philo's theory of creation is an eternal one and therefore both aspects would be simultaneous.

10. The term is taken from Edward Booth, *Aristotelian Aporetic Ontology in Islamic and Christian Thinkers* (Cambridge: CUP, 1983), p. 36.

11. E. Gilson, *Being and Some Philosophers* (Toronto: Pontifical Institute of Mediaeval Studies, 1952), p. 31.

12. For other Augustinian texts on the Ideas, see, e.g., *De Trin.* VI.10.11; *De civ. Dei* VIII.4; *De Gen. ad litt.* IV. 24.41, V.15.33. For an analysis of *De diversis quaestionibus* q. 46, see S. Gersh, *op. cit.*, Vol. 1, pp. 403-13.

13. Clarke, *art. cit.*, p. 115, Cf. Pegis, "The Dilemma of Being and Unity," pp. 158-59.

14. *Iohannis Scotti Eriugenae Periphyseon (De Divisione Naturae). Liber Secundus*, ed. I.P. Sheldon-Williams (Dublin: Institute for Advanced Studies, 1972), p. 83.

15. *Iohannis Scotti Eriugena Periphyseon (De Divisione Naturae). Liber Tertius*, ed. I.P. Sheldon-Williams with the collaboration of Ludwig Bieler (Dublin: Institute for Advanced Studies, 1981), p. 39.

16. E. Gilson, *op cit.*, p. 38.

17. Clarke, *art. cit.*, p. 116.

18. *Ibid.*, p. 118.

19. For some representative texts, see Bonaventure, *In I Sent.* dd. 27, 35-36; *Quaestiones de scientia Christi* qq. 2-4; *De reductione artium ad Theologiam* #15-20. For Meister Eckhart, see his *Comm. in Gen.* (nn. 1-28) and *Comm. in Jo.* (nn. 1-131).

20. For Aquinas on the Ideas, see, e.g., *Summa theologiae* Ia, q. 14, aa. 5-8; q. 15; q. 44, a.3; q. 84, a.5; *De Veritate* q.4, a.6. Norris Clarke, *art. cit.*, pp. 122-24, goes too far when he claims Thomas "deontologized" the Ideas.

21. See de Rijk, *art. cit.*, pp. 208-11; Clarke, *art. cit.*, pp. 124-25.

22. See Pegis, "The Dilemma of Being and Unity," pp. 152-53, 159-70.

23. This is the formulation in Clarke, *art. cit.*, p. 126. Cf. his remarks on John the Scot in this regard (pp. 117-18).

24. Clarke, p. 126, and pp. 118-19, where the conflict between Neoplatonism and Christian personalism is stressed.

A Brief History of the Liar Paradox*

Larry B. Miller

The liar paradox or antinomy, the statement: "What I am saying is false", has occupied the attention of Russell, Wittgenstein, Tarski and many other modern philosophers. As is well-known, it has a long history stretching back to the very beginnings of Western logic.[1] Aristotle, for example, alludes to it in his *Sophistical Refutations*, while other ancient authors associated it with Epimenides of Megara and Eubulides of Miletus, a pupil of Euclid.

It is less well-known that medieval Islamic scholars wrote highly sophisticated and independent discussions of the liar paradox. Virtually no work at all has been done on the subject, and to make matters worse, none of the major works on the paradox has been published. In what follows, I should like to give a brief sketch of the history of the liar paradox in Islamic thought from the tenth through sixteenth centuries highlighting a few important discussions. I should also like to suggest that Islamic philosophers anticipated modern solutions to the paradox.

The first known reference to the liar paradox in Islamic philosophy appears as early as the tenth century. The Christian philosopher Yaḥyā ibn ʿAdī mentions the paradox in a treatise on sophisms deriving from Aristotle's *Sophistical Refutations*.[2] But in theology, authors of the ninth century make use of it in religious disputations. A theological polemic of the early tenth century uses the paradox, in an argument propounded by the theologian Ibrahim al-Naẓẓām (d. 836), to refute Manichaean dualists.[3]

A later discussion, this time by the tenth century theologian al-Baghdādī, mentions the paradox in the context of a discussion on the nature of "*khabar*".[4] By *khabar* al-Baghdādī sometimes means a statement (in a logical sense), sometimes "a report about or stemming from the Prophet" (thereby making it pretty much equivalent to *ḥa-*

173

dīth), and sometimes both. Again, it is an argument against dualists. Baghdādī's argument has a more logical flavor than al-Naẓẓām's:

> A *khabar* is either true or false; the true agrees with its object [*wāfaqa mukhbarahū*] while the false is contrary to it. It is not possible for one report to be both true and false except in one question [*mas'ala*], namely, the man who never lied [*lam yakdhib qaṭṭ*] and then said, "I am lying." For this *khabar* is a lie on his part; but through it he is both lying and telling the truth in that when a liar reports [*akhbara 'an*] about himself that he is lying, he is telling the truth. This is a means [not only] for refuting [*ibṭāl*] the dualists claim [*qaul*] that the person who makes the true does not make the false, nor vice versa; [but also] their claim that the Light is what makes the true, and the Darkness that makes the false; for, whichever of the two Makers caused him to do this [i.e. speak truly and falsely at the same time] it still follows that truth and falsity are simultaneously related to him and this is contrary to their claim.

Though al-Baghdadi criticized the dualists, he admitted that their arguments were of some interest, particularly in their emphasis on intentionality-- i.e. a person has to intend to lie (qasd).

In any event, al-Baghdadi's discussion does not play any role in later Islamic discussions of the paradox. In early Islamic theology the paradox was used as a method for refuting one's opponents and was not seen as something *per se* problematical and worthy of investigation. It does not seem that the three greatest figures of Islamic philosophy-- Farabi, Avicenna, and Averroes-- ever dealt with it.

But by the middle of the thirteenth century, discussions become common. It is mentioned in logical works, particularly those discussing puzzles and paralogisms derived, mainly, from Aristotle's *Sophistical Refutations*. Thirteenth century discussions were sufficiently common to lead later authors, like Muḥammad Bāqir ibn Murtaḍā al-Yazdī,[5] to think that it had been invented in that period. He suggested two inventors. First, the "prince of the sceptics" Fakhr al-Dīn al-Rāzī, and second, that great misleader of men Ibn Kammūnah al-Baghdādī "who brought numerous objections against God's holy word." I cannot corroborate that Fakhr al-Dīn al-Rāzī was interested in the problem. But Ibn Kammūnah's interest in the paradox is well documented; indeed, we have manuscripts of his correspondence with the great logician al-Kātibī, known as Debīrān, in which he discusses and solves, to his own satisfaction at least, the paradox.[6] Other famous thirteenth century logicians and theologians like al-Khunajī

[1194-1249], Shams al-Dīn al-Samarqandī [d.@1300] and Naṣīr al-Dīn al-Ṭūsī [1201-1274] also proposed solutions to the paradox.

The liar paradox was, then, well known to thirteenth century philosophers and theologians. But not until the fourteenth century did it become the focus of serious and often lively philosophical debate. The distinguished theologian, al-Taftāzānī (1322-1390), discussed it in his commentary on a book on Islamic theology, his own *Maqāṣid al-ṭālibīn*.[7] Unlike al-Baghdadī, who, as we have just seen, gave the standard "one-step"[8] formulation of the paradox, al-Taftāzānī presents us with a two-step version:

> If someone says, "What I say tomorrow will not be true" and then the next day limits his speech to saying "What I said yesterday was true", then the truth of each statement implies the falsity of the other. Some of the best scholars were perplexed by this sophism....
> Therefore, I call it the "square root paradox".[9] I have examined several opinions but found no satisfactory solutions. In my opinion the proper thing to do regarding this proposition is to admit that one is unable to solve it.

Important though the *Maqāṣid* of al-Taftāzānī may be for the history of the liar paradox and of Islamic theology in general, the real focus of debate was a work by an even better known theologian--the *Tajrīd al-'Aqā'id* of Naṣīr al-Dīn al-Ṭūsī. The two main antagonists were fifteenth century commentators on the *Tajrīd*, Jalāl al-Dīn al-Dawwānī [1427-1501] and Mīr Ṣadr al-Dīn Muḥammad al-Shīrāzī al-Dashtakī [1425-1497],[10] who conducted an acrimonious debate over the liar paradox. Al-Dawwānī wrote three supercommentaries [*ḥawāshīn*] on the *Tajrīd*, none of which have been published. I have not been able, so far, to study any of them, so all of the following comments rely on information from other contemporary or near contemporary treatises and the bio-biographical literature,

In his first supercommentary on the *Sharḥ* of 'Alī Qushjī on the *Tajrīd*,[11] al-Dawwānī probably mentioned something connected with his own solution to the paradox.[12] Al-Dashtakī wrote a commentary on al-Dawwānī's commentary in which he criticised al-Dawwānī's solution to the paradox.[13] Al-Dawwānī replied with a second commentary on the *Tajrīd*.[14] Al-Dashtakī, in turn, wrote a second commentary in reply. The controversy survived even their deaths, for Al-Dawwānī's last commentary was later refuted by al-Dashtakī's son, Ghiyāth al-Dīn Manṣūr [1465-1542].[15] To complicate matters still further both al-Dawwānī and al-Dashtakī also wrote independent treatises on the liar paradox, which survive in manuscripts.[16] Both include a history of the liar paradox, mentioning earlier discussions and solutions in writings by Ibn Kammūnah, al-Katibī, al-Taftāzānī, al Khunajī, Shams al-Dīn al-Samarqandī, al-Saiyid al-Sharīf al-Jurjānī, al-Ṭūsī, and others.

Let me now discuss al-Dawwānī's treatise. The treatise is in three parts: the first introduces the problem and gives two formulations of the paradox; the second summarizes and refutes solutions proposed by his predecessors; the third part presents his own solution and attacks al-Dashtakī at length.

The first part starts out with the two-step formulation of the paradox:

> It is said that it is possible that the conjunction with respect to truth of two contradictory assertions is actual, since were someone to say: "Everything that I am saying at this moment is a lie" and then not say anything else at this time, then necessarily: either this speech is true in reality or false. But on both assumptions there follows the true conjuction of two contradictory assertions.
>
> [This becomes clear if we look at it in the following way:] In the first case, if it is true, then there would follow the falsity [of the statement] "everything that I am saying at this time" but this speech is his speech at that time. Therefore it is false. But the assumption was that it is true, so it will be both true and false at one and the same time! This also has a consequent that it be in conformity with reality on account of its being true; but it will not be in conformity with reality on account of its being false. And this is the conjunction in truth of two contradictory assertions.
>
> Let us now consider that second case: i.e. if we say that the statement is false. In this case, too, we have the conjunction of two contradictories, because [1] it follows that some of the components of his speech at this moment will be true, since [2] were all the components false, then the statement "everything that I am saying at this time" would not be false, since there are no other components of "his saying at this time" other than this saying. [3] It follows, therefore, that it is true, but the assumption was that it is false. [4] Therefore we have the conjunction of two contradictory assertions.

Al-Dawwānī offers an original solution to the problem. It is that this *khabar* is not really a *khabar*, a statement, but rather a performative, *inshā'*. Here is his argument:[17]

> I say, and may God grant me success, the proper meaning of statement [*al-ikhbār*] is reporting [*hikāya*] the "real relation" [*al-nisba al-wāqi'īya*] either [a] in

the manner of correspondence, in which case it would be true, or [b] in the opposite manner, in which case it would be false.

Now it is the nature of a report [*hikāya*] that *the object of the report be specified in reality*[18] even though we may cease to consider the entire report. For example, were you to say to a sculptor, "Make me a sculpture that imitates itself" [lit. a form that imitates that very form] then your speech would not be definite. For, if the thing itself is not specified to begin with, then you can't make a report about it. This is something a priori.[19]

Secondly, they say[20] "If speech corresponds or does not correspond to reality, then it is a statement [*khabar*]; otherwise it is a performative [*inshā'*]."[21] This means that if speech reports about reality, whether or not it corresponds to it, then it is a statement [*khabar*]; but if it is not of this sort, then it is a performative [*inshā'*]. For example, your saying "One is half of two" is a report about reality that corresponds to it; while your saying "One is not half of two" is a report about reality that does not correspond. The object of report in both cases is the status of "one" with respect to what really is the case. Its status in the first case corresponds to reality while in the second case it does not. If you want to, you could say the first is a report that corresponds to "what really is" while the second is a report that does not correspond to "what really is." Generally speaking *a speech's being a statement depends upon its being a report about a "real relation"*.[22] It is on account of this that you hear the best scholars saying, "In performatives, the utterer creates a relation without referring to any thing.[23] This differs from the relation in statements."[24] For they do refer to reality[25] as we have explained in detail in our supercommentary to the *Tajrīd*. Indeed naming them "*inshā'*" and "*ikhbār*" is a splendid indication of what we explained in detail [there]. Etymologically, "*inshā'*" means "bringing into being [*iḥdāth*]" while "*ikhbār*" means "reporting about something real" [in a sense] that is more general than corresponding or not corresponding....

A learned man has said, "the *significatum* of a statement is the truth, while falsity is something that is theoretically possible."[26] What he means is that its truth is something that is clearly inherent to its *significatum*. For example the meaning of your saying, "Zaid is standing" is his being described as standing vis-à-vis what really is the case. This clearly implicates its being true.

Now if someone says "Everything that I'm saying is false", referring to this very utterance [*kalam*], then this will not be properly speaking a statement since it contains a falsification of the relation between "[everything] that I'm saying" and "false." For the relation between "false" and "the *significatum* of the statement" is the relation of the relation between its *significatum* to "truth," as you well know. So affirming the truth [*al-taṣdīq*] of what it contains implicates affirming its falsity. Thus it follows that what is held true is adjudged false. So the soul will be, at one and the same moment, affirming and denying [the same thing] since to deny the affirmative relation is the same as affirming the negative, as was established in its place. But this is absurd.

Al-Dashtakī was quick to criticize al-Dawwānī. He understands al-Dawwānī to mean that "My speech today is false" cannot be a statement since it refers to itself:[27]

> We do not grant that "there is no real relation" such that it would be possible that the relation that this "speech" contains would be a report about it." There is necessarily a relation between "his speech today" (for that is something existent)-- I mean his saying "my speech today is false" and "false"-- whether this be affirmative or negative, since it is impossible that neither be the case in reality. Next, the judgment that there is a "real relation" between "my speech is composite" referring to this very speech and between "composition"; while there is no "real relation" between "my speech today is false" referring to this very speech and "false" is clearly an arbitrary judgment which would not satisfy even the dullest. How then is there not "real relation"? For "relation" here is more general than being affirmative or negative. It comes about between any two things that we posit. So why is it that there is no "real relation", be it affirming or denying, between "this speech" and "false." That this sort of thing could puzzle an educated man is quite unusual. Thus there is a "real relation" between them. It is clear that "my speech is false" reports it, just as "my speech is composite" reports and states the relation betwen "my speech" and "composition". This sort of construction is posited for the statement about the relation between its two terms. It is true that when it is not used in accord with that for which it was originally posited, as in the forms of oaths, it will not be a statement about it. But in our case, it is used in accord with its original imposition. The predicative character of this statement is so clear as to be a priori. It is on this account that no scholar has denied it although many of the best spent much reflection and effort on this paradox. Its denial is one of the peculiarities of this person.

Al-Dashtakī then continues, much of his argument being *ad hominem*:[28]

> I heard from a man of quality that during a class studying the commentary of the *Tajrīd* with this person, when he mentioned the opinion that the utterance "what I'm saying now is false" is not a statement, the latter insulted him and abused him with names whose repetition would be odious. Then he said, "how could it not be a statement, when he intends to make one?"

Of course al-Dawwānī was not at a loss for a response, also *ad hominem*, but this would take us too far afield.[29]

What needs to be stressed is not the intellectual competitions that the liar paradox aroused but the original arguments that were put forward. Al-Dawwānī's solution to the paradox-- that it is a performative-- is strikingly "modern." It anticipates a similar solution proposed by P.F. Strawson.[30] Like many modern philosophers, al-

Dawwani recognized the problematic status of statements with predicates like "is true" or "is false". On the other hand, al-Dashtakī's criticism is paralleled by modern opposition to solutions that are based on material rather than formal considerations of the sentence. To say that we should exclude sentences with predicates "is true" or "is false" seems arbitrary.

Notes

*. A version of this paper was delivered at a meeting of the American Oriental Society in April, 1986. I have also corresponded with Professor Nicholas Heer who provided me with some additional references.

1. The above formulation comes from Cicero, *Academica*, 2,29 si te mentiri dicis idque verum dicis, mentiris an verum dicis? A similar formulation is found in Alexander of Aphrodisias, CAG, *Comm. in Soph. El.*, p. 171, lines 17 ff. Other references are given in Prantl, *Geschichte der Logik* [1955 Reprint of 1855 Edition] I.50-51 and footnote 83; Bochenski, *A History of Formal Logic*, trans. I. Thomas (South Bend, 1961) pp. 237 ff.

2. Gerhard Endress, *The works of Yaḥyā ibn 'Adī* (Wiesbaden, 1977) p. 44.

3. Al-Khaiyāṭ, *Kitab al-intiṣār*, ed. H. S. Nyberg (Cairo, 1925) pp. 30-31. For other references, see Guy Monnot, *Penseurs Musulmans et Religions Iraniennes*, Etudes Musulmanes 16 (Paris, 1974) pp. 298-301.

4. In his *Uṣūl al-Dīn* (Istanbul, 1927) p. 5. But I see now that Josef van Ess refers to a discussion of the problem in al-Jāḥiẓ in "The Logical Structure of Islamic Theology", in *Logic in Classical Islam*, ed. G. von Grunebaum, (Wiesabaden 1970) p. 31. It is also used by al-Baqillānī in a similar fashion in order to refute "dualists." In al-Baqillānī's version, someone says "I am the Darkness". But who is the speaker, one of the people of Light or Darkness? *Kitāb al-Tamhīd*, ed. Richard McCarthy (Beirut, 1957) p. 67 lines 13 ff. He later refers to the difference between ṣifa, attribute, and waṣf, attribution. The latter is oral [*kalām masmū'*] and is thus either true or false [*qaul yumkin an yadkhulahū-al-sidq wal-kidhb*] while the former is that from which the waṣf originates and is not subject to truth or falsity (p. 214, lines 15 ff.). It later turns out that wasf is ambiguous. Seen as speech, it reflects one of the God's essential attributes, *sifat al-dhāt*. But the difference is such that all *wasfs* are *ṣifas* but not vice versa (p. 216, lines 20-21).

5. In the *Fawā'id* to his *Wasīlat al-wasā'il fī sharḥ al-Rasā'il*, pp. 45-47 in the end of the book. [Teheran Lithograph]

6. Another solution was offered by Ibn Kammūnah in reply to al-Kātibī when he asked him to explain his saying "I say: we do not grant that his "speech" at this time is either true or false. For we object to his division. If someone were to say: this is a statement and every statement must be either true or false since in that [way] predicative constructions are distinguished from the other ones, we would say: We do not grant that it is in that [way], that it is distinguished from every-

thing else. Rather it is distinguished by its being possible [*ihtimāl*] that its truth or falsity be asserted. The possibility of making this assertion is not incompatible with its being neither true or false. For it is not a pre-condition of the above assertion that it be true or false. So to sum up, the possibility of an assertion being true or false is not incompatible with its being per se neither.

7. He was the author of the original work as well, viz., *Maqāsid al-tālibīn*. Cf. Hajji Khalifa s.v.

8. I.e. the one step is where the person says, "I am lying." The difference between the former and the two-step version will be clear from what follows.

9. *Maghlatat al-jadhr al-asamm*.

10. On al-Dashtakī see GAL II, p. 262, SII p. 270.

11. 'Alī b. M. Qushjī [d. 1474] *al-Sharh al-jadīd*.

12. That neither sentence is a statement [*khabar*] and hence neither sentence is true or false.

13. Mīr Sadr al-Dīn al-Dashtakī [d.1497]-- *al-Hāshiya al-jadīda al-Sadriya* and *al-Hāshiya al-thāniya*.

14. Al-Dawwānī [d. 1501] 3 Supercommentaries-- *al-Hāshiya al-qadīma, al-Hāshiya al-jadīda* also known as *al-Tabaqāt al-Jalāliya*, and *al-Hāshiya al-ajadd al-Jalāliya*.

15. See GAL II, p. 545; SII p. 593; I 671. Ghiyāth al-Dīn b. Sadr al-Dīn al-Dashtakī [d. 1542]-- *al-Mawā'id al-urqubiya bil-nuqūd al-Ya'qūbiya*.

16. "Risāla fī hall shubhat al-jadhr al-asamm" by al-Dashtakī and "Risāla fī hall shubhat [or maghlatat] al-jadhr al-asamm" by al-Dawwānī. On these manuscripts see *Fihrist kitābkhāne-yi markazī dānishgāh-i Tihrān*, vol. hashtom, ed. Muhammad Danish Pazhuh [Teheran (1339)]. All citations are from Ms. LI copy of al-Dawwānī's work found in Istanbul's Suleymaniye Library.

17. LI 213a.

18. *an yakūna al-mahkūm 'anhū yu'ayyan fī al-wāqi'*. For *al-mahkūm 'anhu*, perhaps one should read *al-mhky*.

19. See Wittgenstein, *Tractatus* 3.332 "no proposition can make a statement about itself because a propositional sign cannot be contained in itself. From B. Mates, *Sceptical Essays*, p. 22 and notes 16-7.

20. I.e. the grammarians? Dawwani's argument that self-referential sentences are performatives stands on this distinction between statments (*khabar*), which can be true or false, and performatives (*inshā'*), which cannot be either true or false.

21. *Inna al-kalām in kāna li-nisba khārij yuṭābiquhū au lā yuṭābiquhū fa-khabar, wa-illā fa-inshā'.*

22. *Wa-bi-l-jumla, fa-madār kaun al-kalām khabaran 'alā kaunihī ḥikāya 'an nisba wāqi'īya.*

23. *Inna al-nisba fī al-'inshā'īyāt yuḥdithuhā al-lāfiẓ min ghair an yunazzi'uhā an al-wāqi' bi-khilāf al-nisba al-khabarīya.* At LI 217a, he gives the following examples: "I hereby sell", "I hereby buy", "Praise God", "Thank God", "There is no God but God", "God is great," etc. None of the examples is true or false.

24. Or, this differs from predicative relation.

25. *Fa-innahā muntazi'a 'an al-wāqi'.*

26. *Inna madlūl al-khabar, huwa al-ṣidq, wal-kidhb iḥtimāl 'aqlī.*

27. LI 214b.

28. LI 216a.

29. LI 216a.

30. *Analysis* (9) 1949.

The Question of Immortality in Lawrence of Lindores's *Quaestiones in Aristotelis libros De anima*

Olaf Pluta

Michalski has well characterized the discussion of the question of immortality in the later Middle Ages as a 'struggle for the soul'[1]; in fact the question of immortality was a most controversial one in the fight between the *via antiqua* and the *via moderna* at the universities in the fourteenth and fifteenth centuries. Lawrence of Lindores († 1437)[2], the first Rector of St. Andrews, was one of the leading figures taking part in this discussion. His commentaries on Aristotle – especially his lectures on the *De anima* and the *Physics*[3] – were used widely at the universities of continental Europe in the fifteenth century and beyond. As his works on natural philosophy were never printed they were neglected afterwards, and the philosopher Lawrence of Lindores remained unknown until he was rediscovered in the twenties by Michalski and Baxter.[4] In this paper I intend to give an outline of Lawrence of Lindores's discussion of the question of immortality, as it is presented in his *Quaestiones in Aristotelis libros De anima*, and to compare his solution with the answers given by some other leading members of the Parisian faculty of arts, especially John Buridan and Nicholas Oresme. Finally I would like to glance at the *Wirkungsgeschichte* of Lawrence of Lindores's solution at the universities in the fifteenth century.

*

William of Ockham's famous quodlibetal question "*Utrum possit demonstrari quod anima intellectiva sit forma corporis*"[5] in which he states that, if understanding is taken to be an act proper to an immaterial, incorruptible and ingenerable substance, then it cannot be demonstrated – neither by reason nor by experience – that we do indeed understand, and that someone following reason and experience would say that the intellection and volition that we experience in ourselves are operations and passions caused and received in an extended and corruptible and generable form,[6] was the *locus classicus* for the authors of the *via moderna* to discuss the problem of immortality.

In his *Quaestiones in Aristotelis libros De anima*[7] Lawrence of Lindores also considers the question "*Utrum intellectus humanus sit forma corporis humani*"[8]. After introducing some arguments for and against the thesis that the human intellect is the form of the human body[9] he divides the body of the question into two articles: In the first he recites three opinions about the nature of the human intellect, in the second article he offers his own solution to the question.[10]

The structure of the *corpus quaestionis* in detail[11] is the following: In the first article Lawrence of Lindores lays down two *notabilia*: first, he recites three opinions regarding the human intellect, secondly, he distinguishes two different meanings of the term 'form'. In the second article he first gives five general *conclusiones*, secondly, he puts forward two *dubitationes* which raise doubt on some of the conclusions.

According to Lawrence of Lindores – who in this part of his question closely follows John Buridan – there have been three more famous opinions about the nature of the human intellect[12]: Alexander of Aphrodisias's materialistic anthropology, Averroes's theory of the unity of intellect and the doctrine of the church, "quae non est tenenda pro opinione, sed potius pro vera fide catholica". The opinion of Aristotle is not considered, because Aristotle's statements regarding the human intellect are *multum obscura*. The obscurity of Aristotle's theory of the human intellect and the apparent conflict between his statements were commonplace in the later Middle Ages. William of Ockham showed that he was not interested in Aristotle's theory of the human intellect any more by saying: "whatever the Philosopher thought of this does not now concern me, because it seems that he remains doubtful about it wherever he speaks of it".[13]

As Lawrence of Lindores briefly summarizes there is a twofold human intellect according to Averroes: the *intellectus possibilis* and the *intellectus agens*. The *intellectus agens* is unmixed with matter and immaterial, ingenerable and incorruptible, not educed from the potency of matter and unique (unus et idem) for all men. It is an assisting form (forma per assistentiam) like the intelligences that move the celestial spheres. However, according to Alexander the *intellectus agens* is not human but is the divine intellect, and Aristotle speaks of this divine intellect when he speaks of the *intellectus agens* in the third book of his *De anima*. Consequently the human intellect is a material, extended and corruptible form like the form of a horse or a donkey. It is an inherent form (forma per inhaerentiam) like the forms of all animals. The Catholic faith, however, teaches that the human intellect is not educed from the potency of matter, but is an indivisible and inextended form that is not generated but immediately created by God individually for every single man. Though it has a beginning in time the human intellect is everlasting (perpetuus a parte post) and incorruptible.[14]

After pointing out the important distinction between *forma assistens* and *forma inhaerens*[15] and recapitulating the teachings of the Catholic faith in five conclusions[16] Lawrence of Lindores raises the first *dubium*: What has to be said about the question *stando praecise in lumine naturali?*[17]

In responding to this doubt he first gives a definition of 'lumen naturale': "*lumen naturale* is called the truth, to which one can properly attain by one's own powers, without special concurrence of the first cause, but with the general influence of the supercelestial beings".[18]

Lawrence of Lindores's definition of 'lumen naturale' became very popular among the philosophers of the fifteenth century, but it should be noted that it was not the only definition. In an anonymous text, now in the university library of Wroclaw (Breslau), but formerly belonging to the Bibliotheca Milichiana in Zgorzelec (Görlitz) we read: "Ista opinio Alexandri secundum viam philosophorum est probabilior inter opiniones recitatas, unde secundum lumen naturale non possumus attingere notitiam illius, quod intellectus humanus sit perpetuus et ingenerabilis, quia *lumen naturale* dicitur per quod aliquid habere possumus experimentaliter et sensualiter per principia simpliciter nota vel ex illis deducibilia evidenter. Vel etiam *lumen naturale* dicitur esse veritas, ad quam (f.244v) quis potest attingere suis propriis viribus sine speciali concursu primi entis, sed cum influentia supercaelestium. Unde nullus propriis viribus potest attingere notitiam illius, ut pro nunc supponitur."[19]

From this definition it follows that no false proposition can be affirmed *in lumine naturali*. For instance, the proposition 'The human intellect is corruptible' cannot be affirmed *in lumine naturali* since faith shows that it is a false proposition, and every proposition that can be affirmed *in lumine naturali* has to be true per definitionem. Likewise it follows that there are true propositions that cannot be affirmed *in lumine naturali*. For instance, the proposition 'The human intellect is everlasting' cannot be affirmed *in lumine naturali* since it can only be known by revelation, it is to be held by faith alone and it cannot be known by man's own powers.

Therefore it is very important to show precisely whether one speaks 'secundum lumen naturale' or speaks 'secundum viam philosophorum', because many false propositions have to be affirmed *secundum viam philosophorum* such as the statements 'Nothing comes of nothing' and 'The world is eternal', but they are not to be affirmed *in lumine naturali* as follows from the definition of 'lumen naturale'.[20]

Finally Lawrence of Lindores answers this doubt by saying that this matter exceeds the capacity of our reason. Thus the question of immortality is a *problema neutrum* if considered *in lumine naturali*. Therefore one is justified in freeing oneself from answering this question *stans praecise in lumine naturali*.[21]

But another *dubium* remains to be solved: What has to be said about the question *secundum viam philosophorum*?[22]

Lawrence of Lindores briefly answers that the opinion of Alexander *pure philosophice loquendo* is reputed to be more probable than the opinion of Averroes. As many masters hold that Alexander put forward his opinion only *secundum viam philosophorum*, he is even regarded to be *fidelis et catholicus*. Anyone who wants to hold the *opinio Alexandri* can easily solve the arguments of Averroes;[23] thus the *opinio Alexandri* turns out to be probable *secundum viam philosophorum*.[24]

Lawrence of Lindores ends the *quaestio* as usual by replying to the initial arguments opposed to his own *determinatio* given in the body of the question.[25]

*

The positions regarding the question of immortality of the two leading members of the Parisian faculty of arts in the fourteenth century, John Buridan and Nicholas Oresme, are extremely divergent.

According to John Buridan the immortality of the soul cannot be demonstrated: "Puto enim, quod non sit demonstrabilis circumscripta fide nostra catholica."[26] Moreover, for him the *opinio Alexandri* is "multum probabilis".[27] He frankly states: "nisi esset fides nostra, ego crederem Alexandro, cuius opinio prius fuit demonstrata; nec rationes prius adductae convincerent demonstrative propositum".[28] He even believes that every pagan philosopher would hold the opinion of Alexander of Aphrodisias: "ego puto, quod philosophus paganus teneret opinionem Alexandri", and he obviously does so because this is what our natural reason dictates: "puto, quod fide catholica circumscripta ... ratio nostra naturalis dictaret, quod intellectus humanus esset eductus de potentia materiae et esset generabilis et corruptibilis".[29]

In contrast to this, Nicholas Oresme not only holds that the *opinio Alexandri* can be disproved (potest improbari),[30] but in rejecting Alexander's materialism he attempts to prove the immortality of the soul by collecting some *rationes antiquorum*, which he has taken mainly from Cicero. The fact that Nicholas Oresme did not bring forward any original arguments here might be the reason why his *Quaestiones de anima* did not attract many philosophers – John Buridan's *Quaestiones de anima* were by far the more influential ones in the later Middle Ages. It should be noted however that Peter of Ailly, who in his *Tractatus de anima* closely follows John Buridan,[31] moves over to Nicholas Oresme in his *Tractatus super de consolatione philosophiae Boethii* and tries to prove the immortality of the soul by using humanist sources like Cicero and Seneca.[32]

Compared to the positions of John Buridan and Nicholas Oresme Lawrence of Lindores's solution can be described as a conciliant one. He apparently does not want to argue with one or the other, but simply tries to avoid any conflict by stating that the question of immortality exceeds the capacity of our reason. This attitude of compromise, which is only too understandable in the times of the Great Schism and the Hundred Years War, was to become common in the fifteenth century. It is characteristic for the so-called *via communis* in Kraków[33] and especially for the famous Benedict Hesse who heavily relies on

Lawrence of Lindores both in his questions on the *Physics* and on the *De anima*.[34]

*

Among the many *Quaestiones de anima* which follow Lawrence of Lindores quite closely let us take a look at three anonymous works now in the Bayerische Staatsbibliothek, Munich, but formerly belonging to the Benedictine monastery Tegernsee, which are dated 1439, 1452 and 1483.

The first (Clm 19674, old signature: Teg 1674), dated 1439, reads: "Notandum, quod *lumen naturale* est veritas, ad quam quis potest pertingere vel attingere propriis viribus sine speciali concursu primae causae, et veritas non est aliquid nisi propositio.

Item: Haec non est concedenda in lumine naturali 'Intellectus humanus est corruptibilis', quia est falsa. Nec illa est concedenda 'Intellectus humanus est perpetuus'; licet sit vera, tamen nullus potest suis propriis viribus ad talia pervenire in praesenti statu.

Multum refert dicere 'secundum viam philosophorum' et 'secundum lumen naturale', quia secundum viam philosophorum multa falsa conceduntur, non autem secundum lumen naturale, ut patet ex dictis.

Et sic qui dicit secundum lumen naturale, tunc potest se excusare de responsione praesentis quaestionis, cum excedat lumen naturale. Et opinio Alexandri pure philosophice loquendo est probabilior inter alias." (f.275r)

The second (Clm 18794, old signature: Teg 794), dated 1452, reads: "Dubium, quid sit dicendum ad quaestionem stando in puro lumine naturali. *Lumen naturale* est veritas, quam quis potest attingere propriis viribus sine speciali concursu primae causae, ut caelum movetur (est lumen naturale *add. cod.*). Nullum falsum est lumen naturale. 'Intellectus est incorruptibilis', 'Intellectus est perpetuus' stando in lumine naturali praecise non sunt concedendae, quia nullus potest haec attingere propriis viribus. Illa 'Intellectus humanus est corruptibilis' non est de lumine naturali, quia est falsa. Multum refert dicere 'hoc (f.227ra) est loqui secundum lumen naturale' et 'hoc est loqui secundum viam philosophorum'; patet, quia secundum Philosophum conceditur, sed secundum lumen naturale nullum falsum est concedendum. Illa est falsa 'Intellectus humanus est perpetuus', quia quis non potest attingere et cetera.

Per hoc respondetur ad dubium, quod illa materia excedit lumen naturale, igitur stando praecise *in lumine naturali*, tunc quis rationabiliter potest se excusare a quaestione proposita respondendo ad eam.

Dubium, quid sit dicendum *secundum viam philosophorum*. Respondetur, quod in utendo puris naturalibus tunc videtur, quod opinio Alexandri sit verior et probabilior, quia ponit eam secundum fidem philosophorum, quia multi dicunt eum fuisse catholicum, quia Alexander ponit illa concomitanter, scilicet inhaerere materiae, esse eductum de potentia materiae, esse extensum extensione materiae, esse multiplicatum et non unicum in diversis corporibus separatis et distantibus, esse genitum et corruptibilem. Et ita videtur dicendum secundum purum philosophum." (ff.226vb-227ra)

The text of the third (Clm 18892, old signature: Teg 892), dated 1483, runs as follows: "Sciendum est primo, quod forma in proposito debet capi large, non solum pro forma actualiter suum subiectum informante, sed pro forma informante aut appropriate coassistente.

Secundo sciendum est, quod *lumen naturale* est veritas (f.68r), quam quis potest attingere per vires proprias sine speciali concursu primae causae. Nullum falsum est de lumine naturali. Non quodlibet verum est de lumine naturali; patet de propositionibus fide credendis ut 'Deus est trinus et unus'. Non est idem dicere 'lumen naturale' et 'via philosophorum', quia secundum viam philosophorum falsum conceditur ut 'Mundus est perpetuus'.

Consequenter sciendum, quod de ista materia sunt tres opiniones. (...)

Consequenter sciendum, quod capiendo formam large tunc intellectus humanus est forma substantialis hominis; patet, quia alias homo non esset proprie unum.

Quinto dicendum est, quod ista materia excedit notitiam luminis naturalis ita, quod stando praecise *in lumine naturali* quis bene potest se de ista materia excusare. Sed quid est dicendum *secundum modum philosophorum* iam patuit secundum tres modos. Consequenter dicendum, quod secundum viam philosophorum praecise considerando opinio Alexandri fuit probabilior quamvis falsa. Sed Aristoteles et Commentator dicentes intellectum esse indivisibilem et inextensum non loquuntur ut philosophi, sed ut specialiter in hac parte illuminati." (ff.67v-68v)

All these texts follow Lawrence of Lindores quite closely not only in his definition of *lumen naturale* but also in his solution of the question of immortality. They are typical of the widespread influence of Lawrence of Lindores at the universities of central Europe in the fifteenth century.

Lawrence of Lindores even influenced the interpretation of John Buridan. In his *Disputata super quaestionibus magistri Buridani super tribus libris De anima Aristotelis*[35] (Clm 19849, old signature: Teg 1849), dated 1447, Johannes Harrer of Heilbronn closely follows Lawrence in Lindores in defining 'lumen naturale' and then states that John Buridan has taken Alexander of Aphrodisias's opinion to be probable only according to the *via philosophorum*, not according to the *lumen naturale*, which is definitely contrary to what John Buridan actually said: "Sed dicens, quid est dicendum (f.150v) ad quaestionem stante lumine naturali, notandum, quod *lumen naturale* est veritas, ad quam quis potest pertingere propriis viribus absque speciali concursu primae causae.

Nullum falsum est lumen naturale. Illa propositio non est concedenda in lumine naturali 'Intellectus est corruptibilis'. Illa propositio in lumine naturali non est concedenda 'Intellectus humanus est perpetuus a parte post', quia numquam potest aliquis devenire in veritatem propositionis in praesenti vita.

Multum refert dicere 'Haec est concedendum secundum viam philosophorum' et 'secundum lumen naturale', quia secundum lumen naturale nullum falsum est concedendum, sed secundum Philosophum sunt concedenda multa falsa, ut ista 'Mundus est perpetuus', et tamen est falsa.

Et sic ad istam quaestionem nullus habet respondere secundum lumen naturale, quia ista excedit lumen naturale. Sed quod est dicendum secundum viam philosophorum, dicit Buridanus, quod stando praecise (in) viis philosophorum opinio Alexandri est probabilior, quia aliquis dicit, quod Alexander fuit Christianus et eum illam opinionem posuisse secundum viam philosophorum." (f.150r-v)

*

For a detailed study of the significance of Lawrence of Lindores for the history of philosophy, who obviously is one of the most important sources for the history of natural philosophy in the fifteenth century and beyond, it is necessary to have critical editions of both his lectures on the *De anima* and the *Physics*. Lawrence Moonan (Oxford) has announced that he will present a critical edition of Lawrence of Lindores's *Quaestiones de anima* in a few years, Thomas Dewender (Bochum) is at present preparing an edition of his *Quaestiones Physicorum*. With these editions at hand another major lacuna in the history of philosophy in the later Middle Ages will be filled.

Notes

1. See KONSTANTY MICHALSKI, "La lutte autour de l'âme au XIVe et au XVe siècle," *Résumés des Communications présentées au Congrès International des Sciences historiques* (Oslo 1928) 116-118; reprinted in OLAF PLUTA, ed. *Die Philosophie im 14. und 15. Jahrhundert. In memoriam Konstanty Michalski (1879-1947)*. Bochumer Studien zur Philosophie, 10 (Amsterdam: Grüner, 1988) XLIX-L. See also KONSTANTY MICHALSKI, "La lutte pour l'âme à Oxford et à Paris au XIVe siècle et sa répercussion à l'époche de la Renaissance," *Proceedings of the Seventh International Congress of Philosophy held at Oxford, England, September 1-6, 1930* (Oxford: Oxford UP, 1931) 508-515; reprinted in OLAF PLUTA, ed., *loc. cit.*, LIII-LX.

2. On the life of Lawrence of Lindores see LAWRENCE MOONAN, "Laurentius de Lundoris," *Dictionnaire d'histoire et de géographie ecclésiastiques* (forthcoming), and in the meantime JAMES HOUSTON BAXTER, "The philosopher Laurence of Lindores," *Philosophical Quarterly* 5 (1955): 348-354.

3. For a detailed description of the extant manuscripts of these two works see LAWRENCE MOONAN, "The scientific writings of Lawrence of Lindores (d. 1437)," *Classica et mediaevalia* 38 (1987): 217-266 [*De anima* commentary] and 39 (1988): 273-317 [*Physics* commentary].

4. See KONSTANTY MICHALSKI, *Les courantes critiques et sceptiques dans la philosophie du XIVe siècle.*. Extrait du Bulletin de l'Académie Polonaise des Sciences et des Lettres. Classe d'histoire et de philosophie – année 1925 (Cracovie 1927) 5-6. Reprinted in KONSTANTY MICHALSKI, *La philosophie au XIVe siècle. Six études*, ed. KURT FLASCH. Opuscula philosophica, 1 (Frankfurt: Minerva, 1969) 157-158. See also JAMES HOUSTON BAXTER, "Four 'New' Medieval Scottish Authors," *The Scottish Historical Review* 25 (1928): 92-95.

5. *Quodlibeta Septem*, Quodl. I, q. 10; *Opera theologica* IX: 62-65.

6. See *ibid.*, 63-64. See also ARTHUR STEVEN MCGRADE, "Some Varieties of Skeptical Experience: Ockham's Case," *Die Philosophie im 14. und 15. Jahrhundert. In memoriam Konstanty Michalski (1879-1947)*, ed. OLAF PLUTA (Amsterdam: Grüner, 1988) 421-422.

7. All citations from Lawrence of Lindores's *Quaestiones in Aristotelis libros De anima* follow the Würzburg manuscript (Universitätsbibliothek, Ms. M. ch. f.235), which is the earliest copy of the text which is both dated and complete. The copy formerly belonged to the Benedictine Abbey of St. Stephen in Würzburg. (See MOONAN, "The scientific writings ...," *loc. cit.*, 246) The text

was written in Prague in 1408 by Hermann Weylerspacher who was then a scholar at the University of Prague. He later became a monk of the Benedictine Abbey of St. Stephen in Würzburg and presumably took the manuscript there (See *ibid.*, 249-251).

For a summary of the contents of Lawrence of Lindores's *Quaestiones in Aristotelis libros De anima* see LAWRENCE MOONAN, *Lawrence of Lindores (d. 1437) on Life in the Living Being* (Philos. Dissertation: Université Catholique de Louvain, 1966) 6.05-6.38. An abstract of this unpublished dissertation has been given by Moonan himself: LAWRENCE MOONAN, "Lawrence of Lindores on Life in the Living Being," *Classica et mediaevalia* 27 (1969): 349-374.

8. III, q.4: Würzburg, Universitätsbibliothek, Ms. M. ch. f.235, ff.61vb-63ra.

9. "Et arguitur, quod non; primo sic: Intellectus non est actus corporis humani, igitur non est forma corporis humani. Consequentia tenet, quia omnis forma dicitur esse actus illius, cuius est forma. Antecedens patet per PHILOSOPHUM dicentem nihil prohibet quandam partem animae separari, quae nullius corporis est actus, et (et *add.* ut *cod.*) videtur loqui *ibidem* de intellectu humano.

Secundo: Intellectus humanus non est virtus in corpore humano, igitur non est forma hominis. Consequentia est nota. Antecedens patet per COMMENTATOREM tertio *huius* dicentem, quod intellectus humanus non est corpus neque virtus in corpore.

Tertio: Si sic, sequeretur, quod homo esset perpetuus. Consequens falsum, quia quilibet homo est mortuus vel moriturus. Et probatur consequentia, quia intellectus hominis est perpetuus, igitur si intellectus est forma hominis, tunc homo secundum intellectum est perpetuus, et etiam materia hominis est perpetua, quia est ingenerabilis et incorruptibilis primo *Physicorum*.

Quarto: Sequeretur, quod homo esset incorruptibilis. Consequens falsum. Et patet consequentia, quia compositum substantiale non dicitur corruptibile nisi propter eius formam. Modo si intellectus (intellectus *add.* qui *cod.*) est perpetuus, qui est forma hominis, sequitur consequens illatum.

Quinto: Sequeretur, quod tu non esses filius patris tui. Consequens videtur inconveniens. Patet consequentia, quia pater tuus vel tui genuit, si intellectus est forma tua. Patet, quia non generavit materiam tuam, quia illa est ingenerabilis, ut iam dicebatur, nec generavit formam tuam, scilicet intellectum, quia intellectus humanus creatur a Deo.

In oppositum arguitur: Intellectus humanus est anima corporis humani, igitur est forma corporis humani. Consequentia tenet, quia idem est anima hominis et forma. Et antecedens patet, quia sibi convenit definitio animae, quia ipse intellectus est actus corporis et cetera.

Secundo sic: Intellectus humanus est substantia, ut supponitur, et non est totum compositum neque materia, ut notum est; igitur est forma. Tunc ultra: Intellectus est forma; et non est forma nisi corporis humani; igitur est forma corporis humani.

Tertio sic: Homo per intellectum differt (f.62ra) a brutis, igitur intellectus est pars hominis. Consequentia tenet, quia per nullum extrinsecum homo essentialiter differt a brutis. Antecedens est notum. Tunc ultra: Intellectus est pars hominis; et non est materia; igitur est forma hominis.

Quarto sic: Illud est forma, a quo causatur differentia specifica; sed ab intellectu causatur ista differentia specifica 'rationale'; ergo intellectus est forma hominis. Consequentia est nota. Et maior patet, quia talis differentia debet sumi a parte essentiali rei et non a materia, quia illa est eiusdem rationis in omnibus generabilibus et corruptibilibus; igitur debet capi a forma.

Quinto sic: Sequeretur, quod homo non esset felicitabilis. Consequens est contra PHILOSOPHUM in pluribus locis libri *Ethicorum*. Patet consequentia, quia felicitas est operatio ipsius intellectus secundum virtutem perfectam in vita perfecta, ut patet primo *Ethicorum*. Modo si intellectus non sit forma hominis, tunc homo per operationem intellectus non diceretur felix.

Sexto sic: Homo dicitur maxime intellectus per PHILOSOPHUM nono *Ethicorum*, et hoc non haberet veritatem, nisi intellectus esset principalior pars et forma corporis humani.

Septimo: Sequeretur, quod magis deberemus diligere sensum quam intellectum. Consequens falsum. Et patet consequentia, quia magis debemus diligere illud, quod est pars corporis nostri, quam illud, quod non est pars corporis nostri; sed sensus est pars corporis nostri et intellectus non per adversarium et cetera." (Würzburg, Universitätsbibliothek, Ms. M. ch. f.235, ff.61vb-62ra)

10. "In quaestione erunt duo articuli. In primo recitabuntur tres opiniones; in secundo respondebitur ad quaesitum." (Würzburg, Universitätsbibliothek, Ms. M. ch. f.235, f.62ra)

11. For the structure of Lawrence of Lindores's questions in general see MOONAN, *Lawrence of Lindores (d. 1437) on Life in the Living Being*, loc. cit., 6.01-6.04.

12. "Quantum ad primum (articulum) est notandum, quod tres fuerunt opiniones magis famosae de ipso intellectu humano." (Würzburg, Universitätsbibliothek, Ms. M. ch. f.235, f.62ra)

13. "quidquid de hoc senserit Philosophus non curo ad praesens, quia ubique dubitative videtur loqui" (Opera philosophica IX, p. 64, 45-46).

14. "Prima opinio fuit ALEXANDRI, qui primo dixit, quod intellectus humanus esset forma educta de potentia materiae, extensa extensione corporis, corruptibilis ad corruptionem hominis ita breviter, quod ipse dicebat quoad hoc similiter, sicut communiter dicitur de forma equi vel asini. Secundo dixit, quod intellectus divinus quodam modo speciali assisteret intellectui humano illustrando et illuminando ipsum quoad formandum intellectiones; et plus assisteret intellectui humano quam aliis formis propter perfectionem intellectus humani ultra alias formas. Et de tali intellectu divino sic assistente intellectui humano dicit PHILOSOPHUM esse locutum, quando loquitur de intellectu agente in tertio *huius*.

Secunda opinio est commentatoris AVERROIS, qui posuit duplicem intellectum humanum, scilicet agentem et possibilem. De intellectu agente dicit, quod est immixtus, immaterialis, ingenerabilis, incorruptibilis, non eductus de potentia materiae, unicus et idem in omnibus hominibus, ut tactum est in quaestione praecedenti. De (f.62rb) hac opinione postea specialius videbitur.

Tertia via, quae non est tenenda tamquam opinio, sed tamquam vera fides catholica, dicit, quod intellectus humanus non est eductus de potentia materiae nec extensus extensione materiae, sed est forma indivisibilis et inextensa, immediate creata ab ipso Deo, multiplicata ad multiplicationem hominum ita, quod quilibet homo habet intellectum distinctum contra intellectum alterius. Item dicit, quod intellectus est perpetuus a parte post et incorruptibilis; licet enim intellectus humanus possit annihilari per potentiam Dei, tamen numquam annihilabitur, sed manebit aeternaliter a parte post. Item dicit, quod intellectus humanus est forma hominis inhaerens homini et cuilibet parti hominis."
(Würzburg, Universitätsbibliothek, Ms. M. ch. f.235, f.62ra-b)

15. "Secundo nota, quod aliquid potest dici forma alterius dupliciter: uno modo per inhaesionem, scilicet quia inhaeret illi, cuius dicitur forma; alio modo per assistentiam, per motum et operationem et non per inhaerentiam, et illo modo intelligentia dicitur esse forma orbis caelestis." (Würzburg, Universitätsbibliothek, Ms. M. ch. f.235, f.62rb)

16. "Quantum ad secundum articulum sit haec prima conclusio: Intellectus humanus est forma substantialis corporis humani. Patet conclusio per septem rationes factas post oppositum, et omnes opiniones recitatae in primo articulo conveniunt in hac conclusione.

Secunda conclusio: Intellectus humanus est forma inhaerens corpori humano. Ista conclusio patebit in sequenti quaestione. In hac conclusione conveniunt ALEXANDER et fides catholica. Sed commentator AVERROES eam negaret, ut patet ex primo articulo.

Tertia conclusio: Intellectus est virtus immaterialis et inextensa, id est non est virtus materialis, educta de potentia materiae, extensa extensione corporis. In hac conclusione conveniunt COMMENTATOR et fides catholica, sed non ALEXANDER. Ista conclusio est fide tenenda; tamen COMMENTATOR nititur eam probare multis rationibus.

Nam primo arguit sic: Nam illa virtus est immaterialis, quae omnem magnitudinem directa repraesentatione intendit; sed sic est de intellectu humano; igitur est virtus immaterialis. Consequentia est nota. Et maior patet, quia, si haberet magnitudinem, tunc non posset intelligere magnitudinem, quia intus existens prohiberet extraneum per PHILOSOPHUM tertio *huius*. Minor patet, quia repraesentato aliquo magno ipsi intellectui intellectus format in se conceptum repraesentatum cuiuslibet magnitudinis.

Secundo arguit sic: Omnis virtus materialis est corruptibilis, sed intellectus non est virtus corruptibilis, igitur non est materialis. Consequentia nota est. Et maior patet, quia omne materiale disponi potest ad corruptionem per qualitativas dispositiones. Minor patet per PHILOSOPHUM tertio *huius*, qui vult intellectum esse perpetuum.

Tertio arguit sic: Intellectus humanus est immixtus corpori per PHILOSOPHUM tertio *huius*, igitur non est virtus materialis.

Quarto: Intellectus humanus in suis operationibus non utitur organo corporeo; igitur non est virtus materialis. Tenet consequentia, quia potentia cognitiva materialis semper utitur organo, ut patet de sensu et cetera. Antecedens patet, quia tempore somni homo (f.62va) intelligit et non intelligit per organa corporea.

Quinto: Sequeretur, quod, postquam intellectus intellexisset magnum intelligibile, quod tunc non posset intelligere parvum intelligibile. Consequens est contra PHILOSOPHUM tertio *huius*. Patet consequentia, quia sensus sentiens magnum sensibile (sensibile] intelligibile *cod.*), postea non potest sentire parvum sensibile, quia secundo *huius* dicitur, quod maius lumen offuscat minus lumen. Modo si intellectus esset virtus materialis sicut sensus, sequeretur consequens illatum.

Sexto: Intellectus humanus intelligit indivisibilia et inextensa, ut quilibet in se experitur, et cum talia non intelligeret, si esset virtus materialis et extensa (et extensa] inextensa *cod.*), igitur conclusio vera.

Septimo: Sequeretur, quod intellectus non cognosceret per cognitiones reflexas. Consequens est contra PHILOSOPHUM tertio *huius*. Patet consequentia, quia virtus materialis non est reflexiva cognitionis super proprium actum.

Quarta conclusio: Intellectus humanus non generatur proprie loquendo. Patet, quia est virtus immaterialis, quia non educitur de potentiis materiae, et per consequens non generatur.

Quinta conclusio: Intellectus humanus creatur. Patet, quia producitur de novo, ut ex fide supponitur, et non generatur per conclusionem praecedentem; igitur creatur." (Würzburg, Universitätsbibliothek, Ms. M. ch. f.235, f.62rb-va)

17. "Sed hic dubitatur, quid esset respondendum stando praecise in lumine naturali." (Würzburg, Universitätsbibliothek, Ms. M. ch. f.235, f.62va)

18. "Pro isto est notandum, quod lumen naturale dicitur esse veritas, ad quam quis potest pertingere suis propriis viribus sine speciali concursu primae causae, sed cum influentia supercaelestium generali." (Würzburg, Universitätsbibliothek, Ms. M. ch. f.235, f.62va)

19. Uniwersytet Wrocławski, Biblioteka Uniwersytecka, Cod. Mil. IV 90, f.244r-v. The first definition of *lumen naturale* can be found in Peter of Ailly's *Tractatus super de consolatione philosophiae Boethii*, q.1, a.1: "Lumen naturale dupliciter potest capi uno modo magis stricte, alio modo large. Stricte capiendo lumen naturale, illa solum dicuntur deduci in lumine naturali, quae ex illis, quae nota sunt per experientiam effectuum naturalium, clare deducuntur et per consequentias evidentes. ... Alio modo lumen naturale sumitur magis large, et sic illa dicuntur deduci in lumine naturali, quae ex illis, quae nota sunt per experientiam effectuum naturalium vel ex his, quae naturaliter per synderesim, id est per rectum rationis iudicium, ab hominibus iudicantur esse vera, et si non clare, tamen probabiliter deducuntur et per tales consequentias, quod si non sufficiant generare scientiam vel evidentem notitiam, tamen sufficiunt generare probabilem opinionem et assensum in puro philosopho non fideli." (The critical edition of Peter of Ailly's *Tractatus super de consolatione philosophiae Boethii* has been prepared by Marguerite Chappuis, Fribourg, and will soon appear in *Bochumer Studien zur Philosophie*.)

20. "Corollarie sequitur, quod nullum falsum est lumen naturale. Patet, quia lumen naturale dicitur esse veritas; sed nullum falsum est veritas.

Secundo sequitur, quod stando in lumine naturali haec non est vera et concedenda: 'Intellectus humanus est corruptibilis'. Patet, quia nullum falsum est concedendum in lumine naturali; sed ista propositio est falsa, ut ex fide supponitur; igitur corollarium verum. Item: Si illa esset concedenda in lumine naturali, vel hoc esset tamquam principium per se notum – et hoc non, ut notum est – vel tamquam conclusio deducta ex principiis naturalis scientiae – et hoc iterum non, quia falsum non sequitur ex veris principiis.

Tertio sequitur, quod stando in lumine naturali haec non est concedenda: 'Intellectus humanus est perpetuus'. Patet, quia, licet illa sit vera, tamen nullus potest suis propriis viribus attingere ad eius notitiam, ut pro nunc supponitur; igitur corollarium verum.

Quarto sequitur, quod multum refert loqui 'secundum viam philosophorum' et loqui 'secundum naturale lumen'. Patet, quia secundum viam philosophorum multa falsa sunt concedenda, scilicet illud: 'Ex nihilo nihil fit', 'Mundus est aeternus'; et tamen talia in lumine naturali non sunt concedenda per iam dicta." (Würzburg, Universitätsbibliothek, Ms. M. ch. f.235, f.62va)

21. "Per hoc dicitur ad propositum, quod ista materia excedit notitiam luminis naturalis, et ergo stans praecise in lumine naturali potest rationabiliter se (f.62vb) excusare de responsione ad istam materiam." (Würzburg, Universitätsbibliothek, Ms. M. ch. f.235, f.62va-b)

22. "Sed tunc dubitaret aliquis, quid es(se)t dicendum de ista materia secundum viam philosophorum." (Würzburg, Universitätsbibliothek, Ms. M. ch. f.235, f.62vb)

23. "Respondetur: Quamvis de hoc sint duae contrariae opiniones, tamen opinio ALEXANDRI pure philosophice loquendo reputabitur probabilior. Unde ALEXANDER a multis magistris tenetur fuisse fidelis et catholicus, sed quod illam opinionem posuerat secundum viam philosophorum. Et quamvis rationes COMMENTATORIS verum concludant et sint probabiles, tamen non sunt demonstrativae nec aliquid demonstrant contra opinionem ALEXANDRI. Igitur, si quis vellet tenere opinionem ALEXANDRI, faciliter responderet ad rationes COMMENTATORIS." (Würzburg, Universitätsbibliothek, Ms. M. ch. f.235, f.62vb)

24. "Ad primam, quando arguitur, quod 'illa virtus est immaterialis, quae omnem magnitudinem et cetera', breviter negaret maiorem. Ulterius diceret, quod illa auctoritas 'intus existens' solum habet veritatem de sensibus exterioribus, sed de sensu communi non habet veritatem, quare nec de intellectu.

Ad secundam negaret minorem. Ad PHILOSOPHUM dicitur, quod voluit, quod intellectus humanus esset perpetuus secundum speciem, vel quod loquebatur de intellectu divino.

Ad tertiam dicitur, quod PHILOSOPHUS *ibidem* loquebatur de intellectu divino. Aliter potest dici, quod 'intellectum esse immixtum' potest intelligi dupliciter: Uno modo, quod (quod *add.* non *cod.*) sit immixtus ita, quod non in omni sua operatione indiget organo corporeo – illo modo voluit PHILOSOPHUS intellectum esse immixtum; alio modo hoc potest intelligi, quod ipse sit immixtus ita, quod non mixtus vel inhaerens materiae – et hoc est falsum, nec PHILOSOPHUS hoc voluit.

Ad quartam dicitur, quod consequentia non valet, quia, licet in aliqua sua operatione non utatur (utatur] utitur *cod.*) organo corporeo immediate, tamen mediate. Sed dubitetur aliquis, ubi ponitur organum ipsius intellectus. Respondetur secundum istam viam, quod ponitur in organo sensus communis seu in organo phantasiae secundum alios.

Ad quintam negatur consequentia. Nec est simile de intellectu et sensu, quia intellectus intelligit per abstractionem, discursum et ratiocinationem; igitur potest intelligere intelligibilia quantumcumque magna sine eius laesione; sed ita non est de sensu.

Ad sextam dicitur, quod intellectus privative intelligit indivisibilia et cetera, quia habito conceptu divisibili componit cum negatione et fit conceptus correspondens isti termino 'indivisibile'. Item potest dici, quod intellectus solummodo intelligit indivisibilia per discursum, nec hoc est inconveniens de virtute materiali.

Ad septimam negatur consequentia, quia non solummodo intellectus potest se reflectere supra suos proprios actus, sed hoc etiam potest facere sensus communis.

Et sic patet, quod haec opinio ALEXANDRI (f.63ra) secundum viam philosophorum est probabilis." (Würzburg, Universitätsbibliothek, Ms. M. ch. f.235, ff.62vb-63ra)

25. "His praemissis respondetur ad rationes ante oppositum. Ad primam negatur antecedens. Ad PHILOSOPHUM dicitur uno modo, quod loquebatur de intellectu divino. Aliter dicitur, quod nihil prohibet quandam animam et cetera sic, scilicet quod non sit forma educta de potentia materiae, et hoc est verum, ut patet ex conclusionibus secundi articuli.

Ad secundam negatur antecedens. Ad COMMENTATOREM dicitur, quod ipse fuit illius opinionis; vel potest dicere, quod voluit, quod intellectus non est virtus in corpore, supple: educta de potentia materiae.

Ad tertiam negatur, quod homo esset perpetuus. Sed bene conceditur, quod homo est perpetuus; sed de hoc magis pertinet ad logicam.

Ad quartam negatur consequentia. Ad probationem, quid sit dicendum, patet ex secunda dubitatione praecedentis quaestionis.

Ad quintam, quando arguitur 'sequeretur, quod tu non esses filius', negatur consequentia; et dicitur: Licet pater tuus nec materiam tuam nec formam tuam generav(er)it, tamen generavit te totum capiendo li 'totum' categorematice. Aliter dicitur, quod pater tuus praedisposuit materiam ad introductionem animae intellectivae in materia tua.

Rationes post oppositum sunt pro prima conclusione. Et haec de ista quaestione." (Würzburg, Universitätsbibliothek, Ms. M. ch. f.235, f.63ra)

26. JOHN BURIDAN, *Quaestiones in Aristotelis libros De anima*, ed. GEORGE LOKERT (Paris 1516) f.24va.

27. "Tertia opinio non ita concordat clare dictis Aristotelis, licet sit multum probabilis. Et illa declarabitur in quaestionibus." (JOHN BURIDAN, *Expositio libri*

De anima; Erfurt, Wissenschaftliche Allgemeinbibliothek, Ms. Ampl. F.298, f.118rb; Roma, Biblioteca Apostolica Vaticana, Ms. Vat. lat. 2162, f.124ra)

28. JOHN BURIDAN, *Quaestiones in Aristotelis libros De anima*, ed. GEORGE LOKERT (Paris 1516) f.24vb.

29. For these quotations cf. ANNELIESE MAIER, "Das Prinzip der doppelten Wahrheit," *Studien zur Naturphilosophie der Spätscholastik, 4: Metaphysische Hintergründe der spätscholastischen Naturphilosophie* (Rome: Edizioni di storia e letteratura, 1955) 22-24.

30. "Ista opinio potest improbari per rationes positas in alia quaestione, ubi probatum fuit, quod intellectus est immixtus." (NICHOLAS ORESME, *Quaestiones de anima*, III, q.4) Cf. PETER MARSHALL, *Nicholas Oresme's 'Questiones super libros Aristotelis De anima': A Critical Edition with Introduction and Commentary* (Philos. Diss. Cornell University, 1980. Ann Arbor: UMI, 1980) 544.

31. Cf. PETER OF AILLY, *Tractatus de anima*, cap. 6, pars 1; cf. OLAF PLUTA, *Die philosophische Psychologie des Peter von Ailly*. Bochumer Studien zur Philosophie, 6 (Amsterdam: Grüner, 1987), part II, 34-35.

32. Cf. PETER OF AILLY, *Tractatus super de consolatione philosophiae Boethii*, q.1, a.1; cf. MARGUERITE CHAPPUIS, *Le traité de Pierre d'Ailly sur la Consolation de Boèce* (soon to appear in *Bochumer Studien zur Philosophie*). For the question of immortality in Nicholas Oresme and Peter of Ailly cf. OLAF PLUTA, "Die Diskussion der Frage nach der Unsterblichkeit bei Nikolaus Oresme und Peter von Ailly," *Studia mediewistyczne* (forthcoming).

33. Cf. MIECZYSŁAW MARKOWSKI, "Der Buridanismus an der Krakauer Universität im Mittelalter," *Die Philosophie im 14. und 15. Jahrhundert. In memoriam Konstanty Michalski (1879-1947)*, ed. OLAF PLUTA (Amsterdam: Grüner, 1988) 245-260.

34. For Benedict Hesse's questions on the *Physics* cf. BENEDICTUS HESSE, *Quaestiones super octo libros "Physicorum" Aristotelis*, ed. STANISŁAW WIELGUS (Wrocław: Ossolineum, 1984). For his questions on the *De anima* cf. BRIGITTE BURRICHTER and THOMAS DEWENDER, "Die Diskussion der Frage nach der Unsterblichkeit in den 'Quaestiones in libros De anima' des Benedikt Hesse von Krakau," *Die Philosophie im 14. und 15. Jahrhundert*, ed. OLAF PLUTA (Amsterdam: Grüner, 1988) 573-602.

35. "Expliciunt disputata super quaestionibus magistri Buridani super tribus libris De anima Aristotelis, exercitata a venerabili viro magistro Johanne Harrer de Heilprunn [=Heilbronn], sabbato die ante festum ascensionis domini sub anno domini et cetera 1447 per me Ulricum Kergerl de Landaw [=Landau] et cetera." (f.185r)

The Halakha as a Theoretical Construction

Sol Roth

The notion of a theoretical or imaginative construction is philosophically popular today and finds application in the fields of epistemology, metaphysics and the philosophy of science. Betrand Russell wrote, in an attempt to give a satisfactory account of the notion of matter, "Whenever possible, logical constructions are to be substituted for inferred entities."[1] He argued, for example, that the idea of a material object is not inferred from, but theoretically constructed out of the experience of sense data. Ernest Nagel maintained that the ideal entities of physics e.g. the instantaneous velocity of Mars, refer to nothing that exists in the universe. He writes

> It is difficult to interpret expressions which assign real number values to the magnitudes of physical properties as signifying empirically identifiable traits in the explicit subject matter of physics...In using real number expressions to denote the instantaneous velocity of Mars at any given time, we are .... predicating something of Mars which, on the basis of the ordinary use of the term "velocity", it could not possibly have. The expression "the instantaneous velocity of Mars" thus seems to denote nothing in the heavens.[2]

It is a theoretical construction that finds applicability in the science of the motion of bodies.

Rabbi Joseph B. Soloveitchik utilized an identical approach in giving an account of the Halakha. The Halakha, he maintained, is an *a priori* system, a theoretical construction, that is imposed on experience. He wrote

> When halakhic man approaches reality, he comes with the Torah given him from Sinai, in hand. He orients himself to the world by means of fixed statutes and firm principles. An entire corpus of precepts and laws guides him along the path leading to existence. Halakhic man, well furnished with rules, judgements, and fundamental principles, draws near the world with an *a priori* relation. His ap-

proach begins with an ideal creation and concludes with a real one. To whom may he be compared? To a mathematican who fashions an ideal world and uses it for the purpose of establishing a relation between it and the real world.[3]

An ideal creation, in the halakhic domain, is a logical construction which, when put in relation to the realm of experience, results in a world which is perceived to contain value.

I

The first observation that needs to be made in connection with the application of the notion of theoretical construction to halakha is that, by doing so, values, the subject matter of halakha, are placed in the same category as theoretical entities. The electro-magnetic wave, the electron, entities referred to by the theoretical terms of physics, are not values and do not prescribe conduct. They belong to the category of thing, though it is not assumed that instances of these things are exemplified in the non-mental universe. The halakha, on the other hand, is a value system which formulates normative ideals which it translates into rules of conduct. Both values and theoretical entities, however, are theoretical constructions.

Scientists do not require that the theoretical entities of physics reproduce in theory structure that is contained in the non-mental world. Instead, they interpret such entities and the scientific theories of which they are part in terms of models[4]. When a scientist proposes a model, he is declaring, in effect, that if the structure of the universe *were* identical to that of the model, our experience of the world would be precisely what it, in fact, is. He does not maintain that the model is an accurate reflection of existing reality. If it is possible to infer from the theory in which the theoretical terms are embedded, laws that can be used successfully in the task of explaining and predicting phenomena in the experienced universe, there then exists a certain harmony between theory and fact that makes the theoretical terms useful to the enterprise of science.

It is not necessary to argue, at length, that halakhic values do not inhere in the universe. If the Halakha declares that the day which arrives at sunset on Friday has the sanctity of the Sabbath day, the intention is not that the period from sundown on Friday and sundown on Saturday, as a physical span of time, has a character which another day, say sundown Monday to Tuesday, does not have. As physical entities, they are identical and indistinguishable. The value does not reflect any inherent subject matter; it is a theoretical construction.

Jewish thought, in addition to regarding the values of the Halakha as expressions of the divine will, perceives the Torah as finding justification by virtue of its harmony and commensurability with human experience. In biblical terminology, "It is very close to you, in your mouth and your heart to do it."[5] In other words, halakhic values need not be embodied in the world but must be consistent with the facts of nature and human nature in order that they may be judged acceptable.

II

Halakhic values are both ideal and theoretical entities. In science, the two are distinguished. An ideal entity is one that is, in a sense, found in nature, but not in ideal form. Newton's law of inertia, for example, states that a body on which no force is acting, if at rest remains at rest and if in motion continues in uniform motion in a straight line. But there is no body in nature which is unexposed to any force whatsoever. Bodies might be arranged in a declining order in which those further in the sequence are under the influence of weaker forces. One may extrapolate, after studying the behavior of the bodies in the sequence, as to the action of a body under the influence of no force whatsoever; but, as a matter of fact, there is no body that is free of all forces. Such a body is an ideal entity.

A theoretical entity, on the other hand, is not one which differs from an existing one merely in degree; it is rather one which may be entirely fictional. The introduction of the concept of the electromagnetic wave is a heuristic device for the purpose of facilitating the task of explanation and prediction. The most that scientists would say is that light behaves *as if* it consisted of waves of a certain kind, but they do not claim that a counterpart of the theoretical notion of the electromagnetic wave exists in the realm of nature. The electromagnetic wave is a theoretical term.

A halakhic value, on the other hand, is both ideal and theoretical. Such a value, piety, for example, consists of two a priori components. The first is a definition which is the result of an a priori procedure. A number of traits are identified as defining components of piety. Included among them might be the recitation of certain prayers, the contemplation of prescribed thoughts, the adoption of a recommended psychological state such as a sense of intimacy in one's relation with God. Piety is thus defined as a behavioral and psychological state of affairs. The second component is the assertion that this behavioral and psychological condition is of importance, that it is worthy of being prized, that indeed it ought to be pursued. This is the normative aspect of piety. It too is a priori and theoretical.

Piety, in so far as the behavioral-psychological condition which constitues it is concerned, may be regarded as an ideal term. It is exemplified in instances of piety only in degree. It is in the same category as a body on which no force is acting. There is no instance of either in existence. No matter how much enthusiasm an individual might generate in an act of piety, prayer for example, it could be maintained that he has not reached the state of perfect piety. Piety, in ideal form, is nowhere to be found.

But piety, in its normative aspect, is entirely theoretical in nature. The fact that piety is of importance and that it should be prized is not to be found in existence at all -- not even in degree. The appreciation of an act of piety, the obligation sensed by a religious personality to perform acts of piety, do not at all derive from the definition of piety. These attitudes have their source and justification in a realm that transcends empirical experience. They are purely theoretical in nature.

III

The claim that the Halakha is a theoretical construction also means that facts are to be subordinated to halakhic values.

In science, the empirical fact is the court of last resort. If the proposition which formulates the fact is incompatible with some propostition logically implied by the theory which is intended to explain the empirical domain to which the fact belongs, then the theory must be modified. The results of the Michelson-Morley experiment revealed a flaw in the theoretical apparatus of science. This led to the reformulation of the theory of gravity in Einstein's Theory of relativity. If a theory is not in consonance with the facts to which it is relevant, then the theory must undergo transformation.

In the halakhic perspective, on the other hand, the fact must submit to the halakhic value. When a conflict occurs, the halakhic goal is to transform the facts so that they may coincide with the halakhic norm. If, for example, the Halakha projects as a value the sanctity of the marriage bond which is accompanied by a prohibition on adulterous relationships, then though as a matter of sociological fact, adultery may be rampant in the community, it is not the value but the fact that must submit to change. The notion that the halakhic value is a theoretical construction, accordingly, also means, in the halakhic context, that the theoretical value has priority over the fact.

This point needs to be stressed, particularly in the context of the Jewish religion. The fundamental basis of this religion is not so much the belief as the precept of action. Its focus is not essentially the doctrines of faith that must be accepted by those who claim religious commitment as the mitzvah that prescribes patterns of conduct that should characterize the life of the Jew. It is this circumstance that has prompted the judgement that Judaism is this-wordly rather than other-worldly. The judgement is sound. The priority that Judaism assigns to halakhic value over empirical fact implies that the this-worldly character of Judaism, is not expressed in submission to this world (the world of fact), but in a preoccupation to transform it so that it might be in accord with the theoretical world, i.e. the world of norms specified by the Halakha.

IV

The idea of the Halakha as a theoretical construction implies not merely that the fact is denigrated in relation to halakhic value; it also means that the fact, whatever it may be, is often ignored, even contradicted, in order to realize the value.

A prime example of this halakhic tendency is a description by Nahmanides of what is required in the posture of humility. In a letter to his son, he declares, "Let every man be greater than you in your eyes."[6] It is clear that, as a matter of fact, it is not the case that every man is greater than the humble person, no matter what standard of greatness is adopted. The facts, however, are to be ignored. The obligation to be humble requires the adoption of an attitude incompatible with the facts.

A corollary of this precept on humility is the Jewish view on equality. For Judaism, the principle of equality is prescriptive rather than descriptive. The Halakha does not declare that all men are equal as a matter of fact. This is not a tenable proposition either on the basis of experience or halakhic norms. At the very least, Judaism regards the Kohen, the Levite and the Israelite as unequal. At most, it is a prescriptive halakhic propostion. Notwithstanding the facts to the contrary, we are to regard and to treat all human beings as equals.

The arrival of a new lunar month has crucial halakhic consequences. The identification of a day as the first day of Tishri implies that the festival of Rosh Hashana is to be celebrated on that day and that ten days hence, on Yom Kippur, there is an obligation to fast. But it is not that fact of the appearance of the new moon that determines that day as Rosh Hashana, but the declaration of a competent court convened for that purpose. If it is decided by the court that the following day is the first day of Tishri, then notwithstanding the appearance of the moon on the preceding day, Rosh Hashana is observed on the day designated by the court.

Accordingly, the notion of the Halakha as a theoretical construction often requires that the halakhic personality elevate himself above the world of fact, to create a world in his imagination controlled by halachic categories and parameters and to respond to the imaginatively constructed element rather than to empirical fact in determining the course of his life.

V

There are some who have argued, and correctly, that the Halakha's emphasis on the theoretical is manifested in its continued interest in categories and concepts which, because of historical transformations, have no relevance today. In the absence of a Holy Temple, the study of the laws of sacrifices is purely theoretical because they can be put to no practical use. The Halakha does emphasis the primacy of theory over fact in this way; but it does so in other ways as well.

Its emphasis on the theoretical is also and more fundamentally exhibited in the fact that it holds the Halakha to be a theoretical construction, that it regards halakhic values as imposed on rather than as discovered in facts, that it strives to achieve consistency between halakhic norms and facts by transforming the facts if they fail to exemplify the norms, and above all, by requiring in many instances that halakhic personalities live in a world of the imagination even where that which is imagined is incompatible with facts.

Indeed, the Halakha seeks to *create* a world which, in all its particulars, will exemplify halakhic norms.

Notes

1. Bertrand Russell, *Mysticism and Logic* (Garden City: Doubleday, 1917) 150. (A republished work)

2. Ernest Nagel, *Logic Without Metaphysics* (Glencoe: Free Press, 1956) 87.

3. Rabbi Joseph B. Soloveitchik, trans. Lawrence Kaplan, *Halakhic Man* (Philadelphia: Jewish Publication Society, 1983) 19.

4. Richard B. Braithwaite, *Scientific Explanation* (Cambridge: University Press, 1953) 91.

5. *Deuteronomy* XXX, 14.

6. Nahmanides, *Kitvei Ramban* (Jerusalem: Mosad Harav Kook, 1963) 374.

Two Philosophical Passages in the Liturgical Poetry of Rabbi Isaac Ibn Giat

Menahem Schmelzer

Abraham ibn Daud, in his *The Exalted Faith*[1], regularly quotes Scripture to bear testimony to the various philosophical opinions expounded by him. It is quite amazing that Abraham ibn Daud's prooftexts, rarely, if ever, contain references to post-Biblical sources, but, on the other hand, include two passages as prooftexts from Isaac ibn Giat's poetry. This clearly indicates that, in the view of Abraham ibn Daud, Ibn Giat's poetry offers valid and authoritative statements relating to metaphysical themes.

In the nineteenth century, the father of modern research in the history of medieval Hebrew poetry, Leopold Zunz, pointed out that Isaac ibn Giat's religious poetry contains interesting information on Jewish philosophy, as well as on the history of sciences among the Jews.[2] Other nineteenth century scholars, Leopold Dukes,[3] Michael Sachs[4] and David Kaufmann,[5] also used in Giat's poetry as a source of philosophical and scientific knowledge.

In 1962, Ibn Giat's Arabic commentary on Ecclesiastes was published for the first time, although the existence of the work had been known previously. With the publication of this work, new insights were gained into the philosophy of Ibn Giat, and the commentary could now also be utilized for the understanding of some difficult poetic passages in his work.[6]

Ibn Giat's religious poetry received very scant attention in recent times and very little, if anything, is published about him in English.[7] This, of course, is to be regretted, since Ibn Giat was a central figure in eleventh centry Spanish Jewry and was highly regarded as halakhist and as poet.[8]

In the present paper, the two passages quoted by Abraham ibn Daud will be examined.

209

Abraham ibn Daud's first quotation is from Ibn Giat's monumental composition for the morning service of the Day of Atonement. It reads:

'ameru keẓat ḥashuvei 'ummatenu ve-ḥakhameha u-meshorereha: gizrei ḥokhemot gavehu gazar u-mekoreihem gaveru ve-lo' lahu gal 'einoth sekhel yaẓa' menhu ve-hu' re'shit darkhei 'el.[9]

In order to understand this passage, we must look for aid in other places in Ibn Giat's compositions, which will, perhaps, shed light on this rather difficult sentence. Elsewhere in the day of Atonement liturgy, Ibn Giat writes:

ma'asekha: zohorei ḥokhemah re'shit yezirot noẓeru ḥukkei tokhenitam mehasig gaveru to'ameha ta'amu ve-ra'u ve-'ameru l'elohim mah nora' ma'asekha
ma'asekha: yesod sekhel me'or ḥokhemah nimẓa' ke-nogah 'esh u-min ha'-esh barak yaẓa' ...
ma'asekha: mi-noqah ha-sekhel nevunoti nimẓa'u neshamot 'ad lo nimẓe'ti ...[10]

The latter passage can best be understood by comparing it to the following statement that occurs in Isaac Israeli's *Chapter on the Elements*:

"Aristotle the philosopher and master of the wisdom of the Greeks said: The beginning of all roots is two simple substances: one of them is first matter, which receives form and is known to the philosophers as the root of roots. It is the first substance which subsists in itself and is the substratum of diversity. The other is substantial form, which is ready to impregnate matter. It is perfect wisdom, pure radiance, and clear splendour, by the conjunction of which with first matter the nature and form of intellect came into being, because it [intellect] is composed of them [matter and form]. After the nature, form, and radiance of intellect had come into being, a radiance and splendour went forth from it. ... From this the nature of the rational soul came into being. ..."[11]

As shown by S.M. Stern, the above is in accordance with the doctrine of emanation as found in the so-called *Ibn Hasday's Neoplationist*.[12] The author of this treatise as well as Isaac Israeli discuss the degrees of emanation and particularly the gradation of the intensity of light in the process of emanation. Concerning this Isaac Israeli says: "Regarding the quality of emanation of the light from the power and the will, we have already made it clear that its beginning is different from its end, and the middle from both extremes, and this for the following reason: when its beginning emanated from the power and the will, it met no shade or darkness to make it dim or coarse."[13]

We have placed Ibn Giat's verses into the framework of ideas concerning the theory of emanation. We may attempt to paraphrase them as follows:

God split apart loftly Wisdom; its fountains swelled and did not diminish; a wave of the springs of Intellect emanated from Him and this was the beginning of God's works.[14]

The second quotation may be rendered as follows:

Your deeds are: At the beginning You created the splendors of Wisdom. Their nature is beyond comprehension and those who ponder it say: how mighty are Your deeds.

Your deeds are: from the light of wisdom You brought into existence the element of Intellect, which is like the radiance of fire. . . .

Your deeds are: from the radiance of the Intellect You brought forth the Soul. . . .

The similarity with Isaac Israeli's text and with Ibn Hasday's Neoplationist is evident, and it is safe to assume that all three were using a common source, probably an Arabic treatise, as Stern indeed had proposed in connection with Israeli and the Neoplatonist.[15]

Let us now return to the quotation found in *The Exalted Faith*. What is the exact meaning of the root *gazar* in *gizrei hokhemot gavehu gazar*? What did Abraham ibn Daud intend to prove with Ibn Giat's verses?

Solomon ibn Gabirol in his *Royal Crown*, when describing creation, says: *ve-kara' 'el ha-'ayin ve-nivka'* (and He called out to nothingness and it was split).[16] The Hebrew root *gazar* is synonymous with the Hebrew root *baka'*. Accordingly, we may consider Ibn Giat's passage as parallel to Ibn Gabirol's. In both, the process of creation, at its very beginning, is described with the help of a verb that means: to split. Shlomo Pines proved that the verb *baka'* in Ibn Gabirol resembles a usage found in a passage occurring in a treatise by Avicenna. Pines also places the use of the Arabic equivalent, the root *falaka*, in the context of writings, which present the reader with an image of the created universe in its various gradations.[17] This is, of course, also the context of the *Royal Crown*, as pointed out by Pines. We may now add Ibn Giat's poem to this group. This long poem, which consists of many parts, also has as its subject the presentation of the created world as one of gradation, beginning with the loftiest emanation, namely that of Wisdom and descending through various stages to the material world. For the earliest stage of emanation, (for the moment at which it begins), Ibn Gabirol and Ibn Giat use the word: to split, *baka'* or the synonymous *gazar*. Both words are used in the Bible for the splitting of waters, e.g. in Genesis 7:11, Exodus 14:21, Psalms 136:13, etc. In Isaiah 58:8, the passive of *baka'* occurs in connection with the spreading of light. Both poets, indeed, employ metaphors of light and water in describing the process of emanation. In Ibn Gabirol we read: *ha-ḥokhemah mekor ḥayyim mimmekha nova'at . . . sho'ev mi-mekor ha-'or mi-beli deli . . . ve-kara' 'el ha-'ayin ve-nivka'*, (and Wisdom is the fountain of life and from You it streams forth . . . without bucket from the fountain of light it draws . . . and He called out to nothingness and it was split),[18] while Ibn Giat says: *gizrei hokhemot gavehu gazar u-mekoreihem gaveru . . . gal 'einot sekhel* (God split apart lofty Wisdom; its fountains swelled; . . . a wave of the springs of Intellect), and in the second passage: *zohorei ḥokhma* (splendours of Wisdom). It seems, therefore, plausible to suggest that in order to convey the idea of Wisdom emanating from God which bears in itself the diversity of subsequent creation, writers in the Arabic tradition as well as in Hebrew poetry employ the word "to split," implying by this the unity of a first substance "which . . . is the substratum of diversity."[19] "To split" is, then, the beginning of the process of emanation, which is further described through metaphors of sources of light and fountains of water.

If we now return to Abraham ibn Daud, we can clearly see the purpose of his quoting this passage by Ibn Giat. Ibn Daud's chapter, in which this quotation is used to support his thesis (called "*ketuvim me'idim*" "what Scriptural verses testify about the above") deals with the order of the universe and especially with the philosophical problem of "what is called the 'Many from the One.'"[20] Ibn Daud recalls this passage from Ibn Giat to prove that there is a chain of intermediaries between the One (God) and the Many (the diversity of the created universe).

The second quotation from one of Ibn Giat's poems occurs in the same chapter of *The Exalted Faith*. It reads:

> *u-va-'asher ha-ri'shon yithbarekh lo' yakif bo makom u-va-'asher madregat kedushato le-ma'alah mi-madregat 'elleh ha-nikra'im sikhliyyim yo'meru kezat nikhbadeinu:*
>
> *zaru mekomoth me-hakhilekha ve-shahu meromoth mi-sevol godlekha vetukku 'adamoth le-fa'amei raglekha ve-'al gav hokhemoth nitke'u 'oholekha ki 'ein mahanekha be-'ohel ve-'ulam* (Concerning [the claims] that the First, may He be blessed, is not encircled by a place and that the grade of His holiness is above the grades of these [entities] that are called "intellects," some of our venerable people said, Places are narrow from encompassing You and heights are bent down from bearing Your greatness. Lands melt at Your footsteps, and upon Wisdom is Your tent thrust, because Your camp is not in a tent or a hall).[21]

This passage is much simpler than the previous one. In it, Ibn Giat expresses the old Rabbinic doctrine, based on biblical antecedents, according to which the world is not the place of God but God is the place of the world.[22] This idea is found frequently in the poems of the classic Golden Age poets, and as shown by Aron Mirsky, its frequent use is caused by the connection between these poems and the basic philosophic-theological work by Bahya ibn Pakuda, *Duties of the Heart*.[23] It is the cardinal belief in the incorporeality of God and, for that reason, finds its place in many liturgical poems of the Spanish school. Mirsky collected a number of such passages from the poems of Ibn Gabirol and Judah Halevi.[24] Ibn Giat's words, as quoted by Ibn Daud, may now be added to them.

Notes

1. Abraham ibn Daud, *The Exalted Faith*; translated with commentary by Norbert M. Samuelson. Translation edited by Gershon Weiss. London and Toronto: Associated University Presses, (1986).

2. Leopold Zunz, *Literaturgeschichte der synagogalen Poesie*. Berlin 1865, p. 195.

3. Leopold Dukes, Die naturhistorischen Hymnen des Isak ibn Gioth, in: *Monatsschrift für die Geschichte und Wissenschaft des Judentums*, vol 8, (1859), pp. 118-121.

4. Michael Sachs, *Die religiöse Poesie der Juden in Spanien*. 2nd ed. Berlin 1901, pp. 262-263.

5. David Kaufmann, *Die Sinne*, Budapest 1884, pp. 30, 40, 44, 51, 84, 93, 124, 139. Also in his *Gesammelte Schriften*, Frankfurt 1908-1915, vol. 1, p. 246 and in his *Studien über Salomon ibn Gabirol*, Budapest 1899, p. 102 and in his notes to S.J. Halberstamm's edition of Judah bar Barzillai Al-bargeloni's commentary to *Sefer Yezira*. Berlin 1885, p. 345.

6. In *Hamesh megillot 'im perushim 'atikim*, edited by Joseph Kafih. Jerusalem 1962, pp. 161-296. See S. Pines in *Tarbiz*, vol. 33, (1964), pp. 212-213 and G. Vajda in *Historia Judaica*, vol. 2, (1963), p. 450 and S. Abramson, *Rav Nissim Gaon*. Jerusalem 1965, p. 305, note 1.

7. See the brief selections from his poetry in *The Penguin Book of Hebrew Verse*; edited and translated by T. Carmi. (Middlesex, England and New York): Penguin Books, (1981), pp. 103-104; 317-320.

8. See Ibn Daud Abraham. *The Book of Tradition (Sefer ha-Qabbalah)*. Critical edition and notes by Gerson D. Cohen. Philadelphia: Jewish Publication Society, 1967, Hebrew section, pp. 60-61; English section, pp. 81-82 and Moshe ibn Ezra, *Kitab al-Muhadara wal-Mudhakara*; edited by A. S. Halkin. Jerusalem: Mekize Nirdamim, 1975, pp. 72-73.

9. *The Exalted Faith* (see above, note 1), Hebrew section, p. 324 (160b, 11.7-9); English section, p. 179. The translation offered there is based on a complete misunderstanding of the original. The composition begins: *ve'erez 'ikkaf*, see: Israel Davidson, *Thesaurus of Mediaeval Hebrew Poetry*, 4 volumes. New York: Jewish Theological Seminary, 1924-1933 (reprint: New York: Ktav Publishing, 1970), letter vav, number 66. The quotation is from the first section; see also:

Yonah David, *The Poems of Rabbi Isaac ibn Ghiyyat*; a tentative edition. Jerusalem: Ahshav, 1987, p. 7.

10. Davidson, *op. cit.*, letter mem, number 2056; David, *op. cit.*, p. 41.

11. A. Altmann and S. M. Stern, *Isaac Israeli: a Neoplatonic Philosopher of the Early Tenth Century.* (Oxford): Oxford University Press, 1958, p. 119.

12. *Op. Cit.*, p. 98.

13. *Op. cit.*, p. 88 and see also p. 102.

14. The Scriptural verses which are reflected in this passage are the following: Psalms 136:13, Genesis 7:19-20; Genesis 47:13; Job 40:19. The use of the plural in *ḥokhemot gavehu* has a parallel in one of Saadia Gaon's poems where we read: *tevunotekha gavehu*. This was pointed out by M. Zulay in his *Ha-askola ha-paytanit shel Rav Sa'adya Gaon*. Jerusalem, The Schocken Institute, 1964, p. 105. The meaning of the phrase is as in the singular and it was translated accordingly, to avoid using the awkward "Wisdoms."

15. *Op. cit.*, p. 96.

16. Section 9; See *Keter Malkhut*, ed. by Y. A. Seidman, Jerusalem, Mosad Harav Kook, 1950, p. 24.

17. Shlomo Pines, "And He called out to nothingness and it was split" - a note on a passage in Ibn Gabirol's Keter *Malkhut*, in *Tarbiz*, vol. 50, (1980-1981), pp. 339-347.

18. *Kether Malkhut*, section 9, ed. Seidman (see above note 14), pp. 20-24.

19. Altmann and Stern, *op. cit.*, p. 119.

20. *The Exalted Faith* (see above note 1), p. 169.

21. *Ib.*, Hebrew section, p. 323 (162b, 11.5-9); English section, p. 180. The quotation is from a poem beginning: *shiru l-' elohim*; see Davidson, *op. cit.* letter shin (supplements in vol. 4), number 54. The best text of this poem is the one published by Joseph Marcus in *Sinai*, vol. 56, (1965), pp. 22-23. See also: David, *op. cit.*, pp. 474-475. In Ibn Daud's text the word *zaru* became corrupted into *saru*, therefore the mistranslation: "Place turn aside." The translation of *tukku* as "melted" was left intact for lack of a better one.

22. See A. Marmorstein, *The Old Rabbinic Doctrine of God*. London 1927, pp. 92-92 and Altmann and Stern, *op. cit.*, p. 126, note 1.

23. A. Mirsky, Hebrew poems from Spain based on the second gate (*Sha'ar Ha-Behina*) of R. Bahya Ibn Paquda's *Hovot Ha-Levavot*, in *Tarbiz*, vol. 50, (1980-1981), pp. 303-338 and his article on the same subject in *Hebrew Language Studies Presented to Professor Zeev Ben-Hayyim*. Jerusalem: The Magnes Press, 1983, pp. 383-406.

24. Mirsky, in *Tarbiz, ib.*, pp. 333-334.

Art and Imitation: Plato and Ibn Sina*

Fadlou Shehadi

I

In the opening section of Ibn Sina's brief introduction to his book on music, he makes some important points about his approach to the subject. I translate it here in full:

"It is time for us to conclude the mathematical branch of philosophy and set forth the general framework of the science of music, limiting ourselves to what essentially belongs to it and enters into its proper domain, detailing its principles and rudiments. We will not extend the discussion with numerical and arithmetical principles and subdivisions which more properly belong to the science of numbers.

"We shall also leave aside the similarities (*muhakayat*) between the elements of music, on the one hand, and heavenly bodies and human character traits, on the other. This is the way of those for whom the sciences have not been distinguished the one from the other, and it has not become clear to them what is essential and what is accidental. There are ancients whose philosophy has been emulated by those negligent ones who have otherwise understood their instructive philosophy and their truth-seeking analysis. This distractedness brought on by emulation, a heedlessness shielded by the high esteem for the ancients, has led to the (uncritical) acceptance. This habit deflects one from the truth; it is a pliant attitude that blocks careful thought.

"In so far as we are able we shall try to discern the truth itself, and resist the pull of tradition, realizing, however, that care and caution tend to protect one from error most of the time, but not always."[1]

This somewhat lengthy quotation is interesting in many ways. First of all, it formulates a "foreign policy" towards the Greeks, which fits in well with what is true of Ibn Sina's fair measure of independence from the ancients. It may well be his most explicit declaration of (relative) independence. Conscious of this fact, Ibn Sina comments in the introduction about his approach to the subject of music by noting that this introduction is not the usual sort that precedes his discussion of the other sciences. He then proceeds to assure us that his ideas are nonetheless based on reliable experience and sound intuition.[2]

The second thing to note is that Ibn Sina obviously accepts the classification of the theoretical study of music as one of the mathematical sciences. Indeed the preoccupation with music theory and its classification as a mathematical science became common practice in Islam since the translation into Arabic of the works on music by Euclid, Ptolemy, Pythagoras and others. And the title of Ibn Sina's book on music reads: "Chapter Three of the mathematical sciences which is on the science of music."[3]

What Ibn Sina, however, wants to avoid, among other things, is the Pythagorean-type approach to music theory, which regards numbers and the principles of numbers as the key to the study of music. Ibn Sina himself discusses intervals in terms of ratios, but does not consider this central to the understanding or the appreciation of music. Ratio-ability is just a fact about musical intervals.

The third interesting thing about the quoted passage is the way Ibn Sina continues the separation between the musical and the extra-musical, this time on the specific matter of *muḥākāt* or imitation. Two extra-musical phenomena are in question: the forms and movements of the heavenly bodies (*al-ashkāl al-samā'iyya*) and human character traits (*al-akhlāk al-nafsāniyya*).

With respect to the astronomical connection, Farabi had earlier rejected comparison with the sounds of the movements of the heavenly bodies in the study of music, but his grounds were different from Ibn Sina's. Farabi objects to the claim that heavenly bodies make music on scientific grounds. He says that it has been shown in physics that celestial bodies cannot produce sound of any kind, let alone musical sound.[4] This undercuts the possibility of any comparison between human and celestial music.

Ibn Sina seems to be saying that even if it were to turn out that celestial bodies do make sound as they move, and musical sound at that, any similarity between human musical composition and celestial natural music would, at best, be accidentally related to the study of our own music. He puts it thus in the quoted passage: those who make these extra-musical connections confuse what is accidental with what is essential. This of course applies not only to the astronomical, but also to the arithmetical, as we have seen. It also applies to the anthropological comparisons, as we shall see shortly.

Strictly speaking, to draw the boundaries for the study of music by means of the accidental-essential distinction, does not rule out the making of such extra-musical references in the study of music. If accidental rather than essential, comparisons are still possible. In proclaiming the autonomy of the science of music, Ibn Sina is simply preventing these extra-musical connections from playing an essential role in any theory about the nature of music. We have seen that Ibn Sina himself does discuss intervals in terms of ratios as a fact about intervals. We shall now see that Ibn Sina also finds room for talk about the imitation of human character traits, but not by way of offering such imitation as central to the nature of music, nor as source of greatest delight.

Before we get to Ibn Sina on imitation and music, let us recall some of the salient features of Plato's view of art, but particularly of music.

II

The first point about Plato's thought is that the concept of imitation is not limited to his theory of art. Thoughts and arguments are imitations of reality;[5] words are imitations of things;[6] sounds are imitations of divine harmony;[7] time imitates eternity;[8] human government imitates true government.[9] Besides imitation, there are the cousin concepts such as participation, approximation, being an imperfect copy, which are central to Plato's hierarchical ontology. One of the significant ways, then, in which Plato approaches art is as a metaphysician with a theory of the different levels of being. The entities created by art are then assigned a place in the general scheme. Another way of putting this, is that Plato's theory of art as imitation is part of a general ontology in which the hierarchy of being is already stratified in terms of, and connected by concepts such as approximation, participation and imitation.

In Plato's general ontology, furthermore, and in his talk about art in particular, imitation may be said to have either a negative or a positive connotation. Negatively put, in the language and spirit of most of the relevant passages in *The Republic*, and counting downward from true being, art as imitation is thrice removed from true being, and twice as imperfect as the things of this world. Art works rank with shadows.

Imitation, however, can be seen in a more positive light. One might speak of an aesthetic eros that drives one upwards, permitting each of the lower levels of being to suggest or evoke the higher reaches. The true artist, like the true philosopher, has the chance to lead upward. In the *Phaedrus* the philosopher and the artist are grouped together in another way: "the soul which has seen most of truth shall come to the birth as a philosopher or artist, or some musical and loving nature."[10] The crucial difference, however, between artist and philosopher remains; for the artist - and Plato here sits most heavily on the poet - lacking the knowledge of the philosopher, needs divine inspiration, but even when he gets it, he still has to contend with the limitations of his medium.

In either case, whether art is appreciated or criticized, the primacy of the ontological perspective is evident. There is, however, a related and equally important principle that leads to a further characterization of Plato's philosophy of art: the degrees of being are paralleled by the degrees of knowledge. Art is judged by its proper business to tell about reality, and scored for its incapacity to give true knowledge. The artist, the appreciator and the critic, all function within the sphere of cognition. Enjoyment is not the main point of art, nor the angle from which art is to be judged, although Plato tells us[11] that we do derive pleasure from the beauty in art, and in the case of music, especially when the sounds are smooth and clear and have a single pure tone. These are peculiar pleasures, and one is relieved to learn that they are unlike the pleasures of scratching. It is only in such rare passages that Plato speaks more like an aesthetician than the metaphysician or moralist that he primarily is.

There is one further point, and this is about music in particular. As an art music imitates, but since music is not a visual art it cannot imitate physical nature. What does it imitate? Perhaps the clearest and most explicit statement is the following: "Rhythms and music are imitations of good and evil characters in men."[12] It should be obvious which of these music should be allowed to do, for music can affect the character of the listener in accordance with what it is imitating. Plato worried as much, even more, about the more specific form of imitation: the impersonation in poetic recitation and dramatic presentation. The potential danger from the imitative character of music and the problem of its unrestricted access to the public engaged Plato as a moralist and political philosopher.

To the metaphysician, the moralist and political philosopher one should add Plato the educator. Aware of the effects that music can have on the soul by virtue of its imitative potency, Plato wants to put it to good use in his Republic. Both music and gymnastics are for the improvement of the soul. Harmony imparts grace;[13] simple melodies inspire temperance, and will be allowed.[14] Harmony produces both temperance and courage. The same conditions of tightness and release that are fulfilled at the physical level when strings are tuned to the right point are echoed in the soul as the right measure is reached, and the morally aimed-for harmony of the soul is attained. However, Plato recognized that training in music alone might make the soul soft and effeminate, just as the mere athlete might become hard and ferocious. Music and gymnastics together should be right and lead to gentleness and moderation.[15]

III

Ibn Sina's approach to music is different in several ways. First, Ibn Sina's basic premise is that music, that is, what is composed, performed and heard, is a kind of sound. Sound is the parent and primary concept. Music is sound having pitch and duration, arranged in a sequence of intervals forming melodies and having rhythm.[16] Music as a science, *'ilm al-mūsīḳā*, studies these elements that make up the music we hear. It is not simply that these are things that happen to make up music, but rather this is what music essentially is. The elements cited and their interrelationships in composition are the right handles by which to grab the phenomenon of music. For this reason I would venture to characterize Ibn Sina's approach to music as close to what we would nowadays call an aesthetician.

This does not prevent Ibn Sina from acknowledging the therapeutic value of music as a fact about it. Both Plato and Ibn Sina are aware of the effects of music on the listener. Plato as a moralist-educator channels that effective power to produce moral virtues in the soul. Ibn Sina as a physician, noting that music can tranquilize, sadden or brighten one's spirits, would naturally think of using its mood-enhancing and emotion-altering powers.

Since Ibn Sina classifies music as a kind of sound, he begins his study of music with what we might call a philosophy of sound, the general phenomenon of sound, although not so general that it includes the sound studied by the physicist. It is the sound that concerns the biologist. Ibn Sina is here remarking on the function of the articulation of sound in the survival of the species and in the life of its individuals.[17] The environment is often hostile and individuals need to signal for help or to warn of impending danger. Sound is also necessary for members of a species who wish to propagate but are separated by distance. They then call attractively to one another. This functional account of sound in general that is offered by Ibn Sina does not, however, extend to music. Bird songs may attract mates, but human songs and instrumental music have no such function.

There is another function of sound that Ibn Sina says is characteristic of the human species, and it goes beyond the biological need for survival and propagation which humans share with beasts. Man is driven by the need to convey to others what is within himself and to learn what is within the self of the other. This might be called the social function of sound as articulate speech. If this account were to be applied by Ibn Sina to music, we would have the equivalent of a communication theory of music, and it would be just the kind of forum for introducing the similarity between the musical and the anthropological. The elements of music cannot communicate in the abstract way our ordinary language does. Music will have to communicate by elements that in some ways imitate emotions and other psychological traits, in so far as this is possible; moreover, such imitation would have to become an essential part of music in that theory, rather than the accidental part that Ibn Sina wants to assign to it.

Ibn Sina, however, resists extending the social communication function of articulate sound in the analysis of music. Once Ibn Sina is confronted with music, whether vocal or instrumental, his interest switches from the concern with why an activity comes about and what its biological and social functions are, to what it is that we enjoy about it once it is before us. The functional biologist of sound and articulate speech yields to the aesthetician of music. Music is a source of enjoyment, but not accidentally and as a bonus, so that we might happen to prefer it to scratching. Enjoyment is the point of music. Whatever else music might do, for example, its therapeutic function, its distinctive function is to delight the soul. Ibn Sina puts it thus when discussing intervals: one should not choose intervals just because they can be constructed, or because they are correct (by some rule), or beneficial (perhaps he means to the disturbed soul), rather one chooses intervals because they are better, and this means to delight the soul, for that is the business of music (*wa amr al-mūsīkā mabnī 'alā al-afḍal, li-annahu li-ifādat al-ladhdhah al-nafsāniyya*).[18]

The delight in music comes to us from three aspects of the music:

1. The characteristics of musical sound as sound. This might be called the surface or sensuous aspect of music.[19]

2. The order and arrangement of notes and intervals into melodies and rhythm, and their occurrence and recurrence in a composition. This may be called the formal aspect, or *al-niẓām* in Ibn Sina's vocabulary.

3. The similarity between music, on the one hand, and natural processes and human traits, on the other. The second and third aspects, the formal and the imitative, take the listener beyond the qualities of sheer sound which is geared to our ears, and address themselves to his discerning faculty (*al-ḳuwwa al-mumayyiza*). While all three aspects can be a source of delight, it is the second, *al-niẓām* (order organization) that is the most pleasing.[20]

A few things should be said about the third aspect, the similarity between the musical and the extra-musical.

First, according to Ibn Sina the extra-musical here is not just human emotions and character traits, be they good or bad. It includes features of human behavior that are not emotions, features that can also be found in the nature that surrounds us, for example, reduction in loudness, drive or thrust, acceleration, and so on.[21] These can be used in describing the musical as well as the non-musical.

The second point about the aspect of imitation is that Ibn Sina acknowledges that imitation in music is a source of delight to the listener,[22] but this limitation is not the key to the nature of music, as we have already observed.

The third point is that there is a question - familiar in general aesthetics - of whether talk about imitation means anything more than that certain effects are evoked or produced in the listener. Unfortunately we do not have much text to go on. The opening of one passage seems to suggest that similarity and evocation are distinct, but it could also be taken differently. Ibn Sina says: "If the melody resembles one of the qualities, it is as if the soul had conformed to that quality and to whatever pertains to it."[23] The if-clause could be referring to a distinct feature called similarity which then happens to produce certain similar effects on the listener, but then the phrase "it is as if" (*fa-ka'annaha*) is ambiguous as between referring to a fact in addition to similarity, or simply translating what the talk about similarity amounts to, namely talk about its effect on the listener.

In another passage[24], Ibn Sina speaks of the way sounds (and this must include music) tranquilize one if one is sad or pained, and of how those sounds (and melodies) help to release certain intense emotions whether joyous or injurious. Here, where he speaks simply of effects on the listener, the picture could be more complicated, since the cure of a sad or pained soul can be achieved by music similar to a number of emotions, or even to non-psychological events and processes. The sadness may be dispelled without the one to one chamelion-type relationship assumed in the earlier passage where he says "it is as if the soul conforms to that quality" which the music imitates. In terms of effect on the listener, there need be no correspondence in kind. As a matter of fact, one can claim that so many of the effects that music is said to have can be acknowledged as resulting from listening to the music, but without necessarily accepting the view that music can be said to imitate anything.

Both Plato and Ibn Sina recognize the effects that music has on the listener, and in both cases the effects are attributable in their theories to the fact that music is imitative, whether essentially for the one, or accidentally for the other. Ibn Sina, however, unlike Plato, seems to be more preoccupied with how delightful that can be. There is none of the "Sturm und Drang" that grips Plato the educator and political philosopher.

Finally, even as Ibn Sina fits into his aesthetic theory the ideas of the similarity between music and human emotions and character traits, he admits of another source of delight that is super-added upon it. The melodies that carry or evoke those imitative traits and cause us to feel them in ourselves occur in a composition in a certain order. It is the coming and going and coming again of these melodies that give the higher delight. Regardless of whatever else these melodies may do, it is by their organizational occurrence and recurrence that we delight most of all. It is this structural or formal aspect of music (*al-niẓām*) that is the source of the greatest delight.[25] And the very fact that the emotion-bearing, emotion-imitating melodies are submerged into a structure that gives greater pleasure, testifies further to the accuracy of characterizing Ibn Sina's philosophy of music as one that finds a place for the imitative function of music, but considers imitation as neither the key to the nature of music nor its most pleasing aspect. To make the very imitative go under, as it were, in the service of another aspect of music, is to place the imitative aspect at a good distance from its Platonic centrality, in either the definition of music as art or in its evaluation. Ibn Sina, thus, remains true to the promise he made in the opening passage of his introduction.

This takes care if Ibn Sina's view of his difference from at least one of the major figures of antiquity. A similar comparative analysis can be done taking others. I am sure someone will dig up some writer from the Greek masters, perhaps less well-known, who held a philosophy of music exactly like that of Ibn Sina's, and this would deflect the Islamic philosopher's claim of difference and independence from the ancients. I may get excited about that, but I cannot promise that I will.

Notes

* An earlier version of this paper was read at the 1983 meeting of the Society for Ancient Philosophy, in New York City. The theme of the conference was "Plato and Islamic Philosophy". Of those outside the Islamic orbit Plato's type of philosophy of art is one kind of target that Ibn Sina was aiming at. Pythagoras would have been another, yet clearly the exclusive pairing off of Ibn Sina with Plato was in response to the conference theme. The title is about art in general, but the essay is primarily about music.

1 Ibn Sina, *Kitāb al-Shifā'*, 4 vols., ed. Zakhariyya Yūsuf (Cairo: al-Amīriyya, 1956), 3: 3-4.

2 *Ibid.*, 4.

3 *Ibid.*, 3.

4 Al-Farabi, *Kitāb al-Mūsīkā al-Kabīr*, ed. Ghaṭṭāṣ 'abd al-Malik Khashaba, (Cairo: Dār al-Kitāb al-'arabī, 1967), 89.

5 Plato, *Dialogues*, 2 vols., trans. B. Jowett, (New York: Random House, 1937), *Timaeus*, 47 B-C; *Critias*, 107 B-C.

6 *Cratylus*, 423 E - 424 B.

7 *Timaeus*, 80 B.

8 *Ibid.*, 38 A.

9 *Ibid.*, 293 E - 297 C.

10 *Phaedrus*, 248 D.

11 *Philebus*, 51 D.

12 *Laws*, VII, 798 E.

13 *Republic*, III, 402.

14 *Ibid.*, 410.

15 *Ibidem*.

16 Ibn Sina, *op. cit.*, 9.

17 *Ibid.*, 4-7.

18 *Ibid.*, 20.

19 *Ibid.*, 4.

20 *Ibid.*, 8-9.

21 *Ibid.*, 8.

22 *Ibidem.*

23 *Ibidem.*

24 *Ibid.*, 7.

25 *Ibid.*, 9.

Peter Bradlay: "No" to Scotist Univocity?

Edward A. Synan

Two misconceptions have prompted these reflections on a disputed question by Peter Bradlay, an Oxford logician of the fourteenth century's first decade.[1] One of these misconceptions is the impression that every generation of mediaeval thought was so clearly dominated by one or another great figure that all lesser masters fade into merited obscurity. A notable instance of this illusion (although, to be sure, it is one so precious that we cannot decently do less than call it a *felix culpa*) is the poem by Gerard Manley Hopkins, "Duns Scotus's Oxford."[2] There is, of course, a philosophical bias against judgments delivered in metre; Socrates himself has warned us to be chary of poets: "... upon the strength of their poetry they believed themselves to be the wisest of men in other things in which they were not wise." (Plato, *Apology* 22 C, translation, B. Jowett). Still, neither Socrates nor any other true philosopher would deny that poets compose beautifully and, let us hasten to say it, few of them match the beauty achieved by Hopkins.

Our question is pedestrian, even naive: With what right did Hopkins say that Oxford once belonged to the Subtle and Marian Doctor? Is there any sense in which Oxford can have been "Duns Scotus's Oxford"?

Surely Hopkins could not have meant the Oxford of streets and buildings although that is precisely the Oxford evoked by his words: "Towery city and branchy between towers;" the branches a home for the lark, for the rook, the whole "river-rounded". Nor could he have meant the University. If the University did not strictly "belong" to the crown, many a document shows that the king felt responsible for chancellor, masters, and the guild of students, not only of Oxford, but of The Other Place as well.[3] The poet must have had in mind the Oxford of intellect, as beautiful as the "Towery city" and no less real than the corporation of masters and students. If Hopkins were right, the city of intellect belonged for a moment to Duns Scotus "Of realty" the most subtle "unraveller".

One intention of this conspicuously unpoetic paper is to propose some reasons for denying that the Oxford of intellect was ever the personal fief of John Duns Scotus. This does not proceed from an anti-Scotus bias. On the contrary, the genuine eminence of Duns can be given full value only if it be measured against the achievements of a crowd of all but forgotten masters who did their work in the metaphorical shadow he cast, perhaps even in his physical presence. Peter Bradlay was one of those lesser masters.

A second misconception now, it is heartening to note, disappearing from academic circles,[4] was a tendency to ignore the primary role that formal logic played in mediaeval thought. After generations of scholarship during which metaphysics or philosophy of mind or theology held pride of place, research is progressively disclosing to us what was obvious to our ancestors: Mediaeval scholars in every discipline remained logicans first and last. Philosophical and theological issues could hardly have been argued so closely had there not been agreement as to what was the province of logic. If in the past the course of mediaeval thought has been read under the too restrictive rubric of the famous name, a parallel blunder has been to read it within the limits of diciplines that are more ambitious, not to say more pretentious, than is logic. The classical humanists were not victims of these misconceptions. Neither sympathetic to mediaeval logic nor unaware of its pervasive role, they knew well that nothing more properly characterized the intellectual edifice they thought it their duty to dismantle than did the intricate formal logic, held in common by mediaeval scholars of all persuasions. From fifteenth and sixteenth century humanists, mediaeval logicians received sharp reproach; fatuous pedants (as they seemed), those logicians were counted hardly worth refuting and their works rarely worth printing. To cite but one humanist on our theme, Thomas More thundered in a letter to Martin Dorp, A.D. 1515, against the *parua logicalia*, treatises now held in high esteem by modern historians of logic: "By Hercules, may those who teach such stuff to boys, despite their age, get the beating they deserve every time they do so!"[5]

Our point of departure here is the fact that Master Peter Bradlay of Balliol, presumably while still in the faculty of arts, opened his series of disputed questions on Aristotle's *Categories* with an attack on univocity. What gives his effort special interest is that a case can be made for the master of univocity, John Duns Scotus himself, as the opponent Bradlay had in mind. If this identification can be sustained, the two misconceptions will have been corrected, so to speak, in passing: the all but unknown Bradlay facing the great Scotus on univocity and their weaponry formal logic.

Peter Bradlay, in accord with scholastic practice, set out arguments in favor of the univocity he rejected and then responded to each argument under the battle-flag of analogy. The five arguments contend that being is univocal with respect to all ten categories and to caused as well as to Uncaused Being.[6]

For the first of those arguments, Peter introduced an involved paragraph with the remark that a concept on which one is certain differs necessarily from concepts on which one entertains doubt: One can be certain of having seen an animal, yet be in doubt as to whether that animal is a human being or an ass. "Human being" and "ass" express diverse meanings; the doubt bears on how to qualify what is surely an animal. Is it human? Is it a beast? "Animal," on which the observer is certain, can be verified univocally of a human being or of an ass (1.27). Bradlay's illustration echoes the familiar line of *Categories* 1; 1a 6-9: "Things are univocally named when . . . the name has the same definition in each case . . . Thus a man and an ox are called 'animals'." The "ancients" knew that the First Principle of all things is being; they were in doubt, Peter assured us, as to whether that First Principle is a substance or an accident.[7] In his shorthand prose Peter jumped to his opponent's conclusion: Being might be a substance or it might be an accident. Which it is may not be certain; thus, "being" is univocally predicable of substance or of accident (1.27).

Second, in the person of his opponent, Peter asserted that every cognitive power has one univocal object and being is the object of intellect. This object, therefore, cannot be (as partisans of analogy hold) the "quiddity of material substance. Because our understanding extends beyond the material, the object of intellect must be a concept of univocal being" (1.28).

The third approach is similar: Power and the primary habit of a power have an identical object (or, as Peter added, "subject," a revelatory usage to which we shall return). Since metaphysics is the primary

231

habit of the intellective power, and since metaphysics for all Aristotelians deals with "being as being" (*Meta.* 4, 1; 1003a 21, 22), then that being, univocally taken, must be the object/subject of intellect as well as of its characteristic possession, the habit of metaphysics (1.29).

Fourth, our knowledge of the First Cause (acquired through our experience of what evidently has been caused) demands that there be community between Cause and the caused to ground this cognitive passage, whether the caused be substance or accident. This bridge can only be being, rightly conceived to be univocal; "no other path is possible for us" (1.30).

Fifth, as mediaeval Aristotelians were wont to do, Peter adduced The Philosopher (*Meta.* 2, 1; 993b 19-31), but he did so here to support his opponent: "The true" is convertible with "being". If the true were not univocal, syllogisms would always be flawed by the fallacy of equivocation. Hence, the true must be univocal and, since being is convertible with the true, being must be equally univocal (1.31).

If to give an opponent's position a fair presentation was a matter of honor among mediaeval academics, to refute that presentation in detail counted as their professional obligation.

Against the first argument Peter claimed bluntly and briefly that it exhibits the fallacy of the consequent. The pro-univocity reasoning parallels: "A man is running, therefore Socrates is running," an evidently fallacious inference of a determinate consequent from an indeterminate antecedent (1.51). Despite the complexity of the argument for univocity, formal logic had supplied Bradlay with a simple refutation, but he did not bother to "describe" that simple refutation-- a more formal procedure for which Walter Burley, for one, has been extolled. All logicians are "formal," as all the animals in *Animal Farm* are equal, but some logicians were more formal than Bradlay.

To the second, Bradlay's refutation refers to the Aristotelian theory of knowing by abstraction from phantasms. Owing to the material starting point of human knowledge in the sensually acquired phantasm, human knowing reveals, not being in its generality, but rather "the quiddity of material substance," (virtually present in the material singular to which our senses are resonant). Peter was ready to concede that his opponent was right to have held that "nothing is understood by the intellect which was not contained under" the matter that begets our phantasms, but here too he identified a fallacious consequence: That one might see Socrates in no way impugns the role of color as the primary object of sight (1.52). This entails the standard scholastic distinction between the "object which" is known and the "object by which" a knowing power operates. In this lexicon, material quiddity is the "object which" is known whereas being functions as the "object by which" knowing takes place (1.53).

Peter's response to the third argument for univocity (1.54) is based on the same distinction, but introduces an analysis of seeing that goes beyond the "Socrates-color" correlation. Being cannot be in any primary way the "object which" is known; rather it is the "object by which" realities are intelligible. Once more Peter apppealed to the parallel of color as the primary "object which" of sight, but here adduced light as the "object by which" colored items are perceived.

Another useful distinction from the Aristotelian tradition served Peter in responding to the fourth argument. This is the distinction between knowing "that" something is and knowing "what" something may be. With respect to the First Cause, the first sort of knowing alone is possible for us. We know the First Cause solely through our knowledge of what has been caused, for we know that our world is a "caused" reality (1.55).

Fifth and last, in Bradlay's view "the true" convertible with "being" is as analogous as is being, verified diversely of substance and of accident. Nor does an analogous conception of being entail a fourth term in syllogism. Peter formulated a most puzzling syllogism-- perhaps a kind of joke-- which he claimed is "good," *bonus*, that is, valid. All three component sentences are questionable:

> Every being is substance;
> accident is being;
> therefore, accident is substance (1.56).

What Peter perhaps intended may be clarified by adding some qualifying phrases:

> Every being (without reservation, *simpliciter*), is substance;
> accident is being (from some point of view, *secundum quid*);
> therefore, (because not nothing) accident is (by analogy the being that)
>   substance (is).

The middle term "being," Peter asserted, is not univocal, but analogous. Given the major premise, why, we may ask, did he formulate so odd a minor premiss? The answer must be that, since accidents are real determinations of real substances, accidents cannot be denied all positive relation to being; still, since accidents are not independent in their being (as are substances), accidents are not being in an unqualified sense. There is, therefore, an analogous being, possessed variously by independent substance and by dependent accidents. Aristotle had introduced his discussion of this enigma by stating that "There are several senses in which a thing may be said 'to be'" (*Meta.* 7, 1; 1028a 10-30). On accidents generally The Philosopher pointed out that they are "quantities or qualities or affections . . . or other determinations of" substances, and only substances "are" in the primary sense of "being."

A first intimation that Bradlay's question involved Scotus is that the series of arguments and responses forms a sequence of five. In his *Ordinatio* on the *Sentences*, currently appearing in the critical edition from the Scotist Commission, Duns announced that he would argue for the univocity of being "in a five-fold way," *quintupliciter*.[8] This admittedly feeble indication could hardly stand without reinforcement; that reinforcement, however, seems to be both available and adequate.

Although diverse in expression, Peter's first argument for univocity echoes the first of the five proposed by Duns. Where Peter has "animal," "human being," and "ass," Duns had qualified "being" as "finite" or "Infinite" again, as "created" and "Uncreated." Both made the point that in each threefold grouping the first conception, "animal" (Bradlay), and "being" (Scotus), can be the object of certitude while the other two, respectively, Bradlay's "human being-ass," Duns' "finite-Infinite" and "created-Uncreated," remain matters of doubt. Since the first and certain concept in each group is other than those in doubt, yet must be included in their notions, "being" and "animal" must be univocal conceptions.[9] That Bradlay knew and responded to the first argument of Duns is incontrovertible.

The second, oddly enough, presents the reader with a situation in which Peter's response to his own formulation of a pro-univocity argument is closer to the words of Duns than is Bradlay's formulation of the argument itself. For the Subtle Doctor had mentioned phantasm and agent intellect; neither occurs in Peter's report of the argument, but both occur in his response. To complicate the issue further, Peter raised the "quiddity of material substance" to which Duns had not alluded. Still, Peter had seen the force of the Scotist contention that an attempt to move from phantasm to an analogically related concept of God, on Scotist principles, could not succeed. Such a phantasm, given the action of the agent intellect, could arrive at the "quiddity of material substance" only; in a Scotist perspective, there the wayfarer would remain, with the unacceptable conclusion that no natural knowledge of God would be possible.[10]

Like all authentically biblical theologians, Scotus was careful not to claim too much for our knowledge of the Holy One. His third argument is that we have no "proper concept" from which we might hope to deduce all necessary truths about God.[11] Yet Peter realized that the God of Scotus is known to some degree in the concept of "being," univocal to creatures and to the Creator; in some sense too, that univocal Scotist being would be the primary object of intellect. Not so, Peter retorted: Being is not the "object which," but the "object by which" our intellect knows.

Duns in his fourth argument made reference to the notion of "simple perfection," to Anselm's *Monologion*, and to the metaphysical procedure of considering a formal intelligibility, a *formalis ratio*, as found in creatures, denuding it of creaturely imperfection, ascribing to it the summit of perfection, and finally attributing it to God.[12] In the first instance, this concept had been derived from creatures; because univocal, it was susceptible of this infinite elevation. Peter mentioned not a word of all this. He was content to say that we know "that God is," but not "what God is," a distinction which, it must be noted, Duns had accepted in an earlier passage.[13]

The fifth argument for univocity in Bradlay has no connection with the fifth in the *Ordinatio* of Duns. There the Subtle Doctor had introduced a "more perfect creature" and that creature's correspondingly "more perfect concept of God."[14] No hint of this finds an echo in Peter. Bradlay's fifth exchange, however, does echo the clarification of univocity that precedes the series of five arguments in the *Ordinatio*. There Duns set two formal norms for univocity: First, a univocal term must be sufficient for contradicton and second, capable of serving as the middle term of a syllogism "without the fallacy of equivocation."[15] Such a fallacy would be effectively a fourth term in the syllogism that contained it. We have seen how enigmatic was Peter's syllogism designed to exhibit the functioning of an analogous middle term.

In any event, that Peter did not mention the name of Duns was, of course, standard academic practice; living masters were not named. Peter's addition to the "object" of a power and of that power's primary "habit" of the term "subject" (*cuius scientie ens est subiectum vel obiectum*, 1.29) is a characteristically Scotist usage that occasioned an illuminating passage in Gilson's study on Duns.[16] That Bradlay was preoccupied by the five-step case of the *Ordinatio* for univocity can not be doubted. All variations between what Duns had there presented and what Bradlay posed as arguments to be refuted can be accounted for by data provided in the critical edition. There Duns is seen to have made additions and suppressions as he prepared his work for definitive publication. His "Oxford work" had meant lecturing on the *Sentences*, Books 1-3 from 1300 to 1302 and on Book 4 in 1303 and 1304. These are precisely the years when our scanty information puts Peter Bradlay at Balliol, preparing the two short works that happenstance has preserved, the present question included.

History has been right to esteem the work and the reputation of John Duns Scotus rather than those of Peter Bradlay. We shall, however, value the Subtle Doctor all the more and understand him all the better the more we know of those other, lesser "unravellers" of "realty" with whom he shared the Oxford of intellect. Peter Bradlay was not the equal of Duns Scotus, to be sure, but my minimum claim is that the consequence: "Not Duns, therefore a dunce" exhibits the fallacy of the consequent.

Notes

1 On Peter Bradlay, a scholar of Balliol College, see A.B. Emden, *A Biographical Register Of University Of Oxford to A.D. 1500*, 2 vols. (Oxford: Clarendon, 1957, 1959) 1, 311, entry for Adam de Burleye in which Peter is mentioned; two works by Bradlay are extant in a unique manuscript, Gonville and Caius MS 668*; one is a series of questions on the *Categories*, the first of which is examined here, "Master Peter Bradlay on the 'Categories'," ed. E.A. Synan, *Mediaeval Studies*, 29 (1967) 273-327 and the second "A Question by Peter Bradlay on the 'Prior Analytics'," ed. E.A. Synan, *Mediaeval Studies*, 30 (1968) 1-21. The manuscript, it is argued elsewhere, seems to have been completed during the reign of Edward I who died in 1307, see *Works Of Richard Of Campsall*, ed. E.A. Synan, vol. 1 (Toronto: Institute of Mediaeval Studies, 1968) 17-20.

2 *The Poems Of Gerard Manley Hopkins*, edd. W.H. Gardner and N.H. Mackenzie (London, N.Y., Toronto: Oxford University Press, 1967) 79.

3 See *Calendar Of The Patent Rolls*, 33 Edward I, Part I A.D. 1301-1307, (London: H.M. Stationery Office, 1898), entries for July 6, 1304, January 16, 1305, March 12, 1305 refer to allotments of money to Franciscan and Dominican houses at both universities as well as to the defense of masters and scholars against violence.

4 Contrast the then justifiable complaint of I.M. Bochenski, *A History Of Formal Logic*, tr. I. Thomas, (Notre Dame Indiana: Notre Dame University Press, 1961) 148 with the generous allotment to logical materials by *The Cambridge History Of Later Medieval Philosophy*, (Cambridge, London, N.Y., New Rochelle, Melbourne, Sidney: Cambridge University Press, 1982).

5 "*Digni, hercle, qui talia iam senes docent, vt quoties pueros docent, toties ipsi vapulent.*" *The Correspondence Of Sir Thomas More*, ed. E. Rogers (Princeton: Princeton University Press, 1947) 39, 11. 385, 386.

6 "*Circa istum librum, queretur primo de ente quod est commune ad 01 <SIC> predicamenta, et ens causatum et incausatum: utrum ens sit commune univocum ad x predicamenta, et simul cum hoc, ad ens causatum et incausatum?*, ed. cit. 275; in the interest of brevity, references to passages in Bradlay's question, the first of eleven, are given in the text (1.27, 1.28 etc.).

7 Not quite an accurate use of the Aristotelian passage at stake, the "ancients," *pampalaioi*, (*Meta.* 1, 3; 983b 1 ff.) are said to have been at odds over the "principle of all things," *arche panton*, and the "first cause," *prote aitia*, but their

candidates were water, air, fire, and earth, not Peter's "substance or accident," nor, of course, the "created or Uncreated, First or not First" being of Scotus.

8 *"Et univocationem sic intellectam probo quintupliciter."* John Duns Scotus, *Ordinatio* 1, d. 3, p. 1, q. 2, #26 *Opera omnia* t. 3, (Vatican City: Scotist Commission, 1954) p. 18; the corresponding passage in Peter Bradlay's question is: *"Ad 5 raciones, tamen factas pro univocacione entis, dicendum est ad formas, quia in posicione dictum est ad materiam satis."* ed. cit. 1.50, p. 283.

9 *". . . scit quod est animal, dubitat, tamen, an sit homo vel asinus . . . antiqui sciverunt de primo principio, quod fuit ens, dubitabant, tamen, an fuit substancia vel accidens . . ."* ed. cit. 279.

10 Scotus ended his second argument with this result of an analogical conception of being: *" . . . ita non poterit haberi naturaliter aliquis conceptus de Deo, quod est falsum." Ordinatio* I, d. 3, pars 1, q. 2, ed. cit. t. 3, 21, 11. 4, 5.

11 *". . . conceptus proprius . . . sufficiens ratio concludendi omnia conceptibilia quae sibi necessario insunt; nullum autem conceptum habemus de Deo . . ."* Ibidem 24, 11. 8-10.

12 Ibidem 25, 11. 3-26, 1. 9.

13 Ibidem 6, #11, 12; 7, 8, #16; 9, #17.

14 Ibidem 26, 11. 14-19.

15 *"Et ne fiat contentio de nomine univocationis, univocum conceptum dico, qui ita est unus quod eius unitas sufficit ad contradictionem, affirmando et negando ipsum de eodem; sufficit etiam pro medio syllogistico, ut extrema unita in medio sic uno sine fallacia aequivocationis concluditur inter se uniri."* Ibidem 18, 11. 10-17.

16 E. Gilson, *Jean Duns Scot.* (Paris: J. Vrin, 1952) 45, 46.

Theodicy in Ben Sira and Stoic Philosophy

David Winston

It has often been claimed that Ben Sira is engaged in a running polemic with Hellenism. Although Rudolf Smend's view that Sirach "hated Hellenism and the Greeks with all his heart" has been echoed to some extent by M. Hengel and more fully by V. Tcherikover, few modern scholars would now subscribe to that position. As J. Goldstein has pointed out, "the words 'Greek' and 'Greece' nowhere appear in Ben Sira's work.... Ben Sira does not tell his fellow Jews that they must not imitate foreigners, nor does he tell Jews to shun pagans." Goldstein believes that "Hellenism was simply not an issue for Ben Sira, since there were few if any Greeks in the country to imitate."[1] J.T. Sanders has correctly observed that Ben Sira "is entirely open to Hellenic thought as long as it can be Judaized.[2] Nevertheless, one can readily detect in his conception of human knowledge a considerably more modest assessment of the human capacity to master natural science than that espoused by the author of the Wisdom of Solomon. Although Ben Sira's blast in 3:21-24 is probably directed against cosmogonic and extra-terrestrial speculations, which he considered potentially dangerous, he does not seem to share the very bold and enthusiastic confidence which the author of Wisdom has in his ability to attain "an unerring knowledge of existent being" (7:17). In contrast to Ben Sira who alludes to man's inability to count "the days of unending time" (1:2), the author of Wisdom knows "the beginning, and end, and middle of times" (7:17), a phrase with a distinctively cosmogonic ring and one deriving from the Orphic theogony.[3] But this denotes only a difference of degree and in no way indicates any reluctance on Ben Sira's part to adapt Hellenistic learning whenever it suited his purposes.

There can be little doubt that Ben Sira's opus is marked by a consistent effort to effect a new synthesis of ideas. In an age when Hellenic wisdom dominated the civilized world, he did his best to broaden the bounds of the Mosaic Law so that it would encompass every manifestation of wisdom. As Collins has correctly pointed out, Ben Sira's so-called nationalization of wisdom constituted in reality the universalization of the Torah.[4] More than he subordinated wisdom to the Law, he assimilated the Law to universal wisdom. The key note in his writing is that of didactic wisdom rather than the Law. The Torah is refracted for Ben Sira through the lens of wisdom, and the case for its legitimacy is made in wisdom's terms. "All wisdom is the fear of the Lord, and in all wisdom is fulfillment of the Law" (Sir. 19:20).[5]

It is especially, however, in his confrontation with the problem of evil that Ben Sira moves beyond the earlier wisdom tradition and is actively engaged in adapting Stoic arguments for the formulation of his main solution to this puzzling paradox, namely, that nature is to be seen as a harmony of opposites. Although Platonism did not arrive in Alexandria before the first century B.C.E., some knowledge of Stoic philosophy does appear to have penetrated the Alexandrian intellectual scene already in the third century B.C.E., for we are told that when Cleanthes, scholarch of the Stoic School from 263 to 232, refused the invitation of Ptolemy Philadelphus, he sent his pupil Sphaerus there instead (Diog. Laert. 7.185). Sphaerus was later the counsellor of Cleomenes III of Sparta, who ended his days in Alexandria, and it is possible that he returned with him there, although the evidence is very uncertain.[6] The visit of an isolated stoic philosopher does not constitute a major presence and it is therefore unlikely that in the absence of a flourishing Stoic center such as those found in Rhodes and in Tarsus, Ben Sira would have possessed a detailed and technical knowledge of the Stoic philosophy. But the broad outlines of their thought and the chief elements of their major doctrines were probably well known to him. Although he does not speak explicitly of the harmony of the universal order, his words clearly imply it. The unity of creation was a given for biblical monotheism, so that Ben Sira faced the same dilemma that stalked the Stoics, whose single-minded monism was their philosophical trademark. Both he and they were constrained to explain the warring dualities that seem to mar the unity of being. In 33:7-14, he seeks to reconcile the unity of creation with a divine plan which consistently discriminates between pairs of opposites: good and evil, life and death, the sinner and the godly. In his effort to explicate the dietary laws, Pseudo-Aristeas had also noted the paradox that, in spite of the fact that creation was one, some things are regarded by the Torah as unclean for food and some even to the touch, and in the course of his explanation of this surprising fact he pointed out that although all things are to the natural reason similarly constituted, being all administered by a single power, in every case there is a profound logic for our abstinence from the use of some things and our participation in the use of others (129, 143). Ben Sira similarly indicates that although every day has its light from the sun, certain days were by the Lord's decision distinguished and made holy, and though all men were created out of earth, some, in God's great wisdom, were hallowed and brought near to Him, while others were cursed and removed from their place. "Look at all the works of the Most High," he concludes, "they go in pairs, one the opposite of the other" (33:15).[7] All this evidently implies that the universe consists of a harmony of opposites in accordance with a mysterious divine design.

The Stoics taught a similar doctrine. First, like Ben Sira, they declared that divine providence is "chiefly directed and concentrated upon three objects, namely to secure for the world, first, the structure best fitted for survival; next, absolute completeness (*ut nulla re egeat*); but chiefly, consummate beauty and embellishment of every kind" (Cic. *Nat. D.* 2.58).[8] Then too, like Ben Sira, they taught that this is the best possible world that could be produced (Cic. *Nat. D.* 2.87), and that notwithstanding apparent imperfections here and there, Nature so organized each part that harmony is present in the whole.[9] As for the evil of natural disasters, "it has a rationale peculiar to itself, for in a sense it too occurs in accordance with universal reason, and so to speak, is not without usefulness in relation to the whole. For without it there could be no good." (Chrysippus, ap. Plut. *De Comm. Not.* 1065B). M. Aurelius finds comfort in the belief that everything contributes to some grand universal scheme: "Nothing is harmful to the part which is advantageous to the whole. For the whole contains nothing which is not advantageous to itself .... As long as I remember that I am a part of such a whole I shall be well content with all that happens" (10.6) Ben Sira's attitude is quite similar: "No one should ask 'What is this?', or 'Why is that?' Everything has been created for its own purpose" (39:21). Indeed, the very elements that are "good for the godfearing turn to evil for sinners" (39:21; cf. Wisd. 16:24). "Fire and hail, famine and deadly disease, all these were created for retribution; beasts of prey, scorpions and vipers, and the avenging sword that destroys the wicked" (39:29-30). The Stoics had also pointed out that providence either watches over earthly affairs or cleanses them by floods and conflagrations (Origen, *C.Cels.* 4.64=*SVF* 2.1174).[10]

The more recalcitrant problem, however, was presented not so much by natural as by moral evil, and here again both Ben Sira and the Stoics employ the same approach. Logic requires the existence of both good and evil. In the fourth book of his treatise *On Providence*, Chrysippus argued as follows: "There is absolutely nothing more foolish than those men who think that good could exist, if there were at the same time no evil. For since good is the opposite of evil, it necessarily follows that both must exist in opposition to each other, supported as it were by mutual adverse forces; since as a matter of fact no opposite is conceivable without something to oppose it. For how could there be an idea of justice if there were no acts of injustice?" (A. Gellius, *NA* 7.1.2-4)."[11]

Finally, Ben Sira's grateful response to the wonders of creation and his urgent call for man's acknowledging praise of their divine Author (42:15-43:33), goes hand in hand with his optimistic assessment of this best of all possible worlds: "All the works of the Lord are good, and he supplies every need as it occurs. No one should say, 'this is less good than that,' for all things prove good at their proper time. Come then, sing with heart and voice, and praise the name of the Lord" (39:33-35). Precisely the same blend of ideas characterizes the Stoic position. For the latter it is a matter of justice to render thanks for God's innumerable benefactions, and it is therefore man's task to hymn the praises of the deity: "Why, if we had sense, ought we to be doing anything else, publicly and privately, than hymning and praising the Deity, and rehearsing his benefits? .... This is my task; I do it, and will not desert this post, as long as it may be given me to fill it; and I exhort you to join me in this same song" (Epict. 1.16.15.21). The special suitability of hymns for singing the praises of God had already been emphasized by Cleanthes: "Bare prose does not have expressions suitable to the divine majesty, nor the meters, melodies, and rhythms to approach as closely as possible to the truth of the contemplation of divine things" (*SVF* 1.486, cf. Plato, *Resp.* 607A.)[12] In sum, in dealing with the very thorny problem of theodicy, Ben Sira seems to have consciously followed in the footsteps of the Stoics, who had already exerted all their ingenuity in order to resolve the many challenges that must have been constantly hurled at them in the face of their self-satisfied and supremely optimistic faith in a perfect all-embracing Nature.[13]

Another aspect of the theodicy issue in regard to which Ben Sira seems to have followed the Stoic lead is in his formulation of the paradox of freedom and determinism. The older wisdom literature did not feel this contradiction too keenly, and was content to assert that all was determined by the gods in advance, and yet at the same time to insist that success and failure, and punishment and reward were conditioned by man's behavior. In Egyptian writings, not only do the gods inspire men to act in all kinds of situations, but they are also said to cause them to commit destructive actions. In the inscriptions of Petosiris, who lived at the dawn of the Ptolemaic era, we read: "God places it [the evil thought] into the heart of him whomever he hates in order to give his goods to another whom he loves."[14] The same idea is already found, however, in the *Instruction of Ptahhotep* (from the Period of the Old Kingdom): "His guilt was fated in the womb; He whom they guide cannot go wrong, whom they make boatless cannot cross" (12=210ff).[15] In the epilogue to that work it is said: "He who hears is beloved of god, He whom god hates does not hear. The heart makes of its owner a hearer or non-hearer ..." (540-550). An individual's career is similarly predetermined. In the Middle Kingdom *Teaching of Khety* it is said: "Lo, I have set you on god's path, A scribe's Renenet [a goddess of bounty and good luck] is on his shoulder on the day he is born .... The Meshkenet [goddess who presided over births] assigned to the scribe, she promotes him in the council."[16] Thus the deities Meskhenet and Renenet determined at a child's birth how successful he was to be in his professional career.[17] On a larger scale, the social staus of a man is also determined by the god: "Man is clay and straw, The God is his builder. He tears down, he builds up daily. He makes a thousand poor by his will, He makes a thousand men into chiefs, when he is in his hour of life."[18] In the *Admonitions of Ipuwer*, dating from the period after the collapse of the Old Kingdom, a number of deplorable events are explained as having been determined at a very early stage by the gods: "This was predestined for you in the time of Horus, in the age of the Ennead."[19] According to *Ptahhotep*, "people's schemes do not prevail. God's commandment is what prevails; Live then in the midst of peace, what they (=the gods) give comes by itself" (115-18).[20] The Demotic *Instruction of Anchsheshonqy* is particularly emphatic concerning the absolute divine control over all human events: "There is imprisonment for giving life. There is release for killing. There is he who saves and does not find. All are from the hand of the fate and the god" (26.5-8).[21]

One passage in *Ptahhotep* seems to imply that one can immunize oneself from the vice of greed, but once having become infected with this disease, he can no longer free himself from it: "If you want a perfect conduct, To be free from every evil, Guard against the vice of greed: A grievous sickness without cure, There is no treatment for it" (298). This has been taken to indicate the author's attempt to qualify his doctrine of absolute determinism.[22] In fact, however, what this passage asserts is the exact equivalent of Aristotle's similar discussion in *Eth. Nic.* 3.1114a, where it is argued that before a man's disposition is formed, he is apparently in a position to act in different ways, but once it is formed, this is no longer true.[23] What all this amounts to is that even what might be considered the relative freedom men ordinarily possess is no longer available to them once they have allowed themselves to acquire incorrigibly diseased dispositions. The theoretical question, however, of whether their initial freedom of action is to be considered absolute or relative is not explicitly resolved by Aristotle, but is turned aside instead by an *ad hominem* argument (1114a31-b25). In any case, the passage cited above from *Ptahhotep* does not necessarily soften the deterministic sentiments quoted earlier from that work.

It has been pointed out that the Demotic wisdom Instruction known as *Papyrus Insinger* was the first such Egyptian writing to deal consciously and explicitly with the freedom/determinism dilemma. Except for the paradoxical chapter endings, which describe man as totally dependent on God and his emissaries, Fate and Fortune ($\check{S}jy$ and $Shne$),[24] all of *Papyrus Insinger's* teachings affirm man's moral freedom. H. Brunner argued that the belief in the regular connection between deed and result had been abandoned in *Papyrus Insinger*, but as Lichtheim has correctly remarked, if this were the case "it would be impossible to understand the Demotic writer's intention when he composed his long Instruction in which that connection is continuously reiterated." What we find in Papyrus Insinger is very much like the paradoxical formulation of the Stoics that everything is in accord with Heimarmene, yet our actions are in our power (*eph' hēmin*). In the light of the various Hellenistic elements in *Papyrus Insinger* it is very likely that in this case too we are dealing with such an influence. Lichtheim has enumerated the following examples of Hellenistic borrowings: *Papyrus Insinger's* loose aphoristic form combined with an attempt to impose some order; the choice of themes (similarity with Pseudo-Plutarch's *On the Education of Children*); 'character' as a key term and the drawing up of a typology of characters; the concept of disposition and its explanation by examples drawn from three classes of things, substances, animals, and men (similar to Stoic theory); the Greek *topos* "count no man happy till his death;" two kinds of shame; not to slight small things (*oligōria*); the fallibility of the wise man; the teaching of the right mean; and finally, the self-presentation of the author. In view of such a considerable number of striking similarities between *Papyrus Insinger* and Ben Sira, it is reasonable to assume that the similar formulation of the freedom/determinism paradox found in both these authors was due to their common use of Stoic sources.[25]

Although a palpably deterministic strain does run through the book of Proverbs, it nevertheless lacks an explicit and conscious expression of the freedom/determinism paradox. Thus the author of Proverbs teaches that the sage will acquire wisdom, while the fool will hold it in contempt, thereby implying that their life course is fixed in advance (Prov. 14:6; 17:16; 9:7; 13:19; 20:12). There is even a verse that asserts that God has created all, including the fool, for a special purpose (16:4).[26] Nowhere, however, does the book of Proverbs declare unequivocally, as does Ben Sira, that God has determined man's character even before his birth (Sir. 1:14-15), or that man was fashioned by God as clay in the power of the potter, so that in accordance with an eternal cosmic plan, the godly or blessed stand over against the sinner or the cursed (Sir. 33:10-15). Moreover, Ben Sira includes, along with his starkly predestinarian passages, emphatic statements concerning man's freedom to choose his life-path accompanied by explicit warnings against blaming God for causing him to sin.[27] The book of Proverbs, on the other hand, like most of the earlier Near Eastern wisdom Instructions, does not explicitly articulate the contradiction between the all-determining divine will and the apparent freedom of choice enjoyed by man.[28]

It may fairly be said that the Hellenistic elements utilized by Sirach are generally in the service of a conventional wisdom view of things, and there is no sign that he was willing to strike out in radically new directions. He undoubtedly found that the manner in which the Stoics dealt with the problem of theodicy was most congenial to the Jewish approach to things, and was therefore quite happy to adopt a number of their formulations in this regard. The author of Wisdom, on the other hand, was clearly a much greater enthusiast of Greek philosophy and science, bold enough to conceive of Wisdom as an eternal emanation (*aporroia*) of God's glory, and even ready to adopt elements of Stoic physical theory in order to explicate biblical miracles. Much of this new spirit, however, must be ascribed to the new social and intellectual context in which that author found himself.

Notes

1. Jonathan Goldstein, "Jewish Acceptance & Rejection of Hellenism," in *Jewish & Christian Self-Definition*, ed. E.P. Sanders et al. (Philadelphia: Fortress, 1981), II,73, 75; Rudolf Smend, *Die Weisheit des Jesus Sirach* (Berlin: Reimer, 1906), p. xxiv.

2. J.T. Sanders, *Ben Sira & Demotic Wisdom* (Chico: Scholars Press, 1983), p. 58. Cf. J.L. Crenshaw, *Old Testament Wisdom: An Introduction* (Atlanta: John Knox, 1981), p. 159.

3. Otto Kern, *Orphicorum Fragmenta* (Berlin: Weidmann, 1922), pp. 91, 201.

4. See John J. Collins, "The Biblical Precedent for Natural Theology," *JAAR* XLV/I Supplement (March 1977), B, pp. 35-67; and D. Winston, *The Wisdom of Solomon* (Anchor Bible 43. Garden City: Doubleday, 1979), p. 36.

5. See Gerhard Von Rad, *Wisdom in Israel* (Nashville & N.Y.: Abingdon, 1972), pp. 246-47.

6. See P.M. Fraser, *Ptolemaic Alexandria* (Oxford: Clarendon, 1972), I, 481; II, 695, n. 17; R. Pautrel, "Ben Sira et le Stoicisme," *Recherches de Science Religieuse*, 51 (1963), pp. 535-49.

7. Cf. Qoh. 7:14; *T. Napth.* 2:7; *T. Asher* 1:4-5; *Midrash Temurah* chap. 1; Philo, *Op.* 33.

8. Cf. Sir. 42:17, "So that the universe may stand firm in his glory;" 42:23, "Everything liveth and abideth forever;" 42:24, "He has made nothing superfluous;" 42:22, "How beautiful is all that he has made;" 43:1, 9, 11. Cf. also Philo, *Spec.* 3.189; *SVF* 2.1009; Xen. *Cyr.* 8.7.22; Cic. *Nat. D.* 28.93.

9. Epictetus 1.12.16: "Instruction consists precisely in learning to desire each thing exactly as it happens. And how do they happen? As he that ordains them has ordained. And he has ordained that there be summer and winter, and abundance and death, and virtue and vice, and all such opposties, for the harmony of the whole ..."; Sen. *Q Nat.* 7.27.4: "Do you not see how opposite the elements are among themselves? They are heavy and light, cold and hot, wet and dry; all the harmony of this universe is formed out of discordant elements." Cf. M. Hengel, *Judaism and Hellenism* (Philadelphia: Fortress, 1974) I, 147-49.

10. Cf. Philo, *Prov.* 2.31-32: God employs famine, pestilence or earthquake out of his concern for virtue. 2.104: Venomous animals are prepared by God for punishment of the errant.

11. In 17:31 Ben Sira writes: "Is anything brighter than the sun? Yet the sun suffers eclipse. So flesh and blood have evil thoughts." Philo similarly writes: "It must needs be that mortal man shall be oppressed by the nation of the passions and receive the calamities which are proper to created being, but it is God's will to lighten the evils which are inherent in our race." (*Her.* 272-74). Cf. Seneca, *De Ira* 2.28.4: "For it is not by the power of the gods, but by the terms of our mortality that we are forced to suffer whatever ill befalls."

12. The use of hyms to the deity in Ben Sira is paralleled by the employment of a hymn to the creator-god in the *Instruction of Papyrus Insinger*, chap. 24, which is entitled "the teaching of knowing the greatness of the god so as to put it in your heart." According to Miriam Lichtheim, both *Papyrus Insinger* and Ben Sira were influenced by Hellenistic wisdom writings.

13. For a good general treatment of theodicy in Ben Sira, see James Crenshaw, "The Problem of Theodicy in Sirach: On Human Bondage," in *Theodicy in the Old Testament*, ed. J.L. Crenshaw (Philadelphia: Fortress, 1983), pp. 119-40.

14. Gustave Lefebvre, *Le Tombeau de Petosiris* (Cairo, 1923-4), II.91 (inscription 127, line 6): cited by Siegfried Morenz, *Egyptian Religion*, tr. A.W. Keep (London: Methuen, 1973), p. 66.

15. See Miriam Lichtheim, *Ancient Egyptian Literature* (Berkeley: U. of California Press, 1973), I.67.

16. *The Satire of the Trades*, or *Teaching of Khety, Son of Duauf*, in Lichtheim, *Ancient Egyptian Literature*, I, 191.

17. Morenz, p. 67.

18. *Instruction of Amenemope* 10.13-18, in Lichtheim, II, 160.

19. See Morenz, p. 68.

20. Lichtheim, *Egyptian Literature* I, 65.

21. Lichtheim, *Late Egyptian Wisdom Literature in the International Context* (OBO 52. Freiburg: Universitätsverlag; Göttingen: Vandenhoeck & Ruprecht, 1983), pp. 90-91.

22. Lichtheim, *Ancient Egyptian Literature*, I.68. The interpretation is that of Michael Fox, *The Book of Qohelet and its Relation to the Wisdom School* (Doctoral Dissertat. Hebrew University of Jerusalem, 1972), p. 51 (Hebrew).

23. See the excellent discussion of this Aristotelian passage in David J. Furley, *Two Studies in the Greek Atomists* (Princeton: Princeton U. Press, 1967), pp. 184-95.

24. *Papyrus Insinger* 5.9 reads: "There is curse and blessing in the character that was given him."

25. See Lichtheim, *Late Egyptian Wisdom*, pp. 107-96.

26. See Fox, pp. 53-54.

27. See Winston, pp. 48-49.

28. I am therefore unable to accept J.T. Sanders' judgment that the book of Proverbs already contained the freedom/determinism paradox that characterizes Ben Sira. Moreover, his citation of Proverbs 22:2 as an expression of the deterministic view is inapt, since that verse refers not to the divine determination of a man's ethical character, but of his economic status. See Sanders, p. 55, n. 127.

The Centrality of Virtue-Ethics in Maimonides

Walter S. Wurzburger

One of the most striking features of Maimonidean ethics is the pivotal role assigned to agent-morality, which focuses on the ethical quality of the state of mind of the agent rather than the propriety of particular actions. In contradistinction to many other Halakhic authorities[1] who, while recognizing virtue-ethics as a sublime religious idea, either do not include it at all among religious obligations or relegate it to a mere means to virtuous conduct, Maimonides both in his legal and philosophical writings treats the cultivation of moral virtues as an intrinsic value, which is explicitly mandated as an indispensable aspect of Jewish piety.

Although one may be tempted to attribute this predilection for virtue to Aristotelian influences, it must be borne in mind that for Maimonides ethics represents not a quest for personal happiness or self-realization but a response to the religious imperative of *imitatio dei*.[2] In his scheme, even the cultivation of the "middle road" which Hermann Cohen[3] characterized as an outright concession to Aristotle, was viewed not merely as a dictate of prudential ethics but as the fulfillment of the Biblical commandment "Thou shalt walk in His ways."[4]

In view of Maimonides' penchant for systematic arrangement, it is highly revealing that the section dealing with the cultivation of virtues is located in *Sefer Hamada*, The Book of Knowledge, the first of the 14 books comprising the *Mishneh Torah*, rather than in parts of the Code which treat interpersonal or social obligations. This in itself indicates that Maimonides looked upon virtue not simply as an instrumental value conducive to ethical conduct, but as an independent and intrinsic value to be pursued for its own sake. Even more noteworthy is the fact that, although Maimonides considered the commandment

"Love thy neighbor as thyself" as the underlying principle of all norms governing relations "between man and his fellow man,"[5] there is no mention at all of this commandment until the sixth of the seven chapters that comprise his *Hilkhot Deot* is reached. The first five chapters revolve exclusively around the commandment "thou shalt walk in His ways," which is defined as the obligation to cultivate the divine moral attributes (the ways of God) according to one's ability.

The commandment "Love thy neighbour" is introduced only in that section of *Hilkhot Deot* which deals with various factors which impact upon the formation of dispositions and character traits. After describing the power of environmental influences, Chapter 7 addresses itself to the requirement to select proper role models. It is only at this point that reference is made to various commandments, starting with "Love thy neighbour as thyself," which mandate rules of conduct in the realm of interpersonal relationships. Special attention should be focused on the fact that Maimonides' interpretation here sharply diverges from that offered in *Hilkhot Avel*[6] where "Love thy neighbor as thyself" is cited as the source of the obligation to perform *acts* of benevolence. In *Hilkhot Deot*, on the other hand, the commandment is interpreted as an aspect of virtue-ethics, i.e., the obligation to experience love towards fellow Isrealites and to manifest this disposition in our conduct.

This formulation as well as the placement of "Love thy neighbor as thyself" together with the other commandments listed in chapters 7 and 8 of *Hilkhot Deot* suggests that, within this particular context, the social utility of the norms figures merely as a secondary consideration. *Hilkhot Deot* is a treatise on personal morality rather than social ethics. It addresses itself primarily to the ethico-religious task of striving to emulate divine moral attributes. The commandments included in this section of the Code are viewed not as ordinances useful to society but as instrumentalities helpful in engendering virtuous dispositions within agents. The commandments discussed here can fulfill this paradeutic function, because human conduct, even more than surroundings or role models, exert a profound impact upon the formation of character.

The belief that conduct moulds attitudes and dispositions is a cornerstone of the Maimonidean ethics. It comes to the fore already in many of his earliest writings. In his *Commentary* on the Mishnah there is considerable emphasis upon the notion that as the result of frequent repetition in the performance of a Mitzvah, our character is refined and ennobled.[7] He similarly points out in the first chapter of *Hilkhot Deot*[8] that morally desirable dispositions can only be acquired by practice. It is through disciplining oneself to act in the proper manner that one ultimately becomes conditioned to appropriate moral virtues, rendering moral conduct completely natural and effortless. Obviously, this opinion echoes the Aristotelian doctrine that virtue is acquired by acting in accordance with the requirements of virtue.

To be sure, Maimonides is by no means unique among Jewish thinkers in attributing such efficacy to the performance of a Mitzvah. A considerable number of medieval Jewish thinkers refer to the Midrashic statement that the Mitzvot were given *letzaref et haberiot*[9] and interpret it in a manner that it is construed as evidence for the proposition that the refinement of human character was the ultimate purpose of the Mitzvot.[10]

But this by no means detracts from the originality of the Maimonidean approach which regards the imitation of God through the cultivation of moral dispositions as a specific religious imperative. That the Maimonidean view was far from a commonplace is attested by the fact that in *Hilkhot Teshuvah* (7:3) he finds it necessary to engage in sharp polemics against the opinion that Repentance is necessary only for sins involving conduct and to insist that sins involving evil traits of character pose a far greated threat to one's spiritual well-being than wrong actions. It should also be noted that the Sciptural proof text (Isaiah 55:7) adduced by Maimonides hardly constitutes conclusive evidence for his case, since it could easily be argued that when the prophet pleaded for reformation of "the way" and "the thoughts" of the wicked, he was concerned with the elimination of the *causes* of sin rather than mere repentance from sin.

Although Maimonides ostensibly bases his virtue-ethics on a Rabbinic text, it must be realized that the passage of the *Sifre*, which is cited in support of his thesis, actually is not offered as a comment on the Biblical verse invoked as proof text for the obligation to cultivate moral virtues. Whereas Maimonides refers to the verse, Deuteronomy 28:9., he actually adduces a Rabbinic comment offered to a similar but different verse. It is with respect to Deuteronomy 11:22 (not

28:9) that *Sifre* notes that "'to walk in all the ways of God,' refers to the ways of God...God is called compassionate, you shall also be compassionate, God is called gracious, you shall also be gracious."

At first blush it appears rather strange that Maimoinides resorts to the *Sifre's* explanation of the meaning of *imitatio dei* and completely ignores the Talmudic definition (B.T. *Sotah* 14a.) which is formulated in terms of the emulation of divine *Middot* (traits) such as clothing the naked, visiting the sick, comforting the mourners and burying the dead. As I have pointed out elsewhere,[11] Maimonides quoted the latter text in combination with the *Sifre* in the earlier formulation of the Mitzvah in the *Sefer Hamitzvot*. But as agent-morality or virtue-ethics became more dominant in his orientation, he restricted the scope of *imitatio dei* to the cultivation of dispositions and deliberately excluded from it any facet of act-morality.[12]

The increasing prominence of virtue-ethics in the Maimonidean system can also be gauged by the fact that in his earliest major work, the *Commentary* on the *Mishnah*, no mention is made of *imitatio dei* in his exposition of various aspects of virtue-ethics. Even his extensive introduction to *Pirkei Avot*, the *Shemoneh Perakim*, which revolves around moral virtues, is totally devoid of any references to *imitatio dei*. It therefore seems plausible to conclude that in the progressive development of Maimonides' thought, cultivation of moral virtues was transformed form a religious desideratum into an outright religious obligation. But even in the earliest stage of his development, when, in contrast with his more mature writings, he sanctioned deviation from the middle road only as a corrective measure but refused to recommend any form of excess as a moral ideal, he, nonetheless, even in the absence of a formal link between the quest for moral perfection and *imitatio dei*, regarded the obligation to cultivate virtuous dispositions as an essential feature of Jewish piety and as a prerequisite to the attainment of prophecy.

It is therefore readily understandable that in chapter 8 of *Shemoneh Perakim* he finds it necessary to make a basic distinction between the ideal motivation for ritual acts and that for moral conduct. Whereas in the ritual sphere, he operates with the principle that "the reward is proportionate to the effort," he emphasized that, in the realm of moral conduct, those who perform moral actions after an inner struggle between inclination and obligation are inferior to those who are motivated by virtous dispositions and hence need not battle against conflicting inclinations. Professor Eliezer Schweid claims[13] that this distinction reflects the assimilation of Greek categories of thought on the part of Maimonides. But in the light of our preceding analysis it appears that even before he formally linked cultivation of virtues with *imitatio dei*, Maimonides regarded virtue-ethics not simply as a matter of mental health indispensable to the proper functionaing of the human personality but as an integral part of Jewish piety. Greek ethics hardly holds a monopoly on the notion of virtue. There are numerous Biblical and Rabbinic passages which could be adduced in support of the thesis that a religiously developed personality is characterized by truly moral dispositions.

The emphasis upon virtue is by no means incompatible with the statement in *Hilkhot Teshuvah* (7:4.) which extolls the repentant person, who experiences great difficulties in overcoming his proclivity for sin. According to Maimonides, he is spiritually superior to an individual who was never subject to temptation and, therefore, required no effort to curb sinful tendencies. Although Professor Isidore Twersky[14] in his brilliant analysis observes that this passage implies that moral conduct involving struggle against inclinations should be assigned a higher spiritual status than effortless moral conduct that is motivated by virtue, it must, however, be realized that for Maimonides an undesirable ethical disposition, even when repressed to such an extent that it does not manifest itself in overt conduct, still calls for repentance. Hence, an individual who can perform moral actions only after inner struggle, while deserving great praise for his conduct, is, nevertheless, inferior to an individual who posseses desirable traits of character. To be sure, Maimonides, in the spirit of Chapter 7:4 would still contend that an individual who had to struggle to overcome his undesirable dispositions before acquiring virtue is spiritually superior to an individual whose virtuous disposition was attained without any effort on his part.

Maimonides' concern for virtue-ethics also accounts for his ability to dispense with the need for an outright religious commandment to engage in supererogatory conduct. Unlike Nachmanides,[15] who bases the obligation to go beyond the minimal religious obligation and to perform acts of supererogation on the Biblical verse "thou shalt do the good and the right," Maimonides contends that supererogatory conduct is an outgrowth of the development of virtuous dispositions. It is for this reason that instead of prescribing supererogatory conduct, he simply refers to the one "who acts in keeping with the standards of the pious."[16] It is only the virtuous person who is able to perceive the need to go beyond explicit legal commandments in the attempt to imitate the ways of God.

In a similar vein we can also explain why Maimonides, in seeming conflict with the biblical view that the Mitzvot were intended for the good of man, places such extraordinary emphasis upon the selfless service of God that he parts company with numerous other Jewish thinkers by including the desire for spiritual satisfaction in the Hereafter among the ulterior motives which are incompatible with the religious ideal of serving God out of pure love.[17] But once we recognize the centrality of *imitatio dei* in the Maimonidean scheme, it becomes obvious why the desire for spiritual satisfaction is bound to interfere with the attainment of the highest rungs of piety. Any type of self-regarding motivation, however noble and sublime, betrays the lack of an essential component of the higher levels of *imitatio dei*, since the love which God manifests to His creatures is totally other-regarding and completely untainted by selfish motives.

While *imitatio dei* constitutes a universally applicable religious norm, it allows for a variety of responses dependent upon individual psychological and intellectual capacities. Hence, the nature and scope of the obligation varies from individual to individual. Significantly, Maimonides, in defining the commandment, stipulates that the cultivation of the dispositions is mandated "in accordance with the capacity of the individual."[18] As he already made it clear in his Commentary to the Mishnah,[19] whereas the lower levels of ethical perfection can be acquired as the result of conditioning through moral conduct, the attainment of the higher levels (the ethics of the pious) presupposes intellectual achievements. This reflected his basic conviction that the intellectual apprehension of God is a necessary condition of the cultivation of the moral vision and selfless motivation without which the highest rungs of moral perfection cannot be reached. It is for this reason that the concluding chapter of the *Guide of the Perplexed* extolls moral perfection which is grounded on the intellectual apprehension of God as the highest manifestation of piety.

It has been argued by a number of scholars that the ideal of *imitatio dei* as described by Maimonides in the *Guide* refers exclusively to the political function of the prophet, who, like Plato's philosopher-king, must forego purely contemplative activity and assume the burdens of a statesman. Thus L.V. Berman maintains that "the imitation of God which comes after the acquisition of theoretical knowledge refers to political activity in founding and governing a state."[20] Following this approach, Professor Pines maintains that the obligation "to apprehend divine justice, righteousness and charity and to acquire a simiarity to them ...is not laid upon all men endowed with a moral sense, but only upon the philosophers who also have a social and political activity."[21] Especially puzzling is the latter's assertion that "the legislator and the statesmen, should be in his imitation of God be, ..either benificent or cruel, not because he has the corresponding sentiments, but because these modes of action are necessary for... the creation and preservation of the highest possible type of community.[22]

Since the cultivation of virtue is defined by Maimonides as the fulfillment of the commandment "thou shalt walk in His ways," it would hardly make sense to demand less moral perfection from an ideal statesman, who is supposed to pattern himself after the prophet, than from ordinary individuals. It seems far more plausible to adopt Professor Twersky's approach[23] and maintain that the *imitatio dei* described in the concluding chapter of the *Guide*, far from being the exclusive prerogative of the statesman, represents the highest possible level of responding to the divine imperative of "thou shalt walk in His ways," which however can be attained only by the philosopher, irrespective of whether or not he functions as a statesman. To be sure, *some* (but by no means all) divine moral attributes - as is made clear in Part 1 Chapter 54 - have relevance only as models for the statesman, but not for individuals without political responsibilities. But this in no way supports the thesis that the other divine moral attributes, especially those enumerated in Chapter 1 of *Hilkhot Deot*, are irrelevant to the quest for *imitatio dei* on the part of ordinary individuals. It must be realized that in the Maimonidean system "thou shalt walk in His ways," represents a continuous challenge, beginning with the attempt to cultivate moral virtues through moral conduct and pointing to the ever higher dimensions of *imitatio dei* which can be engendered only by intellectual perfection.

Notes

1. Cf. Moses ben Yaacov of Coucy, *Sefer Mitzvot Gadol, Mitzvat Aseh*, 7, where the commandment is defined exclusively in terms of acts of benevolence. In the *Sefer Yereim*, Eliezer b. Samuel of Metz interprets the commandment as 1) an additional general Mitzvah enjoining the observance of the various commandments of the Torah and 2) as a specific Mitzvah mandating the performance of benevolent actions. No mention, however, is made of cultivation of traits of character.
   Upon completeion of the bulk of this paper, Professor Isadore Twersky informed me that he was preparing a paper for publication which will deal with the originality of the Maimonidean interpretation of "Thou shalt walk in His ways" as the obligation to cultivate desirable dispositions. I am looking forward to reading the paper in the hope that it will corroborate my own findings.

2. See the important study of Marvin Fox, "The Doctrine of the Mean in Aristotle and Maimonides", in *Studies in Jewish Religious and Intellectual History*, Stein and Loewy, ed., 1979, pp. 93-120. Cf. Steven Schwarzschild, "Moral Radicalism and 'Middlingness' in the Ethics of Maimonides," *Studies in Medieval Culture*, 11, 1977, pp.65-94.

3. Hermann Cohen, "Charakteristik der Ethik Maimunis," Jüdische Schriften, III, 1924, pp.221-89. See also Shimon Ravidowicz, "Perek Betorat Hamussar Larambam," in *Sefer Hayovel Lichvod Mordechai Menachem Kaplan*," 1953, p.236. See also my article "The Maimonidean Matrix of Rabbi Joseph B. Soloveitchik's Two-Tiered Ethics," *Through the Sound of Many Voices*, Jonathan V. Plaut, ed., 1982, pp.178-80.

4. Deut. 28:9.

5. *Commentary to the Mishnah*, Peah 1:1.

6. *Hilkhot Avel* 14:1. While I disagree with many of his conclusions, I have benefited from Shalom Rosenberg's "Vehalakhta Biderachav" in *Mivchar Maamarim Befilosophiah Kelalit Viyehudit*, Chalamish and Kascher, ed., pp.72-91. Some of his solutions were anticipated in my article "Darkei Shalom," *Gesher*, 1977-78, pp. 80-86.

7. *Commentary to the Mishnah*, Avot 3:17.

8. *Hilkhot Deot*, 1:11.

9. Lev. Rabbah, 13:3 and Gen. Rabbah, 44:1.

10. Nachmanides, *Commentary to the Torah*, Deuteronomy 22;6. See also Crescas to *Guide of the Perplexed*, III:26.

11. Walter S. Wurzburger, "Imitatio Dei in Maimonides' Sefer Hamitzvot and the Mishneh Torah" in *Tradition and Transition*, Jonathan Sacks, ed., 1986, pp.321-24.

12. It should also be noted that the phrase "the way in which you shall walk" (Exodus 18:20) is interpreted in the B.T. (Bava Kamma 100a and Bava Metzia 30b) as a reference *not* to dispositions but to *acts* of benevolence, especially visiting the sick and burying the dead.

    It is highly significant that Maimonides does not quote an obvious Talmudic source that he could be cited in support of virtue-ehtics. Abba Shaul (B.T. Shabbat 133b) interprets the verse in Exodus 15:2 as mandating the imitation of the divine attributes of grace and compassion. The most likely explanation for his reluctance to cite this source relates to his doctrine of attributes of action. For Maimonides it would be the height of absurdity to treat the imitation of God Himself as a religious norm, since His utter uniqueness and unity renders this impossible. Only the imitation of His ways is within the ken of human capacities. It is for similar reasons that Maimonides does not utilize the *Sifra* on Leviticus 19:2, which cites Abba Shaul's interpretation of the Biblical commandment "be holy because God is holy." Although this particular verse in Leviticus is the most obvious source of *imitatio dei*, Maimonides prefers to base himself upon the commandment to walk in the ways of God, lest the radical distinction between God and His creatures be blurred. He categorically rules out any attempt to go beyond the imitation of the *ways* of God. The Sifre cited by Maimonides is eminently suited for Maimonides' purposes, because there is no assertion that God actually possesses various moral attributes, only that He is *called* by these terms.

13. *Iyunim Bi'shemoneh Perakim Le-Rambam*, 1969, Chapter 6.

14. Isadore Twersky, *Introduction to the Code Of Maimonides*, 1980, pp.453-59.

15. *Commentary to the Torah*, Deut. 6:18.
    I have dealt with the differences between Maimonides and Nachmanides in their respective treatments of supererogatory conduct in my essay, "Law as the Basis of Moral Society," *Tradition*,19:1, Spring 1981, pp.48-49. See also my "Law, Philosophy and Imitatio Dei in Maimonides,*Aquinas*, 30, 1987, pp.27-34.

    In my article "Darkei Shalom, *op. cit.*, I have shown how the focus on agent-morality and virtue-ethics is reflected in the Maimonidean attitude towards the treatment of non-Jews. Cf. also my "Law, Philosophy and Imitatio Dei in Maimonides," *op. cit.*, especially, p.33.

16. *Hilkhot Gezeilah Va'aveidah*, 11:17 and *Hilkhot Rozeach* 13:4.

17. *Hilkhot Teshuvah*, 10:2.

18. *Hilkhot Deot*, 1:6.

19. Avot 2:5.

20. L.V. Berman, "The Political Interpretation of the Maxim: The Purpose of Philosophy is the Imitation of God," *Studia Islamica*, 15, 1961, p. 60.

21. Shlomoh Pines, "Spinoza, Maimonides and Kant," *Scripta Hierosolymitana*, 20, 1968, p. 28. For a similar approach, see also Eliezer Goldman, "Ha'avodah Hameyuchedet Be'masigei Ha'amitot," *Bar Ilan Yearbook*, 1968, p. 23 ff.

22. Shlomoh Pines, "Translator's Introduction to the Guide of the Perplexed," in Moses Maimonides, *The Guide of the Perplexed*, 1963, p. 122.

23. Isadore Twersky, *op. cit.*, p.511, note 390. Compare also with the thesis of David Hartman, *Maimonides: Torah and Philosophic Quest*, 1976. See also Alexander Altmann, "Maimonides' Four Perfections," *Essays in Jewish Intellectual History*, 1981, p. 73; Yitzchak Engelard, "Equity in Maimonides," *Israel Law Review*, 21,3-4, note 102, p.329 and Daniel H. Frank, "The End of the Guide: Maimonides on the Best Life for Man," *Judaism*, 34, 4, 1985, pp.485-95.

Works by Arthur Hyman

Books:

Studies in Islamic and Jewish Thought, Washington, D.C., Catholic University Press, 1990

Averroes' De Substantia Orbis, critical edition of Hebrew text, English translation, commentary, introduction, Cambridge, Mass.: Medieval Academy of America and Jerusalem: Israel Academy of Sciences and Humanities, 1986

Ed. and Contr., *Essays in Medieval Jewish and Islamic Philosophy*, New York: KTAV, 1977

(With Saul Lieberman), ed., *Salo W. Baron Jubilee Volume*, Jerusalem: American Academy for Jewish Research, 1975

(With James J. Walsh), ed., *Philosophy in the Middle Ages: The Christian, Islamic, and Jewish Traditions*, New York: Harper and Row, 1967 (Paperback: Hackett, 1973; second edition, 1984)

(With Saul Lieberman et al.), ed., *Harry A. Wolfson Jubilee Volume*, Jerusalem: American Academy for Jewish Research, 1965

Articles:

"Jewish Aristotelianism from the 12th through the 14th Centuries," Proceedings of Conference on Judeo-Arabic Studies held at the University of Chicago in 1984, in press

"Maimonides on Religious Language," *Studies in Maimonides' Thought and Environment*, ed. Joel Kraemer, in press

"From what is One and Supple only what is One and Supple Can Come to Be", *Proceedings* of Conference on Jewish Neophilinism held at the University of Hawaii 1987, in press

"Divine Law and Human Reason", Proceedings of Conference held at Yeshiva University 1987, in press

"Maimonides: the Legal Scholar as Philosopher" *Thought*, (Fordham University publication) in press

"Demonstrative, Dialectical and Sophistic Arguments in the Philosophy of Moses Maimonides," *Moses Maimonides and His Time*, ed. Eric L Ormsby 1989, in press

"Aristotle, Algazali and Avicenna on Necessity, Potentiality and Possibility," *Florilegium Columbianum: Essays in Honor of Paul Oskar Kristeller*, eds. Karl-Ludwig Selig and Robert Somerville, New York, 1987, pp. 73-88

"Maimonides on Creation and Emanation," *Studies in Medieval Philosophy*, ed. John F. Wippel, Washington, D.C., 1987, pp. 45-61

"Maimonides on Causality," *Maimonides and Philosophy*, eds. S. Pines and Y. Yovel, Dordrecht, 1987, pp, 157-72

"Averroes as Commentator on Aristotle's Theory of the Intellect," *Studies in Aristotle*, ed. D. J. O'Meara, Washington, D. C., 1981, pp. 161-90

"Jewish Religious Conceptions and Medieval Philosophy," *Actas del V Congreso Internacional de Filosofia Medieval*, Madrid, 1979, pp. 115-24

"A Note on Maimonides' Classification of Law," *Fiftieth Anniversary Volume* of the American Academy for Jewish Research, Jerusalem, 1979, pp. 323-43

"Jewish Philosophy," *The Jewish World*, ed. E. Kedouri, London, 1979, pp. 209-16

"Interpreting Maimonides," *Gesher* (Yeshiva University Publication), New York, 1977, pp. 46-59

"Philosophy, Jewish," and "Maimonides, Moses, His Philosophy," *Encyclopedia Judaica*, 1972, XIII, 421-65; XI, 767-77

"The Liberal Arts and Jewish Philosophy," *Arts libéraux et philosophie au moyen âge*, Montreal-Paris, 1969, pp. 99-110

"Maimonides Thirteen Principles," *Jewish Medieval and Renaissance Studies*, ed. A. Altmann, Cambridge, Mass., 1967, pp. 119-44

"Jewish Philosophy," *New Catholic Encyclopedia*, New York, 1967, VII, 977-80

"Some Aspects of Maimonides' Philosophy of Nature," *La filosofia della natura nel Medioevo*, Milan, 1966, pp. 209-18

"Aristotle's 'First Matter' and Avicenna's and Averroes' 'Corporeal Form,'" *Harry A. Wolfson Jubilee Volume*, 1965, pp. 385-406

"The Composition and Transmission of Averroes' *Ma'amar be-'Esem ha-Galgal*," *Studies and Essays in Honor of Abraham A. Neuman*, Leiden, 1963, pp. 299-307

"Spinoza's Dogmas of Universal Faith in the Light of their Medieval Jewish Backgrounds," *Biblical and Other Studies*, ed. A. Altmann, Cambridge, Mass., 1963, pp. 183-95

DATE DUE

HIGHSMITH # 45220